DEVELOPMENTAL TRAJECTORIES OF CHILDREN'S ADJUSTMENT ACROSS THE TRANSITION TO SIBLINGHOOD: PRE-BIRTH PREDICTORS AND SIBLING OUTCOMES AT ONE YEAR

Brenda L. Volling, University of Michigan
Richard Gonzalez, University of Michigan
Wonjung Oh, Texas Tech University
Ju-Hyun Song, University of Michigan
Tianyi Yu, University of Georgia
Lauren Rosenberg, Patty X. Kuo, Elizabeth Thomason,
Emma Beyers-Carlson, Paige Safyer, and Matthew M. Stevenson,
University of Michigan

WITH COMMENTARY BY

Nina Howe

Patricia J. Bauer
Series Editor

MONOGRAPHS OF THE SOCIETY FOR RESEARCH IN CHILD DEVELOPMENT

Serial No. 326, Vol. 82, No. 3, 2017

WILEY

Boston, Massachusetts   Oxford, United Kingdom

EDITOR
PATRICIA J. BAUER
Emory University

MANAGING EDITOR
LISA BRAVERMAN
Society for Research in Child Development

EDITORIAL ASSISTANT
STEPHANIE CUSTER
Society for Research in Child Development

DEVELOPMENTAL TRAJECTORIES OF CHILDREN'S ADJUSTMENT ACROSS THE TRANSITION TO SIBLINGHOOD: PRE-BIRTH PREDICTORS AND SIBLING OUTCOMES AT ONE YEAR

CONTENTS

COMMENTARY

I. INTRODUCTION: UNDERSTANDING THE TRANSITION TO SIBLINGHOOD FROM A DEVELOPMENTAL PSYCHOPATHOLOGY AND ECOLOGICAL SYSTEMS PERSPECTIVE

Brenda L. Volling

This article is part of the issue "Developmental Trajectories of Children's Adjustment across the Transition to Siblinghood: Pre-Birth Predictors and Sibling Outcomes at One Year" Volling, Gonzalez, Oh, Song, Yu, Rosenberg, Kuo, Thomason, Beyers-Carlson, Safyer, and Stevenson (Issue Authors). For a full listing of articles in this issue, see: http://onlinelibrary.wiley.com/doi/10.1111/mono.v82.3/issuetoc.

For most children, the birth of an infant sibling is a significant developmental transition (Dunn, 1988; Volling, 2005). Similar to other normative life transitions, the period surrounding the birth of a second child can be stressful for some young children (Dunn, 1988). In response to stress, young children often experience sleep disruptions, increases in temper tantrums, whininess, clinging, and anxiety (Campbell, 2002), but the birth of an infant sibling can also bring about positive changes, as well as opportunities for children to grow emotionally through their daily interactions with the infant (Dunn & Kendrick, 1982). The birth of a second child also marks the very beginning of a child's first sibling relationship, one of the longest lasting social relationships of a person's life. Most firstborn children are usually toddlers between 2 and 3 years of age when a second child is born (Baydar,

Corresponding author: Correspondence concerning the Family Transitions Study should be addressed to Brenda L. Volling, Center for Human Growth and Development, University of Michigan, 300 N. Ingalls, Ann Arbor, MI 48109-5406; email: volling@umich.edu

For those interested in the statistical code used to analyze these data (including growth mixture models, random forest, and CART procedures), please email Richard Gonzalez, gonzo@umich.edu.

DOI: 10.1111/mono.12307

Hyle, & Brooks-Gunn, 1997), a developmental time period when most young children demonstrate noncompliant, aggressive, and demanding behaviors, in general, and dealing with the "terrible twos" is considered normative for parents.

One of the challenges for research on the development of disruptive behavior for very young children, and for the transition following the birth of a sibling, is discerning which behaviors constitute a cause for concern and what distinguishes those children having difficulties with the transition from normative developmental changes in challenging behaviors typical of the toddler and preschool period. Indeed, there appear to be large individual differences in how firstborn children react to the birth of an infant sibling with indications that some children experience stress and a period of disruption, whereas others do not (Volling, 2012). There were three goals to the present report. The first goal was to determine whether firstborn children responded differently to the birth of an infant sibling and to identify those children having a difficult time adjusting to the stresses associated with the infant's arrival. To this end, we took a person-centered approach to examine developmental trajectories of firstborns' behavioral and emotional adjustment across the transition to siblinghood, the period when the firstborn moves from only child to older sibling, in an effort to examine individual differences in children's adjustment across this time. In doing so, we conceptualized several possible longitudinal trajectories that could define different types of psychological adjustment experiences for the young child (e.g., short-term adjustment and adaptation, sudden and persistent maladaptation, delayed impact, growth and maturity, stability and continuity) in the year following the birth of a sibling, and tested for these specific trajectory patterns using a person-centered approach (growth mixture modeling). Due to individual differences noted in children's responses to the birth of a sibling, we hypothesized that we would uncover groups (i.e., latent classes) of children following multiple pathways of adjustment over the course of the year. Once these classes were revealed, a second goal of this report was to use indicators of child, parent, and family characteristics collected at the prenatal timepoint to predict children's developmental trajectories. In so doing, we could identify the risks and protective factors that discriminated adjustment trajectories and would allow us to detect with some precision the areas to be targeted for the development of prevention programs designed to assist families making the transition. To accomplish this second goal, we relied on the developmental ecological systems framework (Volling, 2005) to create a potential pool of predictors, including child (e.g., age, gender, temperament), parent (e.g., depression, self-efficacy), and family (e.g., coparenting, attachment) variables that were used in a series of cross-validated data mining techniques followed by traditional statistical testing procedures. Finally, the third goal was to examine how the different trajectories of children's emotional and behavioral adjustment predicted sibling relationship outcomes (i.e., conflict, positive involvement) 1 year after the infant sibling's birth.

The current report begins with a theoretical discussion of young children's behavioral and emotional difficulties from a developmental psychopathology perspective, arguing that young children's behavior problems after the birth of a sibling must be viewed in relation to behaviors that may be annoying and troublesome in the toddler and preschool years, but are considered normative. We also present our ideas for defining different developmental trajectories of adaptation and maladaptation based on theories of family risk and resilience that will be tested directly in our group-based trajectory analyses. This chapter will also discuss a developmental ecological systems perspective that situates the child within a larger set of family and contextual influences that serve as risk and protective factors and determine which children may develop problems over the course of the transition (Volling, 2005) so that we have the theoretical basis for choosing variables used in our prediction analyses. We will also address how variability in children's adjustment after the birth of a sibling may have developmental consequences for sibling interactions later in the year to establish the basis for examining the relations between behavioral and emotional adjustment trajectories and children's sibling relationships. We then turn to a presentation of the methods and procedures for the current study, the Family Transitions Study, a longitudinal, prospective study designed specifically to address changes in firstborn children's adjustment after the birth of their infant sibling. We will also describe our data analytic strategy in some detail and our thinking about the determination and meaning of classes when examining the development of psychopathology in young children before presenting the results. As for results, we begin with an overview of the developmental models describing mean-level change in the sample before moving to an examination of individual differences in the seven syndrome scales examined, with a chapter devoted to each. We end by discussing the implications of our findings for families undergoing the transition from one child to two, as well as recommendations for professionals wanting to assist parents with the stresses associated with the birth of a second child.

ADJUSTMENT AND MALADJUSTMENT IN TODDLER AND PRESCHOOL CHILDREN: A DEVELOPMENTAL PSYCHOPATHOLOGY PERSPECTIVE

In the current study, we take a developmental psychopathology perspective in understanding children's adjustment after the birth of a sibling and use a developmental ecological systems framework to address the risk and protective factors that predict children's adjustment outcomes.

According to a developmental psychopathology approach to understanding adjustment difficulties, young children's adjustment needs to be understood in relation to normative developmental changes occurring during the toddler and preschool years. As Campbell (2011) notes, many problems of children in this age bracket are age-related and transient, often reflecting difficulties adjusting to a stressful developmental transition such as the birth of a sibling. Some children, however, may exhibit more chronic or severe reactions that impair cognitive and social development, that then negatively impact family relationships and require focused interventions to help alleviate these problems. Even when behavioral or emotional challenges are short-lived or a normative reaction to environmental and family stress, they can still pose considerable concern for parents who have to respond to difficult behavior at a time when they, too, may be overwhelmed with family stress and the care of a newborn.

Knowing that most children experience the birth of a sibling between the ages of 2 and 3 (Baydar et al., 1997), it is imperative to examine normative developmental advances during the period of early childhood in order to comprehend what constitutes maladjustment or to understand what sorts of emotional and behavioral disruptions might be observed. Early childhood is a period of significant developmental advances in social, communicative, cognitive, emotional, and even motor development (Brownell & Kopp, 2007). From 18 to 36 months of age children develop a growing sense of self, evince a theory of mind and understanding of others, express empathic concern, socially engage in pretend play, and learn to regulate emotions and behavior (Brownell & Kopp, 2007). Between 3 and 5 years of age, there are further advances in language used to communicate feelings and experiences, and engagement in more sophisticated forms of joint pretend play with parents, siblings, and friends. Advances in moral development also emerge with a growing capacity to empathize with others, experience guilt in response to wrong-doing, and appreciate rule-governed behavior (Kochanska, 1993). Although many of these advances coincide with brain maturation, support and guidance from adult caregivers shape children's developing trajectories of adjustment. In addition, parents and child-care providers make increasing demands for more mature behavior and dispense more firm control and discipline in response to children's transgressions as they get older. Stressful life events during this period may trigger emotional and behavioral reactions such as temper tantrums, noncompliance and defiance, clinginess and separation anxiety, sleep problems, and regression to earlier forms of behavior (e.g., toileting accidents, use of a pacifier). Many of these childhood difficulties have been documented after the birth of a sibling (Dunn & Kendrick, 1982; Legg, Sherick, & Wadland, 1974; Stewart, 1990; Trause, 1978), but what is less clear is whether these difficulties are already evident before the birth, are transient and normative reactions to stress, or may lay the foundation for more serious problems in the future (Campbell, 2002). When these life events occur, behavioral and emotional difficulties may be exacerbated in families experiencing high levels of stress, with emotionally vulnerable parents who feel unable to control children's behaviors, when there are few emotional supports available to parents, when parents are insensitive to or lack an understanding of their children's emotional turmoil, and when they respond harshly or punitively to their children's misbehaviors (Cummings, Davies, & Campbell, 2000).

Because pathological outcomes must be understood in relation to normative development, a developmental psychopathology perspective is concerned with multiple developmental outcomes that describe normative, at-risk, and pathological groups of children (Cummings et al., 2000). In other words, there is a focus on understanding individual differences in developmental trajectories that reflect normative developmental changes, as well as high-risk trajectories that may set the stage for the emergence of psychopathology at a later point in time. As such, there is an interest in examining both adaptation (i.e. resilience) and maladaptation (e.g., psychopathology) in response to stressful life circumstances, in contrast to traditional psychiatric or pathological approaches that focus predominantly on negative life experiences (e.g., trauma) and negative outcomes (e.g., clinical diagnoses). The earliest research on the transition to siblinghood was deeply rooted in these traditional perspectives underscoring the psychodynamic turmoil and hostile-reactive behavioral patterns of young children to the birth of their infant sibling (e.g., Levy, 1934, 1937; Petty, 1953). These psychodynamic perspectives continue to influence our current thinking about the transition to siblinghood and often lead parents to fear the worst from their firstborn children (Gullicks & Crase, 1993). It is time to apply a developmental psychopathology perspective to understanding young children's reactions to the birth of an infant sibling so parents can understand what to reasonably expect after the birth of a second child, how they can respond to their family circumstances, and how professionals can offer assistance to families undergoing a more difficult transition. The Family Transitions Study (FTS) was designed with these issues in mind.

Conceptualizing Change Trajectories of Adaptation and Maladaptation

The current report relies on theories of family risk and resilience as a starting point for conceptualizing adaptive and maladaptive trajectory patterns after a stressful life event such as the birth of an infant sibling. The idea that there may be different pathways in response to stressful life events was first conceptualized by Koos (1946) in the "roller coaster model" that described three stages that families often underwent when confronted by a stressful life event: (1) an initial period of disorganization, marked by increases in conflict and an overall atmosphere of anger and resentment, as well as a search for a means of coping with the stress; (2) a period of recovery in which the family discovered ways to adjust to the stressful event; and (3) a period of reorganization wherein the family members adapted to the stressful changes and returned to a level of functioning at or below the pre-event level. The initial increase in disruption followed by a subsequent decline reflects the potential ups and downs of a roller coaster ride and also underscores the fact that adjustment and adaptation is a change process that takes place over a period of time. Koos's (1946) model would later be refined by other family stress theorists (Hill, 1958; McCubbin & Patterson, 1983; Burr & Klein, 1994) seeking to uncover how family members adjusted to stressful life events in an effort to prevent stress from turning into a family crisis. This description of the family's adjustment and adaptation in response to stressful life events is also applicable to childhood psychopathology and understanding individual resilience in response to adversity. How is it that some children succumb to the stresses of adversity while others appear to "bounce back" and maintain a course of adaptive behavior? This understanding of the "ups and downs" surrounding a stressful transition is critical for the period of early childhood and the transition to siblinghood because of the transient nature of behavioral and emotional problems to stress, and the normative patterns so typical of early disruptive behavior (e.g., an increase in aggression in toddlerhood with a subsequent decline; see Campbell, 2011).

The idea of consecutive periods of adjustment and adaptation as critical for understanding both the family's and children's responses to stress underscores the need for longitudinal research designs that capture the increases and decreases typical of the *Adjustment and Adaptation Response* (*i.e., resilience*) to stress (Haan, Hawley, & Deal, 2002). Further, longitudinal data beyond a prebirth and postbirth assessment (e.g., 1 month following the birth) are critical if we wish to examine trajectories indicative of short-term adaptation and long-term, persistent difficulties reflecting maladaptation. In an effort to understand children's resilience after the stress of the birth of a sibling, we operationalized a longitudinal pattern indicative of an adjustment and adaptation response using the five timepoints of the current research design (prenatal, 1, 4, 8, and 12 months after birth) in which an initial period of disruption and an increase in problematic behaviors (i.e., a period of adjustment) shortly after the birth (prenatal to 1 month) would be followed soon thereafter with a return to prebirth levels of behavioral functioning (i.e., a period of adaptation) by 4 months (see Figure 1). In line with Haan et al. (2002), we are operationalizing individual resilience as a process that is visible only over time with at least three timepoints coinciding with a period before the stressful event, during the stressful event, and some time (or times) after the stressful event. A resilient child in this framework is one who evinces positive adjustment before the event, shows a period of decline during the

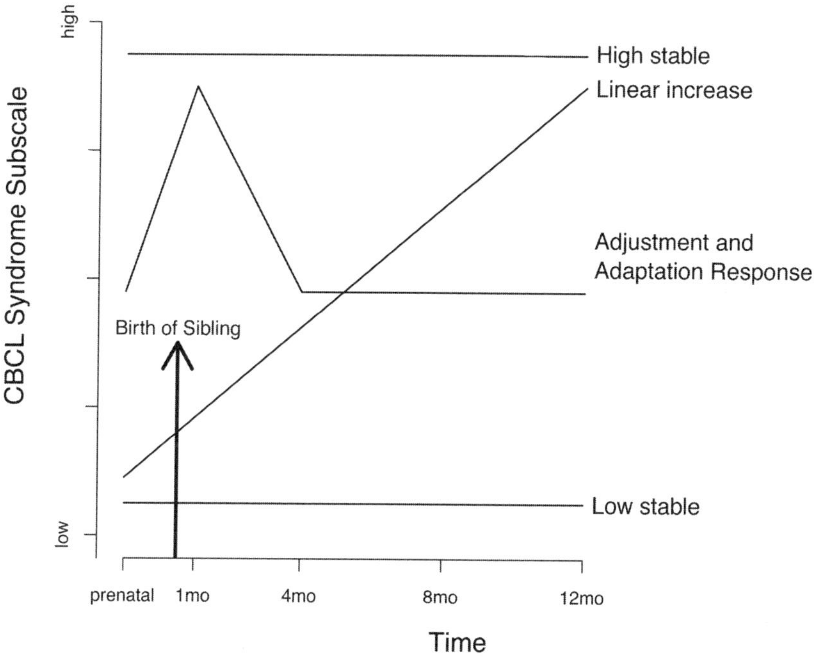

FIGURE 1.—Theorized trajectory patterns of change reflecting adjustment and adaptation, stability, and linear increase.

event, but returns to pre-event levels after the event. In our case, the stressful event is the birth of an infant sibling and the firstborn's adjustment to this event is the focus for understanding resilience to a stressful life event. Resilient children are not simply immune to negative outcomes during stressful periods. Indeed, their initial reactions may be quite immediate, quite negative, and quite intense. Resilient children, however, are able to demonstrate positive adaptation in the face of adversity and risk by eventually returning to their pre-event levels of functioning. The birth of an infant sibling can bring about a period of disruption for the entire family system as a new family member is added, the family structure changes, and family members must learn to adjust and adapt to their new roles as parents, partners, and siblings.

Figure 1 also reveals other potential trajectories reflecting maladaptive or adaptive patterns of behavioral adjustment that may inform us of possible underlying processes explaining children's responses to the birth of a sibling. A *low-stable pattern of no change* would suggest that the birth of a sibling has no or minimal impact on children's behavioral functioning. A *high-stable pattern* would also indicate a pattern of no change as a result of the birth, but the high stable levels of behavior problems over time might very well indicate that family processes already underway before birth are responsible for the high levels of post-birth behavior problems. Of course, the advantages of a pre- and postbirth longitudinal design, in contrast to a postbirth retrospective design, allow one to determine if high levels of postbirth behavior problems were already evident before the birth and not necessarily a result of the birth. Another possible pattern is one of *gradual linear increase* in behavior problems over the year following the infant sibling's birth; a pattern that might occur if there was no immediate change in behavior problems resulting from the birth, but gradual increases that coincided with normative developmental changes of young infants as they progressed from sleeping to crawling to toddling. These social and motoric advances in infant development emerging gradually over time may result in more confrontations between siblings and greater opportunities for the development of disruptive behaviors (Stewart, 1990).

In addition to the Adjustment and Adaptation Response and linear patterns of change, several curvilinear behavioral trajectories may also be apparent following the birth and provide clues as to how children may be

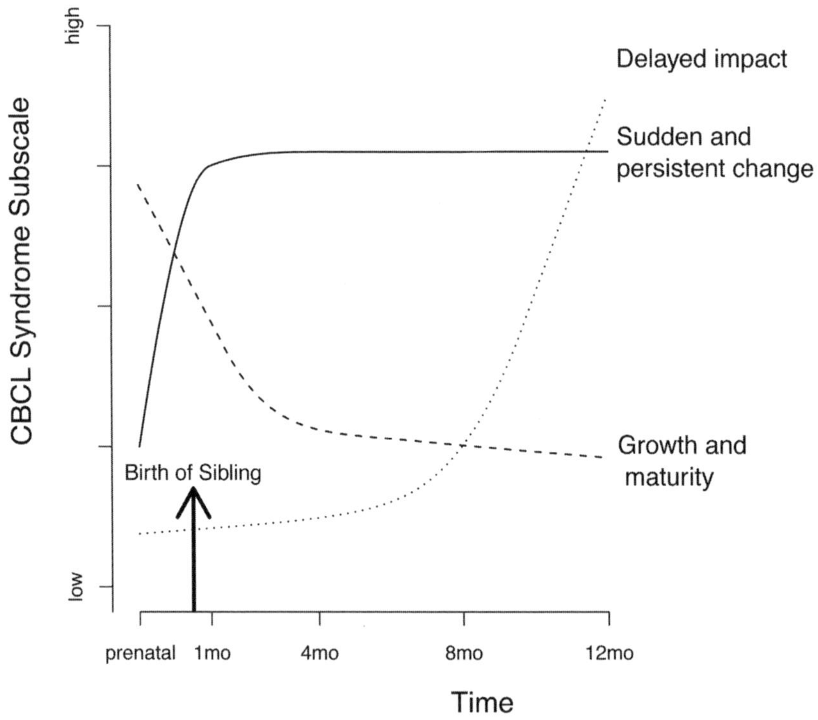

FIGURE 2.—Theorized curvilinear trajectory patterns reflecting sudden persistent change, delayed impact, and growth and maturity.

affected by the birth of an infant sibling. As depicted in Figure 2, one possible maladaptive pattern reflects sudden increases in behavior problems from prenatal to 1 month after birth that would persist over the year. This pattern of *sudden persistent change* that does not return to prebirth levels would reflect a nonresilient, maladaptive pattern of behavior change that would also be consistent with psychodynamic theories underscoring the birth of a sibling as a developmental crisis for the firstborn. Adler (1928) claimed that firstborn children would revert to using any means necessary to regain their parent's attention and love after being dethroned and losing their place in the family to the secondborn infant. This sudden, persistent pattern reflecting a developmental crisis would suggest that the birth of an infant sibling had both an immediate and long-term impact on children's adjustment. Another possible curvilinear trajectory might show a sudden decline in behavior problems that persisted over time, supporting Dunn & Kendrick's (1982) findings that some children evinced *growth and maturity* in response to the birth by becoming more independent and autonomous. Another possibility is reflected in a *delayed impact* curve where behavior problems may remain low over the initial months, but increase suddenly in the latter half of the year as the infant transitions from a dependent, fairly immobile social partner to a walking, talking, and potentially antagonizing brother or sister. In the current study, we tested for all of these potential change trajectories using linear, quadratic, and specialized contrasts in our growth models to capture the various ways children might respond to the birth of a sibling over the course of the ensuing year.

Methodological Limitations of Current Research on the Transition to Siblinghood

There are several serious limitations to the current base of studies on the transition to siblinghood that we believe the Family Transitions Study and our conceptualizations of adaptation and maladaptation can remedy (Volling, 2012). First, few developmental studies actually exist that address children's adjustment after the transition to siblinghood and there has been a noticeable gap over the years (e.g., only one study during the period from 2000 to 2011; see review by Volling, 2012). Second, most studies were conducted and published before the 1984 special issue of *Child Development* was published, in which the developmental psychopathology perspective was clearly laid out for a generation of researchers to follow (see Cicchetti, 1984; Sroufe & Rutter, 1984). None of the extant studies (e.g., Dunn & Kendrick, 1982; Nadelman & Begun, 1982; Stewart, Mobley, Tuyl, & Salvador, 1987; Gottlieb & Mendelson, 1990) was informed by a developmental psychopathology perspective, so many of these studies were focused on children's maladjustment, psychosocial crises (e.g., regression), and distress reactions to the birth of an infant sibling. Third, most studies included assessments of childhood adjustment of unknown psychometric validity, so it was impossible to know whether any changes in children's adjustment were in the nonclinical (i.e., normative) or clinical range and, thus, a cause for concern. Fourth, most studies were unable to examine longitudinal trajectories of behavioral changes because many studies included mothers' retrospective, postbirth reports of change in children's problematic behaviors or only used a simple prebirth (1 month before) and postbirth (1 month after) research design. The ability to detect different trajectory patterns after the transition was not possible because at least three timepoints, preferably more, would be needed to model complex change trajectories. Several studies (Dunn & Kendrick, 1982; Kramer & Gottman, 1992; Stewart, 1990) had repeated assessments spanning the first year and beyond, but the sample sizes ranged from 30 to 41 families and did not allow an extensive examination of individual differences in developmental change trajectories. Despite these limitations, there is some evidence suggesting that individual differences in children's behavioral trajectories after the transition to siblinghood should be expected.

Empirical Evidence of Change Trajectories After the Birth of a Sibling

The work of Dunn and Kendrick (1982) is probably the most relevant and extensive documentation of how children fare after the transition. In this study of 41 working- and middle-class British families, older children had very different reactions to the sibling birth, leading Dunn to conclude that there were wide individual differences in children's reactions and that no single indictor of adjustment could capture these differences. Dunn, Kendrick, and MacNamee (1981), for instance, found that mothers reported a range of problematic behaviors expressed by children, including clinging, withdrawal, opposition, sleep problems, toileting accidents, and feeding difficulties, and these behavioral changes ranged from rarely to frequently in the month following the birth.

Stewart et al. (1987) followed 41 two-parent families in the United States using the same design as the Family Transitions Study in the current report (prenatal, 1, 4, 8, and 12 months). Using maternal reports of children's anxiety, aggression, and confrontations, and regressive behaviors (e.g., using baby talk, wanting a bottle or pacifier) at 1, 4, 8, and 12 months after the birth, they reported that the most frequent (i.e., normative) pattern of behavior problems (51%) was one in which children were high on all problem behaviors 1 month after the birth, high only on anxiety 4 months after the birth, with confrontations remaining high at 8 and 12 months, particularly with the sibling. An additional 12% showed a pattern where children were high on all behavior problems initially at 1 month and continued to remain high only on confrontations throughout the study. Only 10% ($n = 4$) of children evinced few problems after the birth. These initial results examining trajectories in this relatively small sample suggest that we should expect individual differences in trajectories of problem behaviors, that these trajectories may look different depending on the problem behavior being examined, and that most children were initially high on all problem behaviors examined shortly after the infant's birth at 1 month. Unfortunately, in both studies, comparable assessments of children's problem behavior before the birth were not available to know whether those children high after the birth were also high before the birth, or whether there were changes in problem behavior after the birth. Given the stability in individual differences across transitions, such as the transition to parenthood (e.g., Belsky, Spanier, & Rovine, 1983; Cowan & Cowan, 2000), it would not be surprising to see stability in individual differences in children's adjustment after the transition to siblinghood, so a prebirth assessment is critical for this determination.

Volling's (2012) recent review of the longitudinal changes in the firstborn's behavioral adjustment after the birth of an infant sibling did not find strong evidence that most children showed significant increases in problem behaviors. The few studies to date do suggest that some children may indeed have difficulties after the birth of an infant sibling, but the significant limitations of this body of research leave many unanswered questions that the current study was designed to address. The sample of the Family Transitions Study included 241 families preparing for the arrival of their second child, who were assessed initially before the birth in the last trimester of the mother's pregnancy, included information from mothers and fathers using a well-established, psychometrically validated measure of childhood behavior problems, the Child Behavior Checklist (CBCL: 1.5-5; Achenbach & Rescorla, 2000), followed families longitudinally over five timepoints (prenatal, 1, 4, 8, and 12 months), including an initial period shortly after birth (1 month) to capture adjustment and disorganization, and subsequent periods through the year following the birth to capture patterns of resilience and adaptation, as well as long-term persistent behavioral difficulties indicative of maladaptation and developmental crisis.

The first aim of the current study was to examine individual differences in firstborn children's emotional and behavioral adjustment using group-based trajectory analyses that would identify groups (or classes) of children showing different change trajectories starting in the last trimester of the mother's pregnancy with the second child and throughout the year following the sibling's birth. We focused on the seven syndrome scales of the CBCL, rather than the broadband internalizing and externalizing scales, because of the documented variability in children's responses across different domains of problem behavior (see Dunn et al., 1981), as well as our ultimate goal of providing parents and professionals with recommendations for preparing for the transition. We believed it was important to specify precisely which behaviors appeared to be most problematic (e.g., aggression or anxiety), were subject to change across the transition, and might reveal different change trajectories. For instance, one could argue that different patterns of change might describe children's aggression and anxiety, which may have different consequences for children's emerging sibling relationship. Dunn and Kendrick (1982), for instance, found that it was the group of children who showed increases in withdrawal, not angry resistance, shortly after the birth who would later go on to develop problematic sibling relationships at 14 months.

A person-centered approach with longitudinal data allows the integration of several fundamental principles of a developmental psychopathology perspective: (1) the examination of normative patterns of change; (2) the search for individual differences; and (3) the documentation of different developmental pathways indicative of adaptation and maladaptation (Cummings et al., 2000). The modeling of different change trajectories that classifies individuals into groups sharing similar trajectory patterns can distinguish "normative" developmental patterns that may characterize the majority of children, but it can also identify smaller subsets of children following riskier trajectories (i.e., individual differences) indicative of maladaptation (Rutter, 1996). In a community-based sample as the one used in the current research, we would expect few children to fall in the clinical or borderline clinical ranges for problem behaviors, but nevertheless, these smaller risk groups indicative of maladaptation may be the groups we most wish to identify as targets for future intervention efforts. Therefore, even if some groups consisted of few children, we argue that these small groups are important to maintain in analyses because they may be the children displaying the most severe maladaptation after the birth and, hence, deserving of closer scrutiny for purposes of identifying risk and protective factors.

RISK AND PROTECTIVE FACTORS PREDICTING DEVELOPMENTAL CHANGE

Should different groups of children be found based on different change patterns, the second goal of this investigation was to examine child (e.g., age, gender, temperament, social understanding), parent (e.g., parental efficacy, attachment security), and family characteristics (e.g., marital quality, family stress) before the birth as predictors of different patterns of adjustment. Volling (2005) proposed the developmental ecological systems model that described changes in the older child's adjustment across the transition and identified child, parent, and family contextual factors that predicted individual differences in children's adjustment trajectories over the course of the first year after the infant sibling's birth.

The Developmental Ecological Systems Model

Volling's (2005) developmental ecological systems model to explain changes after the birth of a sibling was based on Bronfenbrenner's (1979) ecological model of human development with its focus on multiple levels of ecological contexts impinging on children and their parents, as well as family systems' perspectives with their focus on the interdependencies in family relationships, such as the marital, parent–child and sibling subsystems (e.g., Cox & Paley, 2003). In this model, the child is nested within a larger family system which, in turn, is nested within larger ecological and cultural contexts. Changes in one aspect of the environment and/or individual coincide with changes in other aspects of the ecological context. For instance, changes in children's adjustment may be due, in part, to the changes that are also co-occurring elsewhere in the family system, such as changes in the parent–firstborn relationship, the coparenting relationship, or maternal depression in the postpartum period. Rather than viewing children's adjustment as a direct function of the arrival of the newborn sibling, children's behavior may be indirectly influenced by the changes ongoing in other aspects of the family. This model also incorporates the concepts of multiple determinants (Belsky, 1984) and cumulative risk (Sameroff, 2000) in that the firstborn's developmental outcomes following the birth are related to how many individual (e.g., temperamental reactivity, maternal depression) and contextual (e.g., marital conflict) risk factors are present and changing for better or worse over time. In addition, the presence of promotive factors (e.g., father support) may offset or protect the child from experiencing significant emotional distress and behavioral difficulties (see Volling, 2005, for a thorough discussion).

Similar to the work of Belsky (1984), the developmental ecological systems framework focuses on three domains that are influential in predicting child and family adjustment across the transition to siblinghood: (1) child characteristics (e.g., temperament, age, gender); (2) parent characteristics (e.g., parenting, mental health); and (3) social-contextual characteristics (e.g., partner relationships, social support, work-family relations). Children's temperamental characteristics in the form of negative emotionality and behavioral inhibition have been related to both internalizing and externalizing behavior problems (Leve, Kim, & Pears, 2005; Williams et al., 2009) and so were included in the pool of variables for our prediction analysis. Further, parenting behaviors (e.g., harsh, punitive) and parent–child attachment relationships have been linked repeatedly in prior research on children's problem behavior (Fearon, Bakermans-Kranenburg, Van IJzendoorn, Lapsley, & Roisman, 2010; Groh, Roisman, van IJzendoorn, Bakermans-Kranenburg, & Fearon, 2012; Mackenbach et al., 2014), as has the quality of marital interaction and, more recently, coparenting (e.g., Cummings & Davies, 2011; Schoppe-Sullivan, Weldon, Cook, Davis, & Buckley, 2009) so these family-level variables were also included. Finally, we included work-family stress and social support as social-contextual variables, as well as parental age, education, and family income as demographic characteristics. As a result, we compiled a range of child, parent, and family contextual variables that reflected the social ecology of the developing child over this transition and provided us with the means of targeting risk and protective factors for each of the individual behavioral trajectories uncovered in the following chapters. In each chapter, we review the available evidence pertaining to the specific child, parent, and family characteristics predicting children's behavioral and emotional difficulties. Our goal in the prediction analysis was to uncover targets for intervention that could be identified before the infant sibling's birth so we could eventually assist families undergoing this transition. Although we acknowledge that changes in developmental trajectories may coincide with other changes ongoing in the family before and after the birth, our focus in this monograph is only on pre-birth predictors because of our overriding concern to identify and prevent problems before they occur.

Longitudinal research often follows families over extended periods of time and given the expense and length of time often required to conduct such research, it is often the case that large amounts of information are collected on family members. The Family Transitions Study is no exception. In line with the developmental ecological systems model guiding this research program, we collected large amounts of information on multiple levels of social influence (e.g., parenting, marriage, social networks, work environments) and the individual functioning of two parents (mothers and fathers) and two children (older siblings and infants) using reports from mothers and fathers. Although such an approach allows a wealth of information from which to ascertain developmental determinants of behavioral change, it also poses logistical complications for data analyses and how one should choose the best set of predictor variables from the data available. Even though we pared down the possible predictors to those child, parent, and family variables identified in prior research on young children's behavioral difficulties and the transition to siblinghood, we were still confronted with a mountain of information from which to choose (e.g., mothers' *and* fathers' reports of temperament for negative emotionality and behavioral inhibition). For present purposes, we relied on exploratory data mining procedures (McArdle & Ritschard, 2013) that allowed us to search for the most significant predictors of behavioral change trajectories from a large pool of possible child, parent, and family contextual predictors that were available to us at the prenatal timepoint.

Finding the "best predictors," not just any predictors, was important to accomplish the fundamental goal for developing this study in the first place; to provide a best set of practices for parents and practitioners that would help identify which areas of family life needed to be targeted with respect to sibling preparation or prebirth interventions for children and their parents according to specific needs of the families. Further, we wanted to identify these targets before birth if possible to prevent child adjustment difficulties after the sibling's birth, rather than waiting for problems to emerge once the infant was born. Given that individual differences are the norm in describing children's reactions to a sibling's birth, a one-model-fits-all approach to intervention may not adequately meet the needs of all families. Seidman and French (2004) provided a set of guidelines for determining whether findings supported the need for universal prevention programs offered to everyone experiencing a developmental transition or for more selective programs tailored to the needs and risks of a specific group. Each group of families identified may have unique needs and prevention programs may need to be developed to address these specific needs. Further, different child and family factors may predict different sorts of behavioral and emotional challenges. For instance, what predicts children's withdrawal and anxiety may be different from what predicts children's aggression. By choosing a priori only one child (e.g., gender), one parent (e.g., attachment to mother), and one family variable (e.g., marital conflict) from our existing data set for analyses, we may find what best predicts one group, but not the other. Exploratory data mining procedures allowed us to create one pool of candidate predictors representing child, parent, and family contextual variables based on the developmental ecological systems model, and then to search systematically through all these predictors for each of the seven subscales to identify the best set of predictors for each problem behavior examined.

DEVELOPMENTAL CONSEQUENCES OF CHILDREN'S ADJUSTMENT FOR SIBLING RELATIONSHIPS

Despite the mixed evidence on whether or not there are substantial changes in the firstborn's adjustment from before to after the sibling's birth, there is information pertaining to the development of the sibling relationship in the first year. We view the early interest in the infant and the eventual development of friendly or hostile sibling interaction over the year following the birth as an indicator of children's psychological adjustment to the transition to siblinghood (Oh, Volling, & Gonzalez, 2015; Song & Volling, 2015). Individual differences in the older siblings' reactions to the infant have consequences for the developing sibling relationship and the subsequent development of the children (Dunn, 1983; Song & Volling, 2015). It is widely acknowledged that children develop within a family context and that the quality of the children's family relationships are influential in determining young children's socioemotional development (Cox & Paley, 2003), yet few developmental studies have seriously examined the quality of young children's sibling relationships and the manner in which these relationships contribute to individual outcomes (Bedford & Volling, 2003). This is unfortunate because much of Dunn's earlier work (e.g., Dunn & Kendrick, 1982; Dunn & Munn, 1985; Herrera & Dunn, 1997; Youngblade & Dunn, 1995) documented the importance of the quality of the interaction between young siblings for the development of children's social understanding, cooperative play, and conflict-management skills. For instance, those preschool children who engaged in more pretend play and more positive social exchanges with their older siblings had higher levels of emotional understanding (Dunn, Brown, Slomkowski, Tesla, & Youngblade, 1991; Youngblade & Dunn, 1995).

Even toddlers appear to benefit from nurturant and affectionate interactions with an older sibling. Dunn & Munn (1986) reported that 2-year-old toddlers' sophisticated use of conflict and cooperative behaviors was associated with the older siblings' prosocial behavior 6 months earlier. Moreover, the quality of young children's sibling relationships remained relatively stable over time such that children with highly conflictual relationships in early childhood tended to have similar types of relationships in middle-childhood and adolescence (Dunn, Slomkowski, & Beardsall, 1994; Kramer & Kowal, 2005). Warm and cooperative sibling relationships can be a developmental support and contribute to children's social and emotional development (Dunn, 1988). Yet, aggressive and hostile sibling relationships can be a risk factor for the development of behavior problems that can eventually lead to children's diminished social competence with peers as they enter school (Garcia, Shaw, Winslow, & Yaggi, 2000; McElwain & Volling, 2005). For instance, Tremblay et al. (1999) documented that the presence of an older sibling was a significant risk factor in predicting the developmental trajectories of highly aggressive toddlers. This is also consistent with Patterson's (1986) earlier work finding that coercive sibling relationships in preadolescence and adolescence served as a training ground for the development of aggressive behavior that was then carried over into the children's peer relationships in school.

Early sibling relationship quality appears to predict subsequent sibling relationship quality in several studies. Stillwell and Dunn (1985), for instance, found that those older siblings showing friendly behavior toward their younger 14-month-old sibling made more positive comments about the sibling approximately 3 years later when the older siblings were 6 years old. Interestingly, this friendly sibling behavior at 14 months after the infant's birth could be predicted from children's initial reaction to the newborn sibling within weeks after the sibling's birth. Older siblings who had shown a positive interest in the baby 3 weeks after the birth were also more likely to join positively in interaction between mother and the infant 14 months after the birth, whereas those older children who had initially been difficult and demanding after the birth were also more negative and demanding when mothers played with their younger sibling 14 months later (Kendrick & Dunn, 1982).

Given the developmental significance of the sibling relationship for young children's social and emotional development and the long-term stability of the affective tone of this relationship beginning as early as the first 3 weeks after the infant's birth, it seems especially relevant that the earliest origins of this relationship be examined. Clearly, children's initial reactions to their infant sibling can be viewed as the earliest point in which to observe the development of the sibling relationship. Several small-scale studies have documented the affective quality of interaction between the older sibling and the infant at various timepoints throughout the first year (e.g., Dunn & Kendrick, 1982; Kramer & Gottman, 1992), yet larger, longitudinal studies are needed in order to examine what predicts stability or change in sibling relationship quality and what the developmental consequences are for both the young infant and the firstborn of having either a friendly or difficult sibling relationship at the end of the infant's first year. A final goal of this research program, then, was to determine what the consequences were for children's developing sibling relationship at the end of the first year for children experiencing different developmental trajectories of emotional and behavioral difficulties in the year following the birth. Several recent reviews find strong support of relations between the development of children's externalizing and internalizing problem behaviors, and the quality of the sibling relationship (Buist, Deković, & Prinzie, 2013; Dirks, Persram, Recchia, & Howe, 2015) so we expected to find similar relations between problematic sibling relationships and children's emotional and behavioral adjustment.

The Family Transitions Study

The current study is the first longitudinal examination of children's behavioral and emotional adjustment following the birth of a second child using a large sample of 241 families across five repeated assessments starting in the last trimester of the mother's pregnancy with a second child and following families throughout the year after the birth at 1, 4, 8, and 12 months postpartum. In addition to the sample size and longitudinal design, there were several other unique strengths of the study. First, the study relied on multiple informants for information on children's behaviors. Specifically, fathers' reports of children's problematic behaviors were collected at all time-points, along with mothers' reports, and used to create robust composites of behavioral change so information was not based solely on a single informant. Second, we used a well-validated and widely used measure of children's behavioral adjustment, the Child Behavior Checklist (CBCL 1.5-5; Achenbach & Rescorla, 2000) to assess children's emotional and behavioral difficulties rather than relying on retrospective maternal reports or questionnaires of unknown reliability and validity. Because the CBCL has known cut-offs indicative of clinical and borderline-clinical levels of behavioral and emotional difficulties, we could examine whether changes were a cause of clinical concern. Third, the relatively large sample allowed us to take a person-centered statistical approach in which we were able to identify different patterns of intraindividual change (i.e., developmental trajectories) that were shared by groups of children. Fourth, we used statistical modeling of latent growth curves to test specific theory-driven developmental patterns of adaptation and maladaptation discussed earlier. Fifth, we used prenatal indicators of child, parent, and family functioning to predict the resulting trajectories so that we could isolate those factors found to be most critical for determining risky trajectories in an effort to target intervention and prevention efforts. Finally, we used the trajectory patterns found over the transition and following year to determine whether there were ramifications for the developing sibling relationship at 12 months.

We present the methods and procedures for the study as a whole before moving on to a description detailing the statistical approach used to identify developmental change trajectories for firstborn children. In each of the chapters, one devoted to each of the seven syndrome scales of the CBCL, we review the existing literature on normative patterns and individual differences in the behavioral and emotional problems of early childhood, then move to the risks and protective factors predicting these behaviors before elucidating any links between children's problem behaviors and sibling relationship quality. It should be noted upfront that there is more information for some of these areas (e.g., aggression and sibling conflict) than others (e.g., sleep problems), and this is noted in the presentation and discussion of our findings. We then move to a presentation of the results from the growth mixture modeling of the seven CBCL subscales organizing them with respect to *externalizing* (aggression, attention problems), *internalizing* (anxiety/depression emotional reactivity, withdrawal), and *physical problems* (somatic complaints, sleep problems), with a separate chapter devoted to each. Within each chapter we present the group-based trajectories (i.e., classes) that capture the individual differences in children's adjustment, the child, parent, and family contextual variables from the prenatal timepoint that predict the different groups, and lastly, any findings linking the trajectories of problem behaviors to the sibling relationship outcomes at 12 months of age. In the general discussion, we will return to our decision to analyze individual syndrome scales rather than the broadband internalizing and externalizing dimensions, and what we have learned about children having difficulties after the birth of their infant sibling.

II. METHODS AND PROCEDURES FOR THE FAMILY TRANSITIONS STUDY

Wonjung Oh, Brenda L. Volling, Richard Gonzalez, Lauren Rosenberg, and Ju-Hyun Song

This article is part of the issue "Developmental Trajectories of Children's Adjustment across the Transition to Siblinghood: Pre-Birth Predictors and Sibling Outcomes at One Year" Volling, Gonzalez, Oh, Song, Yu, Rosenberg, Kuo, Thomason, Beyers-Carlson, Safyer, and Stevenson (Issue Authors). For a full listing of articles in this issue, see: http://onlinelibrary.wiley.com/doi/10.1111/mono.v82.3/issuetoc.

PARTICIPANTS

Participants included 241 families, including mothers, fathers, and their firstborn children. Families were initially recruited through flyers posted in local obstetric clinics, hospitals, pediatricians' offices, child care centers, child-birth education classes, and local newspaper advertisements. The majority of participants (64%) were recruited through obstetric clinics; local media provided 30% of our participants, and word of mouth accounted for 6%. To be eligible for the study, families had to meet the following criteria: (1) the mother was pregnant with her second child; (2) the father was the biological father of the second child (98% were also the biological father of the firstborn); (3) the mother and the father were living together (99% were married); (4) the older sibling was between the ages of 1 and 5 years at the time of the infant's birth; and (5) the older sibling did not have chronic and

---

Corresponding author: Correspondence concerning the Family Transitions Study should be addressed to Brenda L. Volling, University of Michigan, Center for Human Growth and Development, 300 N. Ingalls, Ann Arbor, MI 48109-5406; email: volling@umich.edu

DOI: 10.1111/mono.12308

severe physical, mental, or developmental problems. Upon birth, infants with chronic health problems or identifiable disabilities/anomalies, prematurity (<37 weeks) or a birth weight less than 2,500 g were not included. All births were singleton. Of the 408 families who contacted the project office and met study criteria, 241 (59.1%) agreed to participate. Most families cited the time commitment as the major reason for not participating. During the first prenatal home visit, research staff explained the study in greater detail during which parents had the opportunity to ask questions before they signed consent forms for the study, which was approved by the Institutional Review Board of the Medical School at the University of Michigan. Families were compensated $300 for participating in all phases of the study. The attrition rate was 15.8% across the 12 months of the study. The final sample of 241 families was chosen to account for a 15% attrition rate across the study period with the goal of having at least 200 families available for planned analyses. We chose 200 families in order to have an 0.80 power to detect small-to-medium effects using two-tailed alpha $= .05$ (e.g., $r = 0.19$, two groups $d = 0.4$, two times $d = 0.2$, an ANOVA effect size $f = 0.23$ with four groups). At 12 months, 203 families remained in the study.

Characteristics of Family Households

During the prenatal home visit, parents provided demographic information on their education, occupations, family income, age, and race/ethnicity. Parents' length of marriage ranged from 0.58 to 20 years ($M = 5.77$, $SD = 2.74$). Families were primarily middle- to upper-middle class. The mode of household income was $60,000–$99,999 (37.8%); 32.8% of families had a household income greater than $100,000, 27.8% of families earned $20,000–$59,999; and 1.7% of families earned less than $20,000.

Parent Characteristics

At the prenatal timepoint, the mean age of mothers was 31.6 years ($SD = 4.22$) and the mean age of fathers was 33.2 years ($SD = 4.78$). The sample was well educated, with the majority of parents earning a bachelor's degree or higher (83.9% of mothers; 79.2% of fathers).

The racial breakdown of the sample was primarily European American (89.6% of mothers, 89.2% of fathers), followed by African American (5.4% of mothers, 5.0% of fathers), Asian/Asian-American (2.9% of mothers, 3.7% of fathers), and other (2.1% of mothers, 2.1% of fathers). Of the total sample, 3.7% of mothers and 2.9% of fathers were Hispanic. The sample was recruited from four counties in southeastern Michigan. According to the U.S. Census Bureau, families across these counties were, on average, 77% Caucasian/ White (range: 52–97%), 10% African American (range: 0.4–40.5%), 4% Asian (range: 1–8%), and 1% other (range: 0.4–1%); 4% (2–5%) of the population in these counties identified as Hispanic or Latino. Therefore, the racial and ethnic background of the sample was fairly representative of the counties from which they were recruited.

The majority of fathers were employed full-time (92.1%), with 7.8% of fathers being employed part-time, staying home full-time, or unemployed. Nearly a third of the mothers were employed full-time at the prenatal time point (35.7%), 29.9% of mothers were employed part-time ($M = 18.65$ hr/week, $SD = 9.02$ hr/week), 32.8% were staying home full-time, and 1.7% were unemployed.

Parents' occupational prestige was coded according to the National Compensation Survey from the U.S. Department of Labor (Chao & Utgoff, 2003). Mothers who reported they were stay-at-home mothers or unemployed were not asked for a job title. Parents who reported that being a student was their occupation were assigned a code of "student" (2.5% of mothers, 7.8% of fathers). Four mothers and two fathers reported an occupation that was uncodeable (e.g., fundraising, tutor). Most parents (58% of mothers, 47% of fathers) had professional, specialty, or technical careers followed by executive, administrative, and managerial positions (17.2% of mothers, 25.4% of fathers), administrative support positions (10.8% mothers, 2.6% of fathers), service occupations (7.0% of mothers, 4.3% of fathers), sales (2.5% of mothers, 6.0% of fathers), and precision production and repair (0% of mothers and 4.7% of fathers) with less than 1% in occupations classified as handlers, cleaners, and laborers.

Firstborn Children

Of the recruited sample, 54.4% ($n = 131$) of firstborns were girls. On average, firstborns were 2.5 years old at the time of the infant's birth ($M = 31.17$ months; $SD = 10.13$ months). At the prenatal time point, 149 (62%) parents reported their firstborn children were in childcare. Of these families, 87 (58.4%) utilized school-based childcare (e.g., preschool, kindergarten), 7 (4.7%) utilized an in-home care provider, 16 (10.7%) utilized an out of home private provider, 17 (11.4%) utilized a relative, and 22 (14.8%) used a combination of two or more forms of childcare. Of the firstborns in childcare, 72.5% ($n = 108$) were in part-time care (fewer than 40 hr per week) and 27.5% ($n = 41$) were in full-time care (more than or equal to 40 hr per week). The average amount of time per week in childcare was 24.16 hr ($SD = 15.18$).

One month after the birth, parents were asked open-ended questions about how they prepared the firstborn for the birth of the second child, which ranged from sibling preparation classes at the local hospital to showing the child his or her own baby pictures. Table 1 provides detailed information on the different

TABLE 1

ACTIVITIES PARENTS REPORTED TO PREPARE THE FIRSTBORN FOR THE BIRTH OF A SIBLING

Activity	N	$\%$
Media	195	87.8
Books/magazines	160	72.1
Discussion	160	72.1
Changes to the home	55	24.8
Sibling preparation class	47	20.9
Interacted with other infants	31	14.0
Movie/television show	26	11.7
Bought doll	24	11.0
Gifts for child or infant	20	9.0
Took child to prenatal doctor's visits	11	5.0
Tummy interaction	11	5.0
Websites	9	4.1
Arranged for social support	7	3.2
Showed pictures	7	3.2
Religious activity	5	2.3
Specified "nothing"	4	1.8

types of activities families used to prepare firstborns for the birth of their siblings. Most parents (88%) relied on different forms of media (i.e., books, videos, websites) or discussion (72%). Very few families (21%) actually went to hospital-based classes designed to prepare children for the arrival of an infant sibling.

Infant Siblings

Of the 225 families remaining at 1-month, 55% of the infant siblings born were boys ($n = 124$). The gender constellation of sibling dyads (child-infant) consisted of 56 girl–girl, 45 boy–girl, 66 girl–boy, and 58 boy–boy dyads. Gender constellation of the sibling dyad was unrelated to any of the classes identified in our group-based trajectory analyses (all χ^2 nonsignificant), so is not discussed further.

Characteristics of Pregnancy and Birth

The majority of parents reported that both parents wanted and planned for the second child (85.5%), and 11.2% of parents reported that both parents wanted the second child but not right now. Only 3.2% of parents reported that one or both parents had not wanted the second child. Nearly all of the fathers (98%) attended the birth, whereas only 3% of the children attended. Most (96.4%) infants were born at a hospital, 3.1% were born at home, and one infant was born at a birthing center. Mothers were away from home for a mean of 2.28 days ($SD = 1.13$) for the birth. Most of the children

(91.5%) visited their mother and the infant in the hospital at least once. Most infants were born vaginally (75%), and the remainder were born through Caesarean section (25%). All infants were born full-term, were singleton births, and at a healthy weight ($M = 7.96$ lbs, $SD = 1.13$ lbs) and length ($M = 20.38$ inches, $SD = 1.07$ inches).

STUDY DESIGN AND PROCEDURES

Participation in the study began during the last trimester of the mother's pregnancy with the second child ($M = 33.8$ gestation weeks, $SD = 3.3$ weeks) and continued throughout the first year after the infant's birth. Data were collected at five time points (prenatal, 1 month, 4 months, 8 months, and 12 months postpartum) using multiple methods, including behavioral observations of parent–child and family interaction, couple interviews, assessments of children's social-cognitive understanding, and parental self-reports.

These timepoints were chosen to coincide with significant developmental milestones in infant development and to correspond with different phases of the family adjustment and adaptation response based on theories of family stress and resilience (see also Stewart, 1990). These were also the five timepoints used by Stewart (1990) in one of the only longitudinal investigations on the transition with more than two timepoints, which allowed us to compare findings across studies. The prenatal timepoint provided a prebirth (i.e., baseline) assessment point. The period between prenatal and 1 month corresponded to an immediate postbirth period or adjustment phase, whereas the period from 1 month to 4 months corresponded with a restructuring and adaptation period. Further, significant developmental changes occur in infant social behavior and motor develop-ment at both 4 and 8 months of age (e.g., smiling at 4 months and stranger wariness and infant locomotion at 8 months). These social and motoric changes typical of infant development from 4 to 8 months provided more opportunities for infants to engage in family interactions than was possible at 1 month. Finally, the 12-month timepoint marked 1 year after the birth and is also significant for the development of infant–parent attachment relation-ships (Ainsworth, Blehar, Waters, & Wall, 1978).

Home visits were conducted at each timepoint to collect interview data, observations of family interaction, and child assessments of children's social understanding. A set of questionnaires was left for both mothers and fathers to complete after home visits. An additional home visit was conducted at the prenatal, 4- and 12-month timepoints to conduct the Attachment Q-Sort in relation to the older child (Waters & Deane, 1985) with mothers and fathers, and a second social understanding assessment with children. Each home visit lasted approximately 2 hr.

In the first set of analyses, parent reports of children's problem behavior across the five time-points were used to identify developmental trajectories of problematic behavior before and after the sibling's birth. In the second set of analyses, prenatally collected mothers' and fathers' reports of child, parent, and family factors and observations of mother–child, father–child, coparenting and marital interaction during the prenatal home visit were used to predict the different trajectory patterns. In the third set of analyses, trajectory patterns were used to predict children's relationship with their infant sibling at 12 months based on parent reports.

Children's Behavioral and Emotional Adjustment

Both mothers and fathers completed the Child Behavior Checklist (CBCL/$1\frac{1}{2}$–5; Achenbach & Rescorla, 2000) for their firstborn children before and after the sibling's birth (i.e., at prenatal, 1-, 4-, 8-, and 12-month timepoints). The CBCL/$1\frac{1}{2}$–5 is one of the most widely used standardized measures in child psychology for evaluating maladaptive behavioral and emotional problems in preschool children between the ages of $1\frac{1}{2}$ and 5 years (the age of most children in our study), with dedicated clinical cut-off scores at the 97.5th percentile and borderline clinical at the 92.5th percentile. We chose this measure intentionally to capture the extent and severity of maladaptive behavior after the sibling's birth and whether there was evidence to suggest that children were reaching clinical or borderline clinical levels of problem behavior in response to the birth, in contrast to earlier studies using measures with no known standardized norms.

Parents rated 99 items about their children's problem behavior on a 3-point Likert scale from $0 = not\ true$ to $2 = very\ true$. The CBCL/$1\frac{1}{2}$–5 yields seven syndrome scales: (1) *emotionally reactive* (e.g., sudden changes in mood or feelings; α over timepoints $= 0.51–0.69$, $M = 0.62$); (2) *anxious/depressed* (e.g., gets too upset when separated from parents; $\alpha = 0.52–0.68$, $M = 0.59$); (3) *somatic complaints* (e.g., aches or pains without medical cause; $\alpha = 0.35–0.52$, $M = 0.47$); (4) *withdrawn* (e.g., avoids looking others in the eye; $\alpha = 0.48–0.54$, $M = 0.53$); (5) *sleep problems* (e.g., has trouble getting to sleep; $\alpha = 0.70–0.80$, $M = 0.74$); (6) *attention problems* (e.g., quickly shifts from one activity to another; $\alpha = 0.62–0.70$, $M = 0.66$); and (7) *aggressive behavior* (e.g., gets in many fights; $\alpha = 0.85–0.89$, $M = 0.87$). In addition, the CBCL yields two broad band scores: *Internalizing problems* including emotionally reactive, anxious/depressed, somatic complaints, and withdrawn; and *externalizing problems* including attention problems and aggressive behavior. For the current report, though, we examined the individual syndrome scores rather than the broadband emotional and behavioral dimensions because they closely represented problematic behaviors described by parents in prior studies of the transition (e.g., sleep problems, anxiety and clinginess, aggression and opposition) and provided a better means of attempting to replicate these earlier findings. Ivanova et al. (2010) provided further psychometric support for the configural invariance of the factor structure of the seven syndrome scales for 19,106 children aged 1.5–5 years across 23 societies, as well as mean item loadings (0.43–0.72) comparable to the magnitude of the mean alphas reported here across the five timepoints of this study. Further, prior studies examining the emergence of psychopathology in toddlerhood have also relied on many of the individual syndrome scales such as aggression, anxiety, sleep problems, and somatic complaints (e.g., Shaw, Keenan, Vondra, Delliquardi, & Giovannelli, 1997; Shaw, Owens, Giovannelli, & Winslow, 2001; Weinraub et al., 2012; Wolff et al., 2009).

Correlations between mothers' and fathers' reports on the CBCL syndrome scales revealed consistent, significant correlations in the low to moderate range across the five timepoints: (1) emotionally reactive, $r = 0.20$–0.39, $M = 0.29$, all $ps < .01$; (2) anxious/depressed, $r = 0.27$–0.38, $M = 0.32$, all $ps < .001$; (3) somatic complaints, $r = 0.39$–0.53, $M = 0.46$, all $ps < .001$; (4) withdrawal, $r = 0.26$–0.35, $M = 0.31$, all $ps < .001$; (5) sleep problems, $r = 0.57$–0.67, $M = 0.63$, all $ps < .001$; (6) attention problems, $r = 0.38$–0.46, $M = 0.41$, all $ps < .001$; and (7) aggressive behavior, $r = 0.34$–0.48, $M = 0.42$, all $ps < .001$. Because mothers' and fathers' reports were significantly correlated across all timepoints and because we wanted to create robust composites that were not based on a single-reporter, mothers' and fathers' scores were averaged to create one composite score for each child at each timepoint in order to increase construct validity (Rushton, Brainerd, & Pressley, 1983). These composites are subsequently referred to as the CBCL subscales.

CHILD, PARENT, AND FAMILY PREDICTORS AT THE PRENATAL TIMEPOINT

All antecedent variables used to predict the trajectories of problematic behavior were measured at the prenatal timepoint. In line with the developmental ecological systems perspective, prenatal predictors were child, parent, and family contextual characteristics that were potential risk and protective factors that could explain children's adjustment after the birth of a sibling. We used the following conventions when creating child, parent, and family composites. We averaged across mothers' and fathers' reports for child characteristics in order to create more robust composites that were not based on a single informant. We also averaged mother and father reports and behavioral observations for dyadic, couple-level, relationship constructs such as coparenting and marital relationships. Because of our interest in family systems and the role of fathers in supporting children's adjustment across the transition to siblinghood, we kept each of the measures of parenting and parent characteristics separate for mothers and fathers.

Child Characteristics

Children's Temperament

The Child Behavior Questionnaire (CBQ: Rothbart, Ahadi, Hershey, & Fisher, 2001) was used to assess children's temperament. Mothers and fathers completed the anger/frustration and shyness subscales of the CBQ. Each item used a 7-point Likert scale (1 = *extremely untrue* to 7 = *extremely true*). Composite scores were created by averaging mothers' and father's reports on 13 items for "anger/frustration" ($\alpha = 0.77$ for mother, $\alpha = 0.73$ for father) and 13 items of "shyness" ($\alpha = 0.92$ for mother, $\alpha = 0.89$ for father). A higher score on "anger/frustration" reflected more negative affectivity related to interruption of ongoing tasks or goal blocking (e.g., has temper tantrums when s/he does not get what s/he wants; gets quite frustrated when prevented from doing something s/he wants to do). A higher score on "shyness" reflected slower or more inhibited speed of approach and discomfort in social situations (e.g., sometimes prefers to watch rather than join other children playing; gets embarrassed when strangers pay a lot of attention to her/him). We refer to anger/frustration as *negative emotionality* and shyness as *behavioral inhibition* throughout the remainder of the monograph.

Theory of Mind (ToM; Wellman & Liu, 2004)

At the prenatal timepoint, children completed the theory of mind scale to assess children's ability to understand another person's mental states. This scale consists of six subscales that are arranged in developmental sequence (1) *Not-Own Desire*: child judges that two people (the child vs. someone else) have different desires about the same objects; (2) *Not-Own Belief*: child judges that two people (the child vs. someone else) have different beliefs about the same object, when the child does not know which belief is true or false; (3) *Knowledge Access:* child sees what is in a box and judges the knowledge of another person who does not see what is in a box; (4) *Explicit False-Belief*: child judges how someone will search, given that person's mistaken belief; (5) *Contents False-Belief*: child judges another person's false belief about what is in a distinctive container when child knows that it contained something unexpected; and (6) *Hidden Emotion*: child judges that a person can feel one thing but display a different emotion. A composite score summed the number of the tasks for which children provided the correct answer (0–6).

Emotion Understanding

Children's understanding of emotions was assessed at the prenatal timepoint using a series of established tasks to assess nine areas that increased in difficulty level to capture the range of emotional understanding for 1- to 5-year-old children (see Pons, Harris, & de Rosnay, 2004 for a similar strategy for older children): (1) Denham's (1986) *affective labeling* (4 expressive-items: e.g., "Can you show me the happy face?" and four receptive items; e.g., "How does Jenny/Johnny feel when she/he wears this face?"); (2) Denham's (1986) *affective-perspective taking* (stereotypical reactions; four stories); (3) Wellman and Woolley's (1990) *desire-based emotion task* (three stories); (4) Denham's *nonstereotypical reactions* (four stories); (5) Vinden's (1999) *belief-based emotion* tasks; (6) *false-belief explanation*; (7) *false-belief prediction*; (8) *emotion display rules knowledge* (three stories from Jones, Abbey, & Cumberland, 1998); and (9) Gordis's (1989) *mixed emotions* task (three stories). These tasks were administered and coded according to Denham (1986) and Wellman and Woolley's schemes (1990). The Gordis's task was coded following a scoring system used by Maguire and Dunn (1997). A composite score was created by summing across the nine tasks for a total emotional understanding score ranging from 0 to 9. Higher scores reflected greater emotion understanding.

Parenting and Parent Characteristics

Attitudes Toward Physical Punishment

Mothers and fathers completed the 10-item Attitudes toward Physical Punishment Scale (Holden & Zambarano, 1992) to assess parents' attitudes toward spanking their children. Parents rated how strongly they agreed or disagreed with each statement using a 7-point Likert scale (1 = *strongly disagree* to 7 = *strongly agree*; e.g., "Spanking is a normal part of my parenting"). Composite scores were created by averaging the items for mothers and fathers separately (α for mothers and fathers = 0.71).

Parenting Self-Efficacy

To measure mothers' and fathers' parental self-efficacy with regard to their firstborn children, the Parental Locus of Control Scale was used (PLOC: Campis, Lyman, & Prentice-Dunn, 1986). Higher scores indicated that parents felt *less* confident in controlling their child's behavior, whereas lower scores indicated that parents felt efficacious in control of their child's behavior. Mothers and fathers completed the PLOC using a 5-point Likert scale ranging from 1 = *strongly disagree* to 5 = *strongly agree* on the firstborn child (e.g., "what I do has little effect on my older child's behavior"). Composite scores for parental efficacy were created by averaging the subscales "Parental Efficacy (10 items)," "Child Control of Parents' Life (7 items)," and "Parental Control of Child's Life ((10 items)," for mothers and fathers separately (α for mothers and fathers = 0.74 and 0.70, respectively).

Depression

Mothers and fathers completed the 21-item Beck Depression Inventory at the prenatal visit (BDI; Beck, Ward, Mendelson, Mock, & Erbaugh, 1961). The BDI has high internal reliability, well-documented concurrent and discriminate validity, and has been used in many studies of pregnant and postpartum women, as well as with men (Beck, Steer, & Carbin, 1988). Items were summed to create separate composite scores for mothers and fathers ($\alpha = 0.85$ and 0.79 for mothers and fathers, respectively).

Attachment Security

At the second home visit of the prenatal timepoint, mothers and fathers completed the Attachment Q-sort (AQS; Waters & Deane, 1985) to assess the security of the mother–firstborn and father–firstborn relationship. The AQS can be used with a wide age range of children with items appropriate for home observation. The AQS consists of 90 cards, each of which contains a statement about child behavior (e.g., when child returns to mother after playing, she/he is sometimes fussy for no clear reason). Parents had been left the list of the 90 behaviors 2 weeks earlier at the first home visit with instructions to observe their children over the next few weeks with these behaviors in mind. Using a sorting board designed for this purpose, a trained research assistant sat with each parent while they separately sorted the 90 cards into nine piles (10 cards each) ranging from "least characteristic of your child" to "most characteristic of your child." Attachment security scores were calculated by correlating mothers' and fathers' sorts with a criterion sort representing the hypothetically "most secure" child. Higher scores indicate a closer fit to the criterion sort for a securely attached child; correlations were transformed into Fisher's z coefficients. Parent-completed AQS's are a valid measure of attachment in early childhood when conducted according to the criteria established in earlier studies, which were adopted for this study (Moss, Bureau, Cyr, & Dubois-Comtois, 2006; Tarabulsy et al., 2008; Teti & McGourty, 1996).

Family and Social Context

Marital Relationship Quality

At the prenatal timepoint, both parents completed the 25-item Intimate Relations Scale to assess marital quality (Braiker & Kelley, 1979). The measure yields four subscales: (1) *love*: the degree to which spouses feel a sense of love and belonging (10 items, "To what extent do you have a sense of belonging to your spouse/partner?," $\alpha = 0.83$ and 0.80 for mothers and fathers, respectively); (2) *maintenance*: the extent to which spouses attempted to enrich, improve, and maintain their relationship (five items, "How much do you and your spouse/partner talk about the quality of your relationship?," $\alpha = 0.69$ and 0.64 for mothers and fathers, respectively); (3) *conflict*: the extent to which couples engaged in marital disputes (five items, "How often do you feel angry or resentful toward your partner?," $\alpha = 0.78$ and 0.68 for mothers and fathers, respectively); and (4) *ambivalence*: the extent to which spouses reported confusion and were unsure about the future of the relationship (five items, "How confused are you about your feelings toward your spouse/ partner?," $\alpha = 0.75$ and 0.68 for mothers and fathers, respectively). Each item was answered on a 9-point Likert scale ($1 = very little or not at all$; $9 = very much or extremely$). As in prior research, we composited love and maintenance into *positive marital relations* and ambivalence and conflict into *negative marital relations* for mothers and fathers, and then averaged across parents to create dyadic composites of *positive* and *negative martial relationship quality* (Volling, Oh, Gonzalez, Kuo, & Yu, 2015).

Home Observations of Marital Interaction

Husbands and wives engaged in a 10-min, video-taped, marital interaction during which they were instructed to discuss their day. Husbands' and wives' affect and behaviors were coded by trained independent coders using the Interactional Dimensions Coding System (Kline et al., 2004). Each 10-min interaction was separated into three equal segments of 3 min and 20 sec. Within each segment, each spouse was coded for *positive affect*—the positivity of tone of voice, facial expressions, and body language; *negative affect*—the negativity of tone of voice, facial expressions, and body language; *dominance*—one spouse's control over the other; *support validation*—positive listening and speaking skills that demonstrated support of the other spouse; *conflict*—expressed struggle between the two partners; *withdrawal*—avoiding interaction with spouse; and *communication skills*—one person's ability to convey thoughts and feelings in a clear, constructive manner. Each code was rated on a 9-point scale from 1 (*extremely uncharacteristic*) to 9 (*extremely characteristic*). Inter-rater reliability, measured via intraclass correlations, ranged from 0.88 to 0.95 ($M = 0.91$) for wives and 0.78 to 0.92 ($M = 0.88$) for husbands. Means across segments were calculated for each code ($\alpha = 0.76$–0.88 for husbands; 0.77–0.84 for wives). Two composites were then created from these individual mean codes to reflect positive marital interaction (*positive affect + support validation + communication skills*; $\alpha = 0.71$ for husbands, 0.59 for wives) and negative marital interaction (*negative affect + dominance + conflict + withdrawal*; $\alpha = 0.73$ for husbands, 0.71 for wives), which were then averaged across spouses to create a dyadic, relationship composite of *negative* and *positive marital interaction*.

Division of Household Labor

During a couple interview at the prenatal timepoint, both parents jointly reported division of household labor using the Household Task Checklist (HTC: Baruch & Barnett, 1986). Parents had to agree on who did what for each of the nine items of the HTC. Each item was measured on a scale ranging from $1 = almost$ *always wife* to $3 = both equally$ to $5 = almost always husband$. Items included meal preparation, cleaning house, laundry, grocery shopping, meal cleanup, household repairs, yard work, car repairs, and paying bills and were averaged ($\alpha = 0.56$).

Division of Childcare

During a joint couple interview at the prenatal timepoint, both parents jointly reported on who did what for 11 child care tasks using the *Checklist of Child Care Tasks* (CCCT: Baruch & Barnett, 1986; Ehrenberg, Gearing-Small, Hunter, & Small, 2001). Each item was rated on a scale from 1 = *almost always wife*, 3 = *both equally*, 5 = *almost always husband* and averaged (e.g., making snack for child, taking child to the doctor, cleaning up child's room, and supervising child's morning routine; $\alpha = 0.73$).

Coparenting

Mothers and fathers completed the 14-item Coparenting Questionnaire (CQ: Margolin, Gordis, & John, 2001) to assess perceptions of their spouse's coparenting *cooperation* (e.g., "My spouse says nice things to me about our child"; five items), *triangulation* (e.g., "My spouse tries to get our child to take sides when we argue"; four items), and *conflict* (e.g., "My spouse argues with me about our child"; five items). Each item was rated on a 5-point Likert scale ranging from 1 = *never* to 5 = *always*. Dyadic composite scores were created by averaging parents' reports for cooperation ($\alpha = 0.79$ for mothers and 0.66 for fathers), triangulation ($\alpha = 0.50$ for mothers and 0.63 for fathers), and conflict ($\alpha = 0.74$ for mothers and fathers).

Home Observations of Coparenting Behavior

The 15 min of videotaped family freeplay were divided into three equal 5-min intervals coded for coparenting behavior. Trained coders rated couple interaction on a 5-point rating scale (1 = *very low* to 5 = *very high*) according to six dimensions of coparenting behavior, which included cooperation, pleasure, interactiveness, displeasure, coldness, and competition developed by Schoppe-Sullivan and coworkers (Schoppe, Mangelsdorf, & Frosch, 2001; Schoppe-Sullivan, Mangelsdorf, Frosch, & McHale, 2004). Each member of the coding team was randomly assigned to rate positive or negative dimensions of behavior. Based on 20% of the sample, intraclass correlation coefficients that assessed inter-rater reliability ranged from 0.72 to 0.90. Ratings were then summed across the three videotaped segments, and means were calculated for each code. Two composites were created to reflect supportive coparenting and undermining coparenting. *Supportive coparenting* ($M = 8.09$) was generated from the sum of interactiveness ($\alpha = 0.73$), pleasure ($\alpha = 0.74$), and cooperation ($\alpha = 0.78$), and *undermining coparenting* ($M = 6.68$) was calculated from displeasure ($\alpha = 0.76$), coldness ($\alpha = 0.79$), and competition ($\alpha = 0.78$).

Daily Hassles and Stress

At the prenatal timepoint, mothers and fathers reported the extent to which they felt hassled while completing daily tasks of parenting, using the Daily Hassles Scale (DHS: Crnic & Greenberg, 1990). Each item was rated on a

5-point Likert scale ($1 = $ *no hassles* to $5 = $ *huge hassles*). Example items included: "You continually have to clean up after your child's messes," "your child is constantly under foot or in the way," and "having to run extra errands just for your child." Composite scores were created by averaging the 14 items for mothers ($\alpha = 0.84$) and for fathers ($\alpha = 0.83$).

Family Support

Mothers and fathers reported on the 12 items of the Parenting Support Scale (PSS: Bonds, Gondoli, Sturge-Apple, & Salem, 2002) to assess the extent to which parents perceived support with regard to parenting (e.g., "Someone to talk to about things that worry you" and "someone to help you take care of your child"). Each item used a 5-point Likert scale ($1 = $ *never* to $5 = $ *quite often*). An overall composite score for family support was created by averaging mothers' and fathers' reports ($\alpha = 0.86$).

Social Support

Both parents jointly reported on the nine items of the Family Support Scale (FSS: Dunst, Trivette, & Deal, 1988) to assess the helpfulness of people and groups in caring for their firstborn child (e.g., own/partner's parents, friends, parent groups). Each item was or rated on a 5-point Likert scale ($1 = $ *not at all helpful*; $5 = $ *extremely helpful*; $\alpha = 0.77$) or given a "not available" option if it was not applicable. A composite was created by using the mean of all items across both parents.

Work-Family Conflict

Fathers reported on their work-family conflict using the 22 items of the Work-Family Conflict scale (WFCS: Kelloway, Gottlieb, & Barham, 1999). Each item was measured on a 4-point scale ($1 = $ *never* to $4 = $ *almost always*). The WFCS assessed four dimensions of work and family conflict: *strain-based work interference with family* (e.g., "The demands of my job make it hard for me to enjoy the time I spend with my family"); *time-based work interference with family* (e.g., "To meet the demands of my job, I have to limit the number of things I do with family members"); *strain-based family interference with work* (e.g., "I spend time at work thinking about the things I have to get done at home"); and *time-based family interference with work* (e.g., "Family demands make it difficult for me to take on additional job responsibilities"). A composite was created from the average of all items ($\alpha = 0.72$). Mothers' scores on work-family conflict were not used because most mothers were either not working full-time at the time of the prenatal visit and already on parental leave (30%) or were stay-at-home caregivers (32.8%).

Sibling Relationship Quality at 12 Months

Parents reported on the children's behavior toward their younger sibling at 12 months using the Sibling Relationships in Early Childhood scale

(Volling & Elins, 1998). Three subscales were used (1) *positive involvement* (seven items, "Shares play things with baby," $\alpha = 0.87$ for mothers, $\alpha = 0.86$ for fathers); (2) *conflict* (five items, "Is physically aggressive with baby," $\alpha = 0.76$ for mothers, $\alpha = 0.73$ for fathers); and (3) *avoidance* (three items, "Is happy when baby goes away (e.g., on outings, store with parent)", $\alpha = 0.67$ for mothers, $\alpha = 0.69$ for fathers). Each item was rated from $1 = never$ to $5 = always$; higher scores indicated more positive involvement, conflict, or avoidance on each respective subscale. A composite score for each subscale was created by averaging mothers' and fathers' reports.

DATA ANALYSIS OVERVIEW

Recent advances in statistical modeling offer unique opportunities to model developmental trajectories of children's behavioral adjustment over time, and to identify both predictors of those trajectories and their outcomes. A latent growth approach models trajectories through parameters such as slope and intercept, and estimates parameter values for individuals (known as random effects) as well as the sample as a whole (known as a fixed effect). Thus, latent growth models simultaneously provide information about the common pattern in a sample and the individual heterogeneity around that common pattern. Other techniques, such as group-based trajectory analysis (e.g., Nagin, 1999), model heterogeneity by identifying clusters, commonly called classes, of individuals who share common values on the growth parameters (i.e., similar slope and intercept) of the trajectories. Latent growth models and group-based trajectory analysis can be combined (1) to partition the sample into smaller classes that share common parameter values within their class and (2) to allow for heterogeneity within the class by introducing random effect terms. In other words, individuals in the same class share a fixed effect value for each parameter (i.e., common to all individuals in the same class) and also have random effect terms to model individual differences within a class. This combined technique is known as growth mixture modeling (GMM). The benefit of growth mixture modeling is that it combines two approaches to data analysis and theory testing (i.e., individual differences in trajectories and clustering of trajectories), and allows testing of trajectory parameters across classes, as well as individual differences within those classes.

Modeling Developmental Changes Across the Transition

Examination of the linear slope from a latent growth model informs us whether children show steady or dramatic increases in behavior problems over the year. These models can be extended beyond linear trajectories. For example, it is possible to model curvilinear trajectories by testing global quadratic change across the five timepoints (Prenatal, 1, 4, 8, and 12 months) that might reflect changes across the first year of siblinghood where children show a gradual increase in behavior problems with an eventual gradual decline.

Dunn and Kendrick (1982) claimed that most children showed an initial disturbance shortly after the birth, but that this disturbance was short-lived and by 8 months, most children had adapted. This pattern, which we call an "adjustment and adaptation response" (AAR), suggests there may be an initial burst in behavioral problems immediately following the birth of the sibling (i.e., from prenatal to 1 month postbirth), but children would adapt quickly to the new sibling and return to prebirth levels of behavioral functioning by 4 months, with no additional change throughout the remaining year (i.e., at 8 and 12 months). This pattern indicates that the initial period is stressful for the child with rapid increases in adjustment difficulties. Neither the linear nor global quadratic term capture this adjustment and adaptation response pattern of rapid increase and rapid decline because they are typically defined over all available time points. One might conclude erroneously by examining statistical significance of linear or quadratic terms in a GMM that there was no change even though there was an increase at 1 month and a corresponding decrease by 4 months. In the current modeling framework, we tested linear, quadratic, and adjustment and adaptation response patterns in children's emotional and behavioral adjustment by including a local quadratic contrast that tested change specifically from prenatal to 1 month to 4 months.

Growth Mixture Models

The primary research question in this monograph deals with developmental trajectories of children across the first year following the birth of a sibling. We used GMMs to examine individual developmental trajectories with the goal of identifying intrapersonal growth for each individual by estimating latent variables (i.e., the intercept, linear slope, quadratic parameter, and AAR parameter) based on multiple-repeated indicators, and determining classes of individuals exhibiting similar patterns.

Using Mplus Version 7.0 (Muthén & Muthén, 1998–2012), we first tested unconditional models using the entire sample with full information maximum likelihood (FIML) for each of the seven CBCL subscales to determine which of the developmental patterns provided the best fit to the data. We tested three models at the unconditional stage of model testing. The first model was the standard *linear latent growth* model, which served as the baseline model. This model included random effects for both the intercept and slope to model heterogeneity. The second model added an extra term for the fixed effect quadratic defined across all five time points to test the *quadratic latent growth* model. The quadratic model across the first year is

40

flexible and assesses several potential curvilinear patterns depicted in Figure 2 of the Introduction. For example, the quadratic effect can estimate change describing a *sudden and persistent pattern of maladjustment,* which would reflect a sudden increase in problematic behaviors immediately following the birth that persisted across the first year or a pattern of gradual increase that would subside over the course of the year. The quadratic model could also capture change describing the *delayed impact model,* in which there is minimal evidence of disruption in the early months, but more evidence of increases in problematic behavior later in the year that coincides with significant changes in infant development and increasing sibling confrontations. The third model, the *adjustment and adaptation response* (AAR) model, assessed a pattern of immediate change (i.e., increase in problem behaviors from prenatal to 1 month) that subsided by 4 months. Essentially, the AAR effect is a local quadratic term limited to the first three time points; the AAR model does not examine change at 8 or 12 months. This model added an extra fixed effect term to the baseline (linear) growth model involving the AAR contrast. Each of the unconditional models reflecting change for the sample overall is reported in Chapter III.

Once a best fitting unconditional model was selected for each subscale, we then estimated classes within each of the CBCL subscales for the best fitting model using GMM (Muthén, 2004) with FIML using Mplus Version 7.0 (Muthén & Muthén, 1998–2012). This allowed us to identify classes with distinct trajectories of the firstborn child's behavioral adjustment from prenatal throughout the first year after the sibling's birth. This strategy follows the recommendation of Muthén and Muthén (2000) who suggested that GMM should use the best fitting unconditional model as the base model. Across all GMMs, the fixed effects of the latent growth model (i.e., the intercept, linear slope, and when applicable, the quadratic slope and the AAR contrast) were freely estimated for each class and the random variance of growth parameters (slope and intercept) were constrained to be equal across classes. The residual variance was constrained to be equal across time points with the single residual variance estimated freely. When estimating the maximum likelihood mixture models, we followed the recommendation of Nylund, Asparouhov, and Muthén (2007) to increase the number of random start values to ensure confidence in finding a global maximum solution.

To decide on the number of classes for a particular GMM, we estimated fit indices for 1 (unconditional model) to $k+1$ class-solution models. Models with different numbers of latent classes were evaluated to determine which model provided the best fit to the data. Because models with different numbers of classes were not nested, model comparisons were conducted using a set of multiple fit indices, including the Bayesian Information Criterion (BIC), the sample size adjusted *BIC,* and the Akaike Information Criterion (AIC); lower scores represent better fitting models.

We also used the Lo-Mendell-Rubin (*LMR*) likelihood ratio test of model fit and the entropy measure, which refers to the average classification accuracy in assigning individuals to classes; values range from 0 to 1, with higher scores reflecting better accuracy in classification of class membership. The optimal models were chosen based on goodness-of-fit, parsimony, and avoiding degenerate solutions with a class consisting of only one participant. For simplicity of subsequent analyses, we used the class with the modal posterior probability.

To demonstrate the face validity of the resulting classes, we examined the individual trajectories for each child in the sample (i.e., spaghetti plots) by class membership using standard CBCL cutoffs at the mean, 92.5% (borderline-clinical) and 97.5% (clinical) levels as described in the CBCL1.5-5 manual (Achenbach & Rescorla, 2000) to determine whether resulting classes fell within normative, borderline, or clinical ranges and were thus descriptively meaningful. We present the spaghetti plots in Chapter IV on aggression for each of the classes to demonstrate this approach, but all figures for the remaining chapters can be found in the supplemental materials.

Missing Data

Where possible we used FIML to estimate models and their parameters operating under the assumption that data are missing at random (Little & Rubin, 2014; Schafer & Graham, 2002). The pattern of missing for the five time points on the CBCL subscales involve the following: 184 families provided observations at all five timepoints, 16 families provided observations at the first four timepoints, 3 families provide observations at the first three timepoints, 7 families provided observations at the first two timepoints, and 10 families provided observations at only the first timepoint. The other patterns of missingness on the longitudinal design on the CBCL scale were not systematic (e.g., three families missing only the 8 month timepoint, four families missing only the 4 month timepoint). We fail to reject the missing completely at random (MCAR) assumption across all seven subscales using the nonparametric test of Jamshidian and Jalal (2010) as implemented in the MissMech package in R.

Using Prenatal Child, Parent, and Family Characteristics to Predict Change Trajectories

Once the trajectory classes were established, the next step in our analysis strategy was to predict the trajectory classes from child, parent, and family predictors obtained at the prenatal time point. One problem that can occur when adding predictors to a GMM where one simultaneously (1) assesses predictors of class membership and (2) estimates class membership is that the composition of class membership may change as predictors are added to or deleted from the model. We wanted membership in the trajectory classes to remain fixed as we tested for predictors rather than have class membership vary as each predictor was added to or removed from the model. As such, we fixed class membership after conducting the GMM and deciding on the number of classes. In this way, we could guarantee that the trajectory classes were not moving targets as we tested different predictors (see also Petras & Masyn, 2010).

Our analyses were further complicated because we had many potential predictors collected at the prenatal time point based on the developmental ecological systems model where several child, parent, and family variables were the focus. Further, predictors could very well differ across the seven CBCL subscales, so we needed to ensure that we were not using a variable selection procedure that would place constraints on which predictor variables were relevant for each CBCL subscale, for example, a predictor for the aggression scale may not have relevance to another subscale, such as sleep problems. We also wanted to minimize multiple comparison issues when testing many potential predictors across the CBCL subscales.

To address these concerns, we relied on new procedures based on modern methods from the computer science and statistical learning fields for variable selection. We adopted two methods, classification and regression trees (CART, Breiman, Friedman, Stone, & Olshen, 1984) and random forests (Breiman, 2001) to select predictor variables. A detailed explanation of both CART and random forests written for the psychological audience is given in Strobl, Tutz, and Malley (2009) and we provide a brief description here. The first cross-validation criterion used the CART procedure as implemented in the recursive partitioning R package rpart. CART uses a recursive partitioning algorithm to estimate cut points on if-then statements (see Strobl et al., 2009 for a detailed description). For example, if mother's attachment score (i.e., the Q-sort) is greater than an estimated value X, then predict class membership i; if mother's attachment score is less than or equal to value X, then predict class membership j and k. Both the predictor, in the example of mother's attachment Q-sort, and the cut-off value, in the example X, are estimated from data. The algorithm continues estimating such if-then statements with corresponding cut-off values until a convergence criterion is met. The algorithm can also find multiple "if" statements such as "if mother's attachment score is less than or equal to Y AND father's attachment score is less than or equal to Z, then predict class i." In this way, the recursive partitioning algorithm can model complicated interaction patterns. We used default settings within the rpart program. This set of if-then statements was "pruned" using a 10-fold cross-validation procedure where estimation was conducted on 90% of the data and predictive validity was assessed on the remaining 10% (i.e., proportion of correct predicted class membership as assessed by out-of-sample prediction). A particular if-then statement is pruned from the model if it does not predict well as assessed in the cross-validation procedure. This recursive partitioning algorithm with cross-validation criterion typically led to three or four candidate predictors of class membership among the entire set of available prenatal predictors.

The second cross-validation-based criterion emerged from the random forest procedure (see Strobl et al., 2009, for a detailed description). This procedure examines repeated random subsets of predictors, evaluates each variable's predictive validity within that subset and rank orders predictors on the basis of their predictive accuracy using the Gini coefficient. We considered a variable as a candidate predictor if it emerged as a top-three variable in predictive validity based on the measures.

The key criterion we used to select variables was predictive validity, as assessed by cross-validation in both CART and random forests. We opted for estimating GMM and searching for class predictors in two separate steps rather than in one simultaneous procedure (McArdle & Ritschard, 2013). Once these candidate predictors were identified, we then used them in multinomial logistic regressions to assess their significance in predicting trajectory classes. Thus, our approach uses two criteria to select predictors: (1) cross-validation, also known as predictive accuracy, in a hold-out sample to identify predictors and (2) statistical significance in a multinomial logistic regression. These two criteria may lead to different conclusions when applied individually. For example, cross-validation may find that a variable performs well in predicting membership in a relatively small class, say $N = 12$, but the statistical significance criterion in the multinomial logistic regression may find that the same variable does not significantly identify this small class compared to the reference class. We required that a predictor pass both criteria: (1) emerge as a predictor of class membership in cross-validation in either CART or random forest, *and* (2) emerge as a statistically significant predictor of class membership in the multinomial logistic regression.

Across the seven CBCL subscales there was often complete overlap between the variables selected by the random forest and CART procedures. After finding candidate predictor variables that passed the cross-validation criterion, we estimated multinomial logistic regressions to provide standard statistical testing of those candidate predictors. When conducting the multinomial logistic regression models, we used traditional maximum likelihood estimation and interpreted each beta coefficient as a unique predictor controlling for the other predictors in the model. The reference class in the multinomial logistic regressions for each CBCL subscale was the largest "normative" class; for some subscales we also report additional tests involving comparisons between pairs of classes that shared similar prenatal starting points, but different developmental outcomes (multifinality) or different prenatal starting points with similar outcomes (equifinality). Given the post hoc and exploratory nature of these additional tests, we identify them in the relevant chapters and recommend that a more conservative Type I error rate be used for those tests (e.g., $\alpha = .01$). For all multinomial logistic regression models, we compared the baseline main effect model using candidate predictors that emerged from our selection process to a model that included all possible higher-order interactions between the candidate predictor variables. This allowed testing of potential interactions beyond main effects. Testing of higher-order interactions would likely lead to overfitting of data and potentially spurious results, so we limited our analysis to an omnibus test of higher-order interactions using the standard difference in a Chi-square test to compare nested models (i.e., the main effect model compared to the model that includes all higher-order interactions). Only one of the seven subscales (somatic complaints) exhibited significant higher-order interaction effects in the multinomial logistic regression. Even though we tested for all higher-order interactions, we limited interpretation to statistically significant two-way interactions to minimize the chance of interpreting spurious interactions.

Using Class Membership to Predict Sibling Outcomes

To determine whether there were meaningful differences across the classes that would predict sibling relationship quality, we examined whether and how class membership predicted sibling relationship quality one year following the birth of a sibling. Here we used restricted maximum likelihood regression (REML) on three dimensions of sibling relationship quality: positive involvement, conflict, and avoidance. Because the classes are categorical variables, we used dummy coding designating the largest normative class as the reference class for each of the seven CBCL subscales. We report regression coefficients and standard errors for these analyses.

Across our analyses we used modal class membership in both the multinomial logistic regressions and the outcome regressions. More advanced procedures for including uncertainty information about class membership (such as class membership probability) in the context of traditional distal outcome regression and multinomial logistic regression to assess class predictors and variable selection methods are still in development, so we thought it would be premature to use those fledging methods in this monograph. Some preliminary sensitivity analyses where class membership was sampled according to class membership probability as one preliminary attempt to address uncertainty in class membership in the context of regressions yielded similar conclusions, so we felt reassured moving forward with using modal class membership throughout our predictor and outcome regressions.

III. STABILITY AND CHANGE IN CHILDREN'S EMOTIONAL AND BEHAVIORAL ADJUSTMENT AFTER THE BIRTH OF A SIBLING

Brenda L. Volling, Wonjung Oh, and Richard Gonzalez

This article is part of the issue "Developmental Trajectories of Children's Adjustment across the Transition to Siblinghood: Pre-Birth Predictors and Sibling Outcomes at One Year" Volling, Gonzalez, Oh, Song, Yu, Rosenberg, Kuo, Thomason, Beyers-Carlson, Safyer, and Stevenson (Issue Authors). For a full listing of articles in this issue, see: http://onlinelibrary.wiley.com/doi/10.1111/mono.v82.3/issuetoc.

To begin our investigation of the developmental patterns of children's emotional and behavioral adjustment after the birth of an infant sibling, we have organized the presentation of the seven CBCL syndrome scales into three sections corresponding to *externalizing* (aggression, attention problems), *internalizing* (anxiety/depression, emotional reactivity, withdrawal), and *physical problems* (somatic complaints, sleep problems). Descriptive statistics for each of the scales across the five timepoints can be found in Table 2.

We then calculated cross-time correlations to determine whether there was stability in individual differences in children's behavioral, emotional, and physical symptoms over the course of the study. Indeed, on all subscales, there were stable individual differences (all ps significant at $<.05$) from the prenatal-to 12-month timepoint on aggression ($r = 0.65$–0.76, $M = 0.72$), attention problems ($r = 0.66$–0.76, $M = 0.71$), anxiety/depression ($r = 0.47$–0.79, $M = 0.64$), emotional reactivity ($r = 0.54$–0.68, $M = 0.61$), withdrawal

---

Corresponding author: Brenda L. Volling, University of Michigan, Center for Human Growth and Development, 300 N. Ingalls, Ann Arbor, MI 48109-5406; email: volling@umich.edu

DOI: 10.1111/mono.12309

TABLE 2

MEANS AND STANDARD DEVIATIONS FOR THE SEVEN SYNDROME SCALES OF THE CHILD BEHAVIOR
CHECKLIST, 1.5–5 YEARS

Scales	Prenatal ($n = 229$) Mean (*SD*)	1 Month ($n = 218$) Mean (*SD*)	4 Months ($n = 208$) Mean (*SD*)	8 Months ($n = 206$) Mean (*SD*)	12 Months ($n = 199$) Mean (*SD*)
Aggressive behavior	8.55 (4.53)	9.91 (4.91)	8.93 (4.75)	8.86 (4.56)	8.63 (4.99)
Attention problems	2.25 (1.46)	2.26 (1.48)	2.15 (1.51)	2.09 (1.56)	1.89 (1.46)
Anxious/ depressed	1.66 (1.32)	1.60 (1.27)	1.55 (1.36)	1.56 (1.43)	1.57 (1.43)
Emotional reactivity	2.07 (1.34)	2.27 (1.55)	2.23 (1.55)	2.07 (1.50)	2.19 (1.57)
Withdrawal	1.12 (1.03)	1.28 (1.14)	1.38 (1.19)	1.52 (1.16)	1.51 (1.11)
Somatic complaints	1.68 (1.39)	1.61 (1.44)	1.56 (1.42)	1.37 (1.34)	1.42 (1.30)
Sleep problems	3.11 (2.61)	2.86 (2.25)	2.94 (2.41)	2.89 (2.43)	2.85 (2.20)

($r = 0.47$–0.64, $M = 0.57$), somatic complaints ($r = 0.47$–0.70, $M = 0.58$), and sleep problems ($r = 0.63$–0.76, $M = 0.70$).

To examine change in children's adjustment over time for the sample as a whole, we ran unconditional latent growth curve models to examine (1) which of the possible effects (linear, quadratic, Adjustment and Adaptation Response [AAR]) best described the overall trajectory pattern for each of the subscales; and (2) whether there was significant variance in the different growth parameters providing evidence of individual differences in the level of initial problem behavior at the prenatal timepoint (intercept) and the patterns of trajectories tested (linear, quadratic, AAR). Recall that the quadratic term would capture several different curvilinear patterns (e.g., delayed impact, gradual increase and decline, and sudden, persistent change). We were particularly interested in whether there was any evidence of a maladaptive pattern of sudden, persistent change (i.e., developmental crisis) in problem behavior in which children's behavior increased suddenly from prenatal to 1 month and did not return to prebirth levels by 1 year after the birth.

Across all models, time was centered at the prenatal timepoint. Following standard practice in the structural equations modeling (SEM) approach to latent growth curve modeling, the intercept paths were constrained to be 1 for each timepoint. The paths from the latent linear slope to the observed items were constrained to be 0, 1, 2.5, 4.5, and 6.5, which corresponded to the prenatal, 1-month, 4-month, 8-month, and 12-month timepoints, respectively. The rationale for the unequal spacing of the linear contrast values was because the timepoints themselves were not equally spaced. For the quadratic model, a new contrast was created involving the squared terms of the linear contrast and added to the model as a fixed effect term. The paths from the latent AAR factor to the observed items were constrained to be $-1, 2.5, -1, 0$, and 0. The AAR contrast is orthogonal to the linear contrast, but not to the grand mean contrast (i.e., the intercept). The reason we settled on orthogonality to the linear contrast was because we wanted to ensure that the AAR contrast modeled properties of the trajectory over and above the linear slope.

For the unconditional models, we used Chi-square difference tests for nested models (e.g., comparing the quadratic latent growth model to the linear growth model). For non-nested models, such as comparing the quadratic model to the AAR model, we used multiple criteria including the Bayesian Information Criterion (BIC; Schwarz, 1978), the sample size adjusted BIC (SSA BIC; Sclove, 1987), and the Akaike Information Criterion (AIC; Akaike, 1987); lower scores represent better fitting models. To be noted, we removed one extreme outlier from the growth mixture modeling analysis in three cases, anxiety-depression, attention problems, and emotional reactivity, because they were more than 5 SD above the mean, resulting in an n of 229 for these analyses.

In the section that follows, we examine which of the models tested (e.g., linear, AAR, quadratic) best fit the data for each of the problem behaviors and referred to this model as the best fitting unconditional model. We then interpreted the overall general pattern (i.e., mean level) for each subscale based on the best fitting model. Because each unconditional model also indicated significant variance (i.e., individual differences) around the growth parameters, each subsequent chapter focused specifically on modeling the individual variability in growth trajectories using growth mixture modeling.

EXTERNALIZING PROBLEMS

Aggressive Behavior

Chi-square tests between the unconditional latent linear model, the unconditional quadratic model, and the unconditional AAR model for aggression indicated that the unconditional quadratic model, $\Delta\chi^2$ $(1) = 3.927$, $p < .05$, and the unconditional AAR model, $\Delta\chi^2$ $(1) = 30.085$, $p < .001$, were better fitting models than the unconditional latent linear model. Model comparisons between the unconditional quadratic and unconditional AAR model indicated the unconditional AAR model was a better fitting model (i.e., non-nested model comparisons: the unconditional AAR model, AIC = 5507.988 vs. the quadratic model, AIC = 5534.146, smaller AIC indicates a better fitting model).

The growth parameters for the unconditional AAR model are presented in Table 3. The fixed effects (mean) for the intercept and AAR contrast for aggression are significant, suggesting that for the sample overall there was an increase in aggression from prenatal to 1 month, with a decline by 4 months. This effect contrasts with the fixed effect for the linear slope, which is nonsignificant, showing no overall linear change in aggressive behavior after the birth of a sibling. The random effects (variance) do indicate, however, that there is substantial variability around the intercept and the linear slope. The unconditional AAR model was chosen as our final model to be used in the Growth Mixture Modeling (GMM) of aggression trajectories presented in Chapter IV.

TABLE 3

Growth Parameters for the Unconditional Latent Growth Models for the Seven Syndrome Scales of the Child Behavior Checklist, 1.5–5 Years (Achenbach & Rescorla, 2000)

Growth Parameters	Intercept		Linear Slope		Quadratic Slope		AAR Contrast	
Aggressive behavior								
M (SE)	9.026***	(.29)	−.026	(.04)	–	–	.349***	(.06)
Variance (SE)	16.047***	(1.79)	.113**	(.04)	–	–	–	–
Attention problems								
M (SE)	2.276***	(.09)	−.059***	(.01)	–	–	–	–
Variance (SE)	1.652***	(.18)	.010*	(<.01)	–	–	–	–
Anxious/depressed								
M (SE)	1.615***	(.08)	−.006	(.01)	–	–	–	–
Variance (SE)	1.143***	(.14)	.017***	(.01)	–	–	–	–
Emotionally reactive								
M (SE)	2.124***	(.09)	.006	(.01)	–	–	–	–
Variance (SE)	1.442***	(.17)	.014**	(.01)	–	–	–	–
Withdrawal								
M (SE)	1.112***	(.07)	.143***	(.04)	−.013*	(.01)	–	–
Variance (SE)	.733***	(.09)	.008**	(.00)	–	–	–	–
Somatic complaints								
M (SE)	1.659***	(.09)	−.044**	(.01)	–	–	–	–
Variance (SE)	1.279***	(.16)	.010*	(.00)	–	–	–	–
Sleep problems								
M (SE)	3.012***	(.16)	−.020	(.02)	–	–	–	–
Variance (SE)	4.758***	(.53)	.044***	(.01)	–	–	–	–

Note. AAR = adjustment and adaptation response. The random effects (variance) of the quadratic slope and the AAR contrast were constrained to be 0.
*p < .05, **p < .01, ***p < .001.

Attention Problems

Chi-square tests indicated that the unconditional latent linear model was a better fitting model than the unconditional AAR model, $\Delta\chi^2$ (1) $= 0.797$, $p = 0.372$, and the unconditional quadratic model, $\Delta\chi^2$ (1) $= 0.419$, $p = 0.517$, so the unconditional latent linear model was chosen as the final model to be used in the GMM.

The growth parameters for the unconditional latent linear model for attention problems are presented in Table 3. The fixed effects for the intercept and linear slope are significant, highlighting that, on average, there is a linear decrease in attention problems from prenatal to 12 months for the sample. In addition, the random effects indicate substantial variability around the intercept and linear slope that can be modeled in our analyses looking at individual differences in trajectories for attention problems.

INTERNALIZING PROBLEMS

Emotional Reactivity

Chi-square tests indicated that the latent linear model was the better fitting model, in comparison to the unconditional AAR model, $\Delta\chi^2$ (1) $= 1.912$, $p = 0.167$, and the unconditional quadratic model, $\Delta\chi^2$ (1) $= 1.384$, $p = 0.239$.

Growth parameters presented in Table 3 for the unconditional model show the fixed effect for the intercept was significantly different from zero, yet there was no average change in emotional reactivity, that is, the fixed effect for the slope was zero. The random effects for both the intercept and the linear slope were significant. The unconditional latent linear model was chosen as the final model for the GMM presented later.

Withdrawal

Chi-square tests indicated the unconditional latent linear model for withdrawal was a better fitting model, $\Delta\chi^2$ (1) $= 0.716$, $p = 0.397$, than the unconditional AAR model, but the unconditional quadratic model was a better fitting model than the unconditional latent linear model, $\Delta\chi^2$ (1) $= 6.471$, $p < .05$. Thus, the unconditional quadratic model was chosen as our final model in the GMM.

The growth parameters for the unconditional quadratic model presented in Table 3 show the fixed effects for the intercept, linear slope, and quadratic slope are significant. Overall, there was a moderate increase in withdrawal with a decelerating rate of curvature in the growth trajectory over time. The random effects indicate that there is significant variability around the intercepts and linear slope.

Anxiety-Depression

The Chi-square tests between the unconditional latent linear model and the unconditional AAR model and the unconditional quadratic model indicated the unconditional AAR model, $\Delta\chi^2$ (1) = .050, $p = 0.823$, and the unconditional quadratic model, $\Delta\chi^2$ (1) = 2.062, $p = 0.151$, were not better fitting models than the unconditional latent linear model, which we chose for the final model for the GMM.

Table 3 shows the growth parameters (fixed and random effects for intercept and slope) for the unconditional latent linear model. There was no significant change in anxiety-depression, on average (i.e., the linear slope was nonsignificant), but there were significant random effects for both the intercept and linear slope.

PHYSICAL PROBLEMS

Somatic Complaints

Chi-square tests between the unconditional latent linear model and the unconditional AAR model for somatic complaints, and the unconditional quadratic model, indicated that neither the unconditional AAR model, $\Delta\chi^2$ (1) = .005, $p = 0.944$, nor the unconditional quadratic model, $\Delta\chi^2$ (1) = 1.668, $p = 0.197$, were better fitting than the unconditional latent linear model. The unconditional latent linear model was chosen as our final model for the GMM analyses.

The growth parameters for the unconditional latent linear model presented in Table 3 reveal the fixed effects for the intercept and linear slope are significant. For the sample overall, there is a linear decrease in somatic complaints from prenatal to 12 months. In addition, the significant random effects indicate there is substantial variability around the intercept and linear slope.

Sleep Problems

Chi-square tests between the unconditional latent linear model and the unconditional AAR and unconditional quadratic models for sleep problems indicated that neither the unconditional AAR model, $\Delta\chi^2$ (1) = 1.419, $p = 0.234$, nor the unconditional quadratic model, $\Delta\chi^2$ (1) = 1.092, $p = 0.296$, were better fitting models than the unconditional latent linear model, which we chose as our final GMM model. The growth parameters show that the fixed effect for the intercept is significant, but the fixed effect for the linear slope is nonsignificant (see Table 3); there is no overall linear change in sleep problems after the birth of a sibling. The random effects are significant for both the intercept and linear slope.

Having now established the general trajectory pattern for each of the subscales for the entire sample and finding variability in the growth parameters for each subscale, we now proceed to discuss the search for individual differences in growth trajectories using growth mixture modeling for each of the CBCL subscales.

IV. DEVELOPMENTAL TRAJECTORIES OF CHILDREN'S AGGRESSIVE BEHAVIORS AFTER THE BIRTH OF A SIBLING

Brenda L. Volling, Richard Gonzalez, Tianyi Yu, and Wonjung Oh

This article is part of the issue "Developmental Trajectories of Children's Adjustment across the Transition to Siblinghood: Pre-Birth Predictors and Sibling Outcomes at One Year" Volling, Gonzalez, Oh, Song, Yu, Rosenberg, Kuo, Thomason, Beyers-Carlson, Safyer, and Stevenson (Issue Authors). For a full listing of articles in this issue, see: http://onlinelibrary.wiley.com/doi/10.1111/mono.v82.3/issuetoc.

Dunn and Kendrick (1982) reported that some children were quite aggressive toward mothers and their infant siblings shortly after the birth. These early behaviors 3 weeks after the birth predicted the quality of sibling relations at 14 months after the birth, which, in turn, continued to predict early sibling relationship quality when the younger sibling was 6 years old (Stillwell & Dunn, 1985). Stewart (1990) also found that 36.5% of the 41 children in his study were involved in physical confrontations with the infant at 1 month, whereas 47.5% were aggressive with mothers and 40% were aggressive with their fathers at 1 month after the birth. Although the number of children in physical confrontations with family members decreased substantially by 4 months, the number increased again by 8 months after the birth, with most physical confrontations focused on the sibling at 12 months. Thus, understanding early patterns of aggression after the birth of a sibling takes on added significance given the long-term continuity of aggression and

---

Corresponding author: Correspondence concerning the Family Transitions Study should be addressed to Brenda L. Volling, University of Michigan, Center for Human Growth and Development, 300 N. Ingalls, Ann Arbor, MI 48109-5406. email: volling@umich.edu

For those interested in the statistical code used to analyze these data (including growth mixture models, random forest, and CART procedures), please email Richard Gonzalez, gonzo@umich.edu.

DOI: 10.1111/mono.12310

sibling relationship quality from the earliest months after the birth and from early childhood (Hay et al., 2014; Song & Volling, 2015).

Development of Aggression in Early Childhood

Numerous studies have examined the development of aggression in early childhood, finding that aggression and other disruptive behaviors such as noncompliance and defiance are quite common in toddlerhood (i.e., terrible twos) and the preschool years (Campbell, 2002). In general, physical aggression increases from 2 to 3 years and begins to decline around 4 years of age (Alink et al., 2006; NICHD Early Child Care Research Network, 2004; Tremblay et al., 1999), a time during which many children experience the transition to siblinghood (Baydar et al., 1997). When aggressive behavior does not decline from toddlerhood into elementary school, children are considered at risk for numerous social-emotional problems and maladjustment (Campbell, 2002). Despite the decline in children's aggression over early childhood, there are notable individual differences in young children's aggression that are fairly stable over the preschool period (e.g., Alink et al., 2006). Several investigators have now examined individual differences in longitudinal trajectory patterns across toddlerhood, preschool, and into elementary school in an effort to identify those children most at risk for developing persistent patterns of aggressive behavior.

Individual Differences in Young Children's Aggression

There are now numerous studies using mixture modeling to examine group-based trajectories of aggressive behavioral patterns. We focus here on those studies that have examined the early toddler and preschool years as this is the period that coincides with the transition to siblinghood and thus, our findings need to be understood within this developmental framework. In a sample of 572 children followed longitudinally from 5 to 42 months, Tremblay et al. (2004) identified three physical aggression trajectories across the 17-, 30-, and 42-month time points. The first was a group who exhibited little or no physical aggression over the course of time and accounted for 28% of the sample. The largest group of children (58%) followed a pattern in which children started relatively low but increased modestly in their physical aggression from 17 to 42 months. The final group consisting of 14% of children started out higher on aggression than the other two groups and continued to increase in their aggression from 30 to 42 months.

Other researchers examining trajectories of externalizing behavior problems, which includes aggression, during the toddler and preschool years, reveal similar longitudinal trajectory patterns; generally finding three or four groups of children who often differ with respect to their starting points (intercepts) and rates of change (i.e., linear slope). These groups often consist of a relatively large group of children with low externalizing problems over time, a smaller group of children with generally high and persistent externalizing problems, and groups who start at different points and show declines starting around 2 years of age (e.g., Hill, Degnan, Calkins, & Keane, 2006; NICHD Early Child Care Research Network, 2004). Tremblay et al. (2004) documented that the largest risk factor for distinguishing the relatively small number of children in their high aggression trajectory group was the presence of young siblings in the family. Having a sibling as the target for physical aggression increased the odds of membership in the high-aggression group by more than a factor of 4.

Based on these earlier findings, we hypothesized there would also be variability (i.e., individual differences) in children's trajectories of aggressive behavior after the birth of a sibling and that we could identify distinct groups of children. We anticipated a large normative group of children with low aggression across the course of the year following the birth (i.e., low-stable). We also hypothesized that there may be a smaller, yet high-risk, group of children who would be persistently higher in their aggression over time and who may very well increase in aggression under the stress of the transition (e.g., high-stable or high-increasing). In her study of hard to manage preschoolers, Campbell (2002) noted that these children reacted strongly to the birth of a younger sibling. As noted earlier, we also tested for an adjustment and adaption response and a maladaptive response (i.e., sudden persistent change) in line with theories of family risk and resilience, and the emphasis on the transition to siblinghood as a psychosocial crisis for firstborns based on psychodynamic theorizing (Adler, 1928; Levy, 1934). Specifically, we tested whether increases in aggression from prenatal to 1 month after the birth increased and if so, how long-lived this increase was. Dunn and Kendrick (1982) claimed that emotional upset and disruptive behavior had diminished by the end of the first month after the birth and most children appeared to have adapted shortly thereafter. Thus, if aggression did increase, we expected to see an adjustment and adaptation response, in which increases in aggression from prenatal to 1 month would have returned to prebirth levels by 4 months after the birth, indicating that children had adapted to changes in their families. The adjustment and adaptation response would provide evidence of potential disturbance in response to the stresses of change brought about by the birth, but this effect would subside by 4 months once the family had adapted to the arrival of the new family member and adjusted to the change in roles and expectations.

In contrast to these stable and adaptive patterns, we also tested for several other trajectory patterns that might manifest and reflect increases in problem behavior over time. One maladaptive response reflecting a sudden increase from prenatal to 1 month that persisted and remained high throughout the year could be tested with a quadratic polynomial or curvilinear pattern whereas a second pattern would show a gradual linear increase in aggression over time. Because no prior study has examined individual differences in growth trajectories of aggression across the transition to siblinghood, our modeling of trajectory patterns is based both on theories of family stress and resilience and prior research examining linear patterns of change in aggression over early childhood.

Risk and Protective Factors in the Prediction of Early Aggression

Potential risk factors that maintain stable aggressive tendencies in early childhood are generally grouped into child, parent, and family characteristics, which are also consistent with the developmental ecological systems perspective (Volling, 2005). With respect to child characteristics, temperamental difficulty or negative emotionality has been examined frequently and seems to be a developmental precursor to the emergence of externalizing behavior problems, although the exact process by which this occurs is not entirely clear (Bates, Maslin, & Frankel, 1985; Gartstein, Putnam, & Rothbart, 2012; Morris, Keane, Calkins, Shanahan, & O'Brien, 2014; Shaw, Keenan, & Vondra, 1994). High negative emotionality is posited as a central feature of psychopathology because difficult and fussy infants, and young children, often have difficulty regulating their anger and may be prone to the use of aggression in their social interactions (Hay et al., 2014).

In the parenting domain, hostile, power-assertive, and rejecting maternal behavior, or the lack of maternal acceptance and warmth, have been related consistently with the development of externalizing behaviors in young children (Choe, Olson, & Sameroff, 2013; Dishion & Patterson, 2006; Miner & Clarke-Stewart, 2008; Towe-Goodman & Teti, 2008), although the relations between maternal and child behaviors most likely reflect a transactional process of increasing coercion and punishment over time (e.g., parental reactivity hypothesis) rather than a simple unidirectional relation (Collins, Maccoby, Steinberg, Hetherington, & Bornstein, 2000; Combs-Ronto, Olson, Lunkenheimer, & Sameroff, 2009; Kochanska & Kim, 2012). Further, children with insecure avoidant and disorganized attachments to their mothers are more likely to have externalizing behavioral difficulties (Fearon & Belsky, 2011; Fearon et al., 2010), whereas positive father involvement and children with secure father–child attachments are less likely to have externalizing problem behaviors in early childhood (Boldt, Kochanska, Yoon, & Koenig Nordling, 2014; DeKlyen, Biernbaum, Speltz, & Greenberg, 1998; DeKlyen, Speltz, & Greenberg, 1998; Herbert, Harvey, Lugo-Candelas, & Breaux, 2013).

Maternal depressive symptoms have also been linked to the development of children's disruptive behavior, whether this link is direct or mediated by its effect on ineffective parenting practices and inconsistent discipline (Dix & Yan, 2014; Owens & Shaw, 2003; Tremblay et al., 2004). Parents, both mothers and fathers, reporting lower parental self-efficacy also reported their children had more behavior problems (Gross & Tucker, 1994; Hill & Bush, 2001), although it is not clear if this association is a reflection of parent's feelings of ineffectiveness in the parental role or an actual increase in problematic child behaviors. In an earlier report, we found that mothers' and fathers' parental self-efficacy at 1 month after the infant's birth, specifically their inability to control and discipline their older child when naughty, predicted the older sibling's antagonistic interactions with the younger sibling later in the year following the birth (Oh, Volling, & Gonzalez, 2015). When parents felt ineffective in disciplining the older sibling shortly after birth, their children were engaging in aggressive and antagonistic behavior with their 4-month-old infant siblings.

Interparental or marital conflict has been consistently tied to young children's disruptive behavior (Amato & Cheadle, 2008; Lindsey, Caldera, & Tankersley, 2009; Peterson & Zill, 1986) and externalizing behavior problems (Cummings & Davies, 2011; Cummings, Goeke-Morey, & Papp, 2004; Davies, Cicchetti, & Martin, 2012; Kaczynski, Lindahl, Malik, & Laurenceau, 2006). Coparenting between mothers and fathers in the form of either supportive or conflictual relations also predicts externalizing and disruptive behaviors in young children (Belsky, Woodworth, & Crnic, 1996; Schoppe-Sullivan et al., 2009). We have also found that home observations of coparenting (low support and undermining) between parents during triadic interaction with the firstborn before the birth predicted increases in externalizing behaviors 1 month after the birth, and that supportive and undermining coparenting interacted so that the greatest increases in externalizing behavior problems occurred when mothers and fathers were high on undermining coparenting and low on supportive coparenting (Kolak & Volling, 2013). Parenting stress (Shaw et al., 2001) and the social support parents receive from family and friends may play a role in the emergence of disruptive behaviors, most likely due to the fact that reliance on others for emotional, financial, and instrumental support can alleviate much of the caregiving stress, reduce role overload, and enhance parental mental health (DeGarmo, Patras, & Eap, 2008; Guralnick, Hammond, Neville, & Connor, 2008; Hoagwood et al., 2010; Leahy-Warren, McCarthy, & Corcoran, 2012; Lee, Anderson, Horowitz, & August, 2009).

In the current study, we considered children's temperamental characteristics (e.g., negative emotionality), parent characteristics (e.g., depression, parenting behaviors, feelings of efficacy, attitudes toward spanking), and family and social contextual factors (e.g., marital quality, social support, coparenting, parenting hassles) before the birth as predictors of our aggression trajectories as part of the variable selection algorithms. Variable selection procedures are preferable when the goal is to pinpoint which factors are most strongly related to outcomes and can provide the evidence base needed to target effective interventions. Should a high-risk group of children showing clinically significant levels of aggression be identified, either before or after the birth of their infant sibling, this approach lets us identify those child, parent, and social-contextual factors most relevant for targeted interventions for these families.

Sibling Relationships and Early Aggression

According to Patterson (1986), coercive sibling interaction in childhood serves as a "training ground" for the development of aggressive behavior (i.e., the sibling training hypothesis). The strongest risk factor in predicting the trajectories of a highly aggressive group of toddler boys was the presence of a sibling in the household (Tremblay et al., 1999). The family is the first place that many young children encounter conflict and sibling conflict is commonplace in most households with two or more young children. Dunn and Munn (1986) reported that sibling conflict in early childhood occurred approximately 7 times an hour; similar to the 6.3 times per hour reported by Perlman and Ross (1997) with a sample of 2- and 4-year-old siblings. Although ubiquitous, sibling conflict can be both mild (e.g., argumentative) or severe (e.g., violent) and involve both destructive and constructive conflict resolution. Destructive conflict-resolution during sibling conflict, even for very young children, predicted aggressive behavior problems among preschool boys (Garcia et al., 2000). Early sibling conflict and aggression seems to play an influential role in the development of preschool children's emerging emotion regulation and aggression. Further, sibling conflict is strongly associated with the development of children's externalizing and internalizing difficulties (Dirks et al., 2015). Therefore, we examined whether the resulting aggression trajectories would predict sibling relationship quality, specifically more conflict and less positive involvement 1 year after the birth. We hypothesized that trajectories of aggression should predict the quality of the children's sibling relationship at the end of the year, particularly levels of sibling conflict. Children expressing high levels of aggressive behavior over the course of the year would be engaged in more sibling conflict and less positive sibling relationships at 12 months.

In the current study, we used a group-based trajectory analysis (growth mixture modeling) to ascertain different patterns of children's aggressive behavior across the transition, hypothesizing that children who evinced increased aggression or who had been highly aggressive before the infant's birth and continued to remain high over the course of the year would be engaged in more sibling conflict 1 year after the birth compared to children who were low on aggression or experienced minimal change in aggression over the course of the transition.

58

RESULTS

Individual Differences in Trajectories of Aggressive Behavior

Having determined in Chapter III that the unconditional Adjustment and Adaptation Response (AAR) model fit the aggression data better than both the unconditional latent linear and unconditional quadratic models, we used growth mixture modeling (GMM) to model the variability in the growth parameters and identify the patterns of aggression trajectories across the five timepoints of the study. We determined that the five-class Adjustment and Adaptation Response model (we will use AAR throughout the Results section for ease of presentation) solution with the fixed effects (i.e., intercept, linear slope, and AAR contrast) and the random effects (i.e., intercept, linear slope) of growth parameters was considered the best fitting model based on fit indices; the five-class model had a lower BIC and AIC, AIC = 5495.30, BIC = 5,588.13, than both the four-, AIC = 5,497.03, BIC = 5,576.11, and six-class models, AIC = 5,497.94, BIC = 5,604.52, and higher entropy (0.705) than the four-class model (0.673). Table 4 presents estimates and standard errors for the fixed effects of each class, which provide interpretation of the changes observed within each class, in addition to the random effects. Figure 3 shows the different trajectory patterns for the five classes. In determining class labels, we used a naming convention in which we denoted the starting value (intercept) first (e.g., high, mid, low) and then the pattern of change most characteristic of this class (e.g., decreasing, AAR).

The largest class was denoted as the *low-increasing* class and represented 40% of the sample ($n = 92$). As can be seen in Table 4 and Figure 3, children in this class showed the lowest levels of aggressive behavior at the prenatal time-point with a gradual linear increase over the first year after the birth of the sibling. A second class of children showed a significant increase in their aggressive behavior from prenatal to 1 month and then a decrease by 4 months (i.e., AAR effect). This *low-AAR class,* comprising 29.6% of the sample ($n = 68$), had low levels of aggressive behavior at the prenatal time point, followed by an increase from prenatal to 1 month, but a decrease from 1 to 4 months, and then remained stable for the rest of the year. A third class was labeled the *mid-stable* class (19.1%; $n = 44$) and showed moderate levels of aggressive behavior at the prenatal time point that remained stable throughout the first year after the birth of the sibling. The fourth, *mid-AAR-decreasing* class, accounted for only 7.8% of the sample ($n = 18$) and started out with mid-to-high levels of aggressive behavior at the prenatal time point, followed by a fairly dramatic increase from prenatal to 1 month in aggression, then a subsequent decrease from 1 to 4 months, with a further decrease in aggressive behavior for the rest of the year. The smallest class, *high-decreasing,* by contrast, accounted for 3.5% of the sample ($n = 8$) and showed

TABLE 4

GROWTH MIXTURE MODEL RESULTS FOR AGGRESSIVE BEHAVIOR: PARAMETER ESTIMATES AND STANDARD ERRORS FOR FIXED EFFECTS

Classes Parameters	Low-Increasing $n=92$ (40%)	Low-AAR $n=68$ (29.6%)	Mid-Stable $n=44$ (19.1%)	Mid-AAR-Decreasing $n=18$ (7.8%)	High-Decreasing $n=8$ (3.5%)
Intercept	5.222*** (.483)	9.363*** (.854)	12.565*** (.786)	13.385*** (.813)	19.376*** (1.142)
Linear slope	.254** (.081)	−.143 (.139)	−.109 (.195)	−.431* (.177)	−.736** (.251)
AAR	.060 (.105)	.710*** (.215)	−.241 (.239)	1.831*** (.224)	−.044 (.312)

Note. Standard errors in parentheses. AAR = Adjustment and Adaptation Response. The random effect (variance) of intercept est. = 2.949, SE = 1.386, p = .033; the random effect of linear slope est. = .037, SE = .048, p = ns; the random effect of the AAR contrast was constrained to be 0.
*p < .05, **p < .01, ***p ≤ .001.

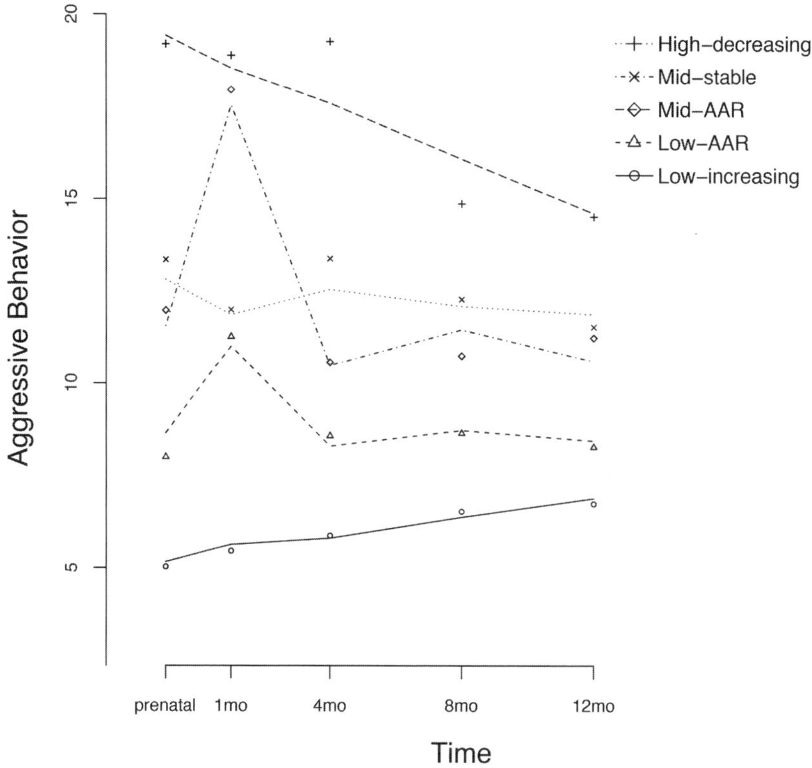

FIGURE 3.—Trajectory classes for aggressive behavior from Growth Mixture Model ($n = 230$).

the highest level of aggressive behavior at the prenatal timepoint with a significant linear decrease over time. Thus, results are consistent with theoretical patterns indicative of linear increase, stability and no change, as well as adjustment and adaptation as presented in Figure 1 in the Introduction and with none of the curvilinear patterns of change in Figure 2, including sudden, persistent change reflecting a psychosocial crisis model.

Spaghetti plots showing the individual trajectories for each child by class membership can be found in Figure 4. For each plot, the lower line represents the normative mean for the CBCL aggression subscale (1.5–5: Achenbach & Rescorla, 2000), the second line represents the 92.5th percentile, which indicates the borderline clinical range cut-off, and the top line represents the 97th percentile, which denotes the clinical range cut-off. What these figures clearly show is that the five classes fit precisely within these cut-off ranges, and are in line with what we would expect for a community-based low-risk sample in which most children were low and fell well below the borderline or clinical cut-offs for aggressive behavior,

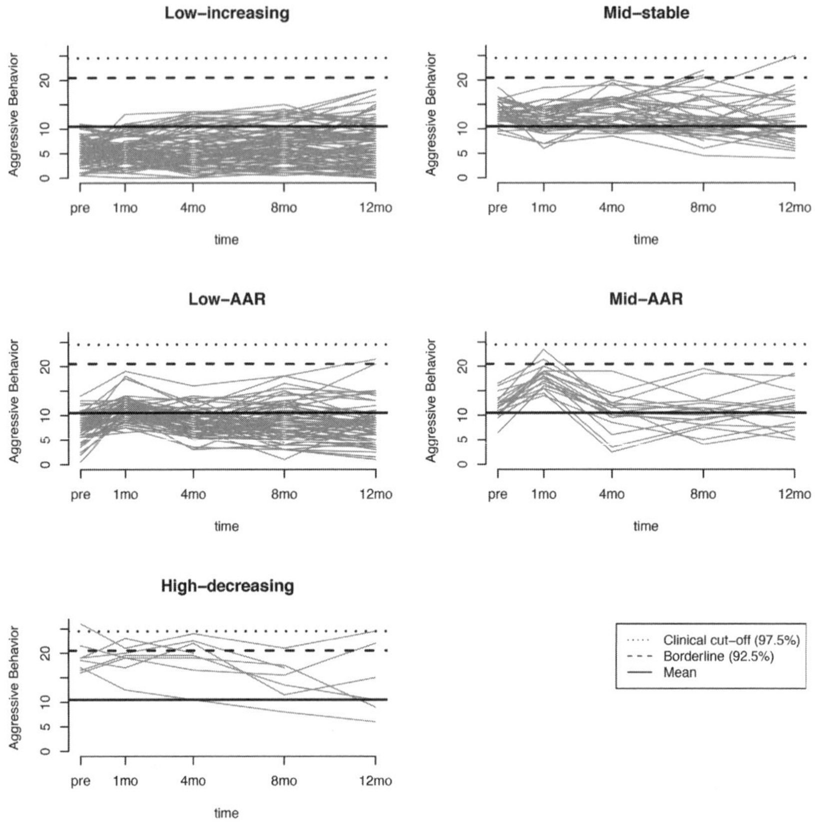

FIGURE 4.—Spaghetti plots of individual trajectories for each of the five aggression classes showing the mean (lowest line), borderline-clinical (92.5%; middle line), and clinical (97.5%; highest line) levels.

and only a few children were identified in the clinical cut-off range. For instance, all children within the low-increasing class were well below the normative mean, whereas all the mid-stable children fit within the borderline clinical range. Only the eight children in the high-decreasing class were near or above the clinical range cut-off. These figures demonstrate that the identified classes represent distinct and meaningful classes of children who fall within the normative, borderline, and clinical ranges established for the CBCL. Also, the mid-AAR-decreasing class differs from the low-AAR class, with the low-AAR starting in the low range and reaching the borderline range after the birth, and the mid-AAR starting in the borderline range and hitting the clinical range cut-off. Thus, the GMM analyses identified two classes of children, both having an AAR effect, but one actually experienced clinical levels of problem behaviors in response to the sibling's birth. This group of children is of particular interest because even though small in number there is evidence that they are experiencing behavioral changes severe enough to be clinically significant. Although several of the resulting classes have few children and could be considered statistical outliers or too few for class enumeration, these children are most deserving of our attention and should not be dismissed for purely statistical reasons.

Predicting Aggressive Trajectories

The combined recursive tree and random forest variable selection procedure identified four candidate predictors of the five classes of the aggression trajectories. These predictors were children's negative emotionality, attachment security to mother, fathers' parental-self efficacy, and observations of undermining coparenting during prenatal home visits. We then tested whether these four variables were statistically significant predictors of the five aggression classes by conducting a multinomial logistic regression with each predictor entered as a continuous, centered, additive predictor using the low-increasing class as the reference class. We computed a second multinomial logistic regression that also included all possible higher-order interactions between the five predictors. The full model with all higher-order interactions was not significantly better than the reduced model, *LR Chisq* ($df = 44$) $= 51.15$, $p = 0.21$, so we report the results of the reduced model with additive main effects.

Table 5 presents the coefficients, the standard errors, the odds ratios, and z tests for the multinomial logistic regressions using the large, low-increasing class as the reference class. The z tests show that children's negative emotionality is a significant predictor of differences between each of the four classes and the low-increasing reference group (all z's > 1.96). In all cases, there is a greater probability of being in the low-AAR, mid-stable, mid-AAR-decreasing, and high-decreasing class for children higher in negative emotionality compared to the low-increasing class. Children's attachment security to mother significantly predicted the difference between the high-decreasing class and the low-increasing reference class such that lower attachment security to mother is associated with a higher probability of being in the high-decreasing class relative to the low-increasing reference class. Father's parental efficacy was a significant predictor of the mid-stable and the high-decreasing class, with higher scores (i.e., greater feelings of ineffectiveness in disciplining) predicting a greater probability in both the mid-stable and high-decreasing classes relative to the low-increasing class.

Because of our interest in discerning differences between classes hitting different levels of clinical significance, we also conducted exploratory multinomial logistic regressions using several of the other classes as the reference class. Using the high-decreasing class as the reference class, in which children started near the clinical or above the clinical range on

TABLE 5

RESULTS OF MULTINOMIAL LOGISTIC REGRESSION ANALYSIS EXAMINING CLASS DIFFERENCES FOR AGGRESSIVE BEHAVIOR WITH THE LOW-INCREASING CLASS AS THE REFERENCE CLASS

Predictor	Low-Increasing vs.	b	SE	z	p	OR
Child negative emotionality	Low-AAR	1.07	0.34	3.14	0.002	2.92
	Mid-stable	2.56	0.50	5.13	<0.001	12.97
	Mid-AAR	1.54	0.56	2.77	0.006	4.66
	High-decreasing	6.88	2.15	3.21	0.001	976.31
Undermining coparenting	Low-AAR	0.11	0.10	1.05	n.s.	1.11
	Mid-stable	−0.19	0.15	−1.25	n.s.	0.83
	Mid-AAR	−0.32	0.19	−1.67	n.s.	0.72
	High-decreasing	1.14	0.71	1.60	n.s.	3.13
Attachment security to mother	Low-AAR	−1.38	0.99	−1.40	n.s.	0.25
	Mid-stable	−1.58	1.24	−1.27	n.s.	0.21
	Mid-AAR	−2.17	1.57	−1.39	n.s.	0.11
	High-decreasing	−23.24	10.2	−2.43	0.023	0.00
Fathers' parental efficacy[a]	Low-AAR	0.75	0.49	1.52	n.s.	2.12
	Mid-stable	2.49	0.70	3.59	<0.001	12.11
	Mid-AAR	0.65	0.79	0.83	n.s.	1.91
	High-decreasing	7.09	2.92	2.43	0.015	>1000

Note. n.s. = nonsignificant; *OR* = odds ratio; AAR = Adjustment and Adaptation Response.
[a]Higher scores indicate lower sense of efficacy as a parent.

aggression before the birth, we found that children's negative emotionality, attachment security to mother, undermining coparenting during triadic observations, and fathers' parental self-efficacy significantly predicted class membership in the high-decreasing compared to the mid-AAR-decreasing class. Specifically, children in the high-decreasing class were more negatively emotional, $b = -5.34$, $z = -2.463$, $OR = .005$, had parents engaged in more undermining coparenting, $b = -1.47$, $z = -2.014$, $OR = 0.231$, had fathers with low parental efficacy, $b = -6.44$, $z = -2.172$, $OR = .002$, and had less secure attachments to their mothers, $b = 21.06$, $z = 2.06$, $OR > 1,000$, than children in the mid-AAR-decreasing class. Actually, children in the high-decreasing class were higher on negative emotionality (all z's less than -1.96) and had less secure attachments to their mothers than any of the four comparison classes (all z's greater than 1.96). Further, fathers of children in the high-decreasing class felt less effective as a parent than fathers of children in the low-AAR class, $b = -6.34$, $z = -2.178$, $OR = .002$.

We were also interested in the comparisons between the mid-stable and mid-AAR-decreasing classes because these two classes were similar at the prenatal time point, but evinced different patterns of change, with one showing an AAR and the other remaining stable over time. Using the mid-stable class as the reference class, father's parental efficacy predicted the likelihood difference of being in the mid-AAR-decreasing class, $b = -1.85$, $z = -2.110$, $OR = 0.158$, indicating that fathers who felt more ineffective as a parent were more likely to have children in the mid-stable class. In addition, father's parental efficacy, $b = -1.74$, $z = -2.60$, $OR = 0.175$, children's negative emotionality, $b = -1.49$, $z = -3.15$, $OR = 0.225$, and observed undermining coparenting, $b = 0.294$, $z = 2.05$, $OR = 1.34$, predicted the low-AAR class relative to the mid-stable class, with greater feelings of ineffective fathering, more negatively emotional children, and less undermining coparenting associated with greater probability of membership in the mid-stable class compared to the low-AAR class. Finally, we were interested in the mid-AAR-decreasing and low-AAR classes. Both showed an adjustment and adaptation response, but they differed both with respect to their intercepts (i.e., prenatal scores) and the extent of the response, with one showing a modest increase, and the other showing an increase hitting clinical levels. Only the observations of undermining coparenting predicted the difference between class membership, $b = -.432$, $z = -2.22$, $OR = 0.649$ (using low-AAR as reference), with parents in the low-AAR more likely to use undermining coparenting during home observations than parents in the mid-AAR-decreasing class.

Consequences of Children's Aggression for Sibling Relationships at 1 Year

To determine whether children's aggression trajectories predicted the quality of the sibling relationship at 12 months after the birth, we conducted a series of regression analyses across the three dimensions of sibling relationship quality (i.e., positive engagement, conflict, and avoidance) using the low-increasing class as a reference group because our predictor, the aggression trajectory classes, was categorical. Results revealed that at 12 months, parents of children in the mid-stable (est. $= 0.243$, $SE = 0.108$, $p = .026$) and mid-AAR-decreasing classes (est. $= 0.382$, $SE = 0.143$, $p = .008$) reported significantly more sibling conflict at 12 months than the low-increasing class. The mid-stable group was also significantly less likely to be positively engaged with their younger siblings at 12 months (est. $= -0.213$, $SE = 0.104$, $p = .041$) than the low-increasing class.

DISCUSSION OF CHILDREN'S AGGRESSION TRAJECTORIES

In this chapter, we examined the overall pattern of children's aggression after the birth of a sibling, as well as subgroups of trajectories that captured individual differences within the overall sample. Additionally, we explored the predictors of these trajectories and tested whether distinct trajectory subtypes were associated with differences in sibling relationship quality when the younger sibling was 1 year of age.

Results examining the overall pattern of aggressive behavior across the sample indicated that the adjustment and adaptation response, with an initial increase in aggression from prenatal to 1 month and a subsequent decline in aggression from 1 to 4 months, best described children's aggressive behavior after the birth of an infant sibling. Thus, firstborn children, in general, do appear to show an initial increase in aggression after their infant sibling's birth, but this increase is short-lived and children return to prebirth levels by 4 months. Testing the AAR contrast in our statistical models provides solid evidence for what we are referring to as an adjustment and adaptation response after a normative stressful life event (the birth of an infant sibling) that underscores the resilience of many children, and stands in contrast to a pattern of sudden and persistent change indicative of maladjustment that would have been captured by the quadratic effect. Thus, our results provide far more support for resilience in the face of stress and change for children undergoing the transition to siblinghood than any evidence of psychosocial trauma or a developmental crisis underscored in some of the earliest psychodynamic accounts of children's reactions to the birth of a sibling (Levy, 1937; Winnicott, 1964) in which children supposedly would resort to any means necessary to recapture the lost attention and love of their parents.

Despite evidence of an adjustment and adaptation response to their sibling's birth, heterogeneity in children's aggression trajectories was further evident, and we were able to identify five trajectory patterns that described children in the present sample; several in line with current studies looking at trajectories of aggression and externalizing behavior in the toddler and preschool period. The largest class of children (40%) was low on aggression initially at the prebirth time point and gradually increased (linear) in their aggression over the year following the sibling's birth. This pattern may reflect a normative developmental trajectory in that children are known to increase over the toddler years in their aggressive behavior before aggression declines around 3–4 years of age. Children in the current study were 31 months of age, on average, so increases in aggressive behavior throughout the year following the birth due to normative age changes would not be completely consistent with extant findings.

In contrast, these gradual increases in aggressive behavior over the months after the birth may coincide with normative developmental changes in the infant during the first year after birth. Maturation in infant mobility with advances in exploratory play and social interest in others as the year progresses means greater social contact between older and younger siblings, yet infants are also limited in their social abilities. These sorts of encounters of invading on the older siblings' play space, while grabbing toys and destroying carefully planned fantasy worlds may often be upsetting to older siblings who themselves are still relatively unsophisticated in their own abilities to resolve conflict. Dunn and Munn (1986) provided detailed descriptions of the conflict between young siblings of this age and the frequent number of conflicts in which parents must intervene over the course of a day (approximately 7 per hour). This interpretation of increasing aggression coinciding with developmental changes in the infant is substantiated by our findings showing that the different aggression trajectories predicted the quality of children's relationships with their younger sibling 1 year after the birth. Children in the mid-stable class exhibited more conflict and were less positively engaged with their infant siblings than children in the low-increasing class. The largest class of children showing low, but linearly increasing, aggression over the year following the birth of their younger siblings appears to describe most children in this sample. Thus, a modest linear increase in children's aggressive behavior may be expected during the year following the birth of a second child.

Because of our interest in identifying the effects of the transition on children's behavioral adjustment and whether these effects were short- or long-lived, we tested different trajectory patterns indicative of no change and linear change (increases and decreases), as well as more specific patterns we hypothesized to reflect different patterns of adjustment and adaptation, one in which children would exhibit initial behavioral disruption in response to the stress of the transition, but adapt over time to the changing family circumstances and return to prebirth levels of behavioral functioning, and a second, more indicative of behavioral maladjustment or difficulties with the transition that would reflect sudden increases in problematic behavior in response to the transition that persisted over time (quadratic model) and did not return to prebirth levels. The quadratic model would also allow testing of other possible developmental trajectories that might coincide with changes in the family and the infant's developmental milestones over time, such as the gradual impact and decline model wherein children increased but returned gradually back to prebirth levels over the year, or the delayed impact model wherein children show little to no change immediately after the birth, but showed significantly greater increases by 8 and 12 months when infant mobility and social intrusions become more frequent (Stewart, 1990). The unconditional latent growth curve model indicated that the model testing the adjustment and adaptation response was a better fit to our data than either the linear or quadratic models suggesting that, on average, there was evidence of initial increases in children's aggression shortly after the birth that subsided by 4 months of age. This model was a better fit to the longitudinal patterns than a maladaptation or developmental crisis model, the delayed impact model, or the gradual impact and decline model. These findings are consistent with Dunn and Kendrick's (1982) work reporting that changes in children's problematic behavior after the sibling's birth were short-lived and most children appeared to adjust to the birth by 8 months of age, although our data suggest that most children have adjusted already by 4 months after the birth.

Regardless of this general pattern, though, there was evidence of heterogeneity in children's aggression trajectories. There was a very small group of children ($N = 8$) who evinced very high levels (clinical and borderline-clinical cut-off range) of aggression even before the birth and actually showed significant declines in their aggression over time. This pattern may reflect the normative developmental decreases in aggression often reported in the literature, but based on our prediction analysis examining the most discriminating prenatal predictors, we offer another possible interpretation focusing on family processes interacting with children's temperament. These eight children differed from the low-increasing class in that they were higher in negative emotionality, had lower attachment security scores to their mothers, had fathers who felt more ineffective in their abilities to parent and discipline the older sibling, and had parents engaged in more undermining coparenting during prenatal home observations. Once the infant was born and mothers were busy with the care of a newborn infant, these insecurely attached children's aggression actually decreased over time, suggesting the possibility that children's behavioral adjustment may have far more to do with family dynamics and changes in the family brought about by the birth of the infant than the actual infant per se. One possible explanation is that children fare better and engage in less aggressive behavior once their mothers' attention is redirected to another child, and the older child is no longer the recipient of the insensitive or intrusive parenting that gave rise to the insecure attachment to their mothers. It is also possible that these children expressed their aggressive tendencies and emotional distress through other means, perhaps becoming more emotionally reactive once the infant was born. Of these eight aggressive children, five were in the mid-increasing group of emotionally reactive children to be described later, suggesting that decreases in aggressive behavior were accompanied by increases in emotional distress over the year. We do not know if these children may have turned to their fathers during this time for security and comfort and whether a secure father–child attachment may account in some ways for this decrease in aggressive behavior. It should be noted, however, that fathers of these children reported feeling less efficacious in their parenting skills, so even if children did turn to their fathers for support, it is not clear that their fathers were able to provide the emotional comfort and security needed to ameliorate their distress.

A similar picture emerged for some of the other trajectory patterns wherein children's negative emotionality and family relationship functioning before the sibling's birth played a large part in predicting class membership. For instance, most children in the three classes that fell within the borderline clinical and clinical cut-offs of the aggression scale, the high-decreasing, mid-stable, and mid-AAR-decreasing classes, were higher on negative emotionality than children in the low-increasing class. Children in the mid-stable class also had fathers who felt less effective in their discipline than those in the low-increasing class, yet had higher attachment security scores with their mothers than children in the riskier, high-decreasing class.

We were particularly interested in comparisons between groups where children were comparable at the prenatal visit, but showed a different pattern of change after the birth, specifically comparisons of the mid-stable group with the mid-AAR-decreasing group, where children had a large increase (some hitting clinical levels) in their aggression after the birth that subsequently declined by 4 months, and comparison of the low-increasing with the low-AAR group, where there was a more modest increase in aggression from prenatal to 1 month that eventually declined by 4 months. Children in the mid-AAR-decreasing group were distinguished from the mid-stable class in that their fathers reported feeling more efficacious in their parenting abilities than those in the mid-stable class. Perhaps the more efficacious fathers of the mid-AAR-decreasing class were able to effectively respond and discipline their children in response to aggressive behavior that allowed children to return to prebirth levels of functioning during a particularly stressful developmental transition.

Most children in the low-increasing and low-AAR classes were low on negative emotionality, yet children in the low-AAR class did have higher scores on negative emotionality than children in the low-increasing class, suggesting that these children may have been more temperamentally reactive to changes in the family after the sibling's birth. It is interesting that children in the low-AAR families had parents who engaged in more undermining coparenting during prenatal home observations than parents in both the mid-stable and mid-AAR-decreasing classes underscoring that mothers and fathers in these families had difficulties working together as coparents and this may have played some role in why the low-AAR children had the significant increase in aggressive behaviors that they did. The low-AAR class represented 30% of the sample and was the second largest class after the larger, low-increasing class. Some have argued that the father's involvement during this transition is critical for children's adjustment (Kreppner, Paulsen, & Schuetze, 1982; Stewart, 1990), and the current findings suggest that children may experience little to no disruption after the birth when their fathers are actively involved in the family either because of their active role as a coparent or their feelings of competence as an effective father. No study before ours has examined fathers' feelings of parental efficacy or coparenting in predicting children's adjustment after the birth of a sibling, but our findings are consistent with earlier research underscoring the strong connections between marital quality, father–child relationships, and children's behavioral adjustment (Booth & Amato, 1994; Cummings, Merrilees, & George, 2010; Davies, Sturge-Apple,

Woitach, & Cummings, 2009; Goeke-Morey & Cummings, 2007; Jouriles & Farris, 1992; Schacht, Cummings, & Davies, 2009; Stevenson et al., 2014).

Two of the five classes revealed a period of adjustment (i.e., the initial response to a potential stressor) and adaptation (i.e., a period in which the child reorganizes and resumes family life much as before the stressful life event). We believe our research program is the first to explicitly test for an adjustment and adaptation response after a normative life event using latent growth curve and growth mixture modeling. The timing of our assessments was critical in capturing this response, given that children had already returned to prebirth levels by 4 months after birth. Had our first postbirth assessment not occurred at 1 month, so soon after the birth, we would have missed the adjustment and adaptation response for children's aggression and most likely concluded that children's aggression remained stable, when in fact the results clearly suggested a perturbation in the family system that eventually resolved itself. Because our analysis strategy was guided by our desire to identify prenatal predictors that would be useful targets for prebirth intervention, we were unable to delineate what family processes after the birth may be responsible for these different change patterns. Future reports will be able to provide more fine-grained analyses addressing the family processes and developmental cascades between child, parent, and family context over time.

Overall, the results examining children's aggression after the birth of a second child indicate that for most children, parents can expect a gradual linear increase in the firstborn children's aggression that more than likely coincides with developmental changes in the infant's growing capacity to socially engage others, both negatively and positively. There is also evidence, however, that there are significant individual differences in how children react to the birth of their infant sibling and that family processes occurring before the birth forecast these individual differences in aggression trajectories over the first year. Temperamentally difficult children with insecure attachments to their mothers in families where fathers felt ineffective in disciplining the firstborn, with more undermining coparenting observed during home observations, were at greatest risk for being aggressive before and staying aggressive after the birth of their infant sibling, or evincing a period of initial disruption that eventually subsided by 4 months. Most children appeared to be resilient and returned to prebirth levels by 4 months after the birth. Intervention efforts targeting the mother–child relationship, fathers' effectiveness in managing the older child's behaviors, and the coparenting relationship before the birth may assist these children and their families with the transition. These results are consistent with prior research finding that preschool children with externalizing or aggressive behavior problems often have difficult temperaments, have insecure attachments to their mothers and fathers, and have parents engaged in more coparenting conflict (Fearon & Belsky, 2011; Fearon et al., 2010; Gartstein et al., 2012; Kochanska & Kim, 2012; Rothbart & Bates, 1998). In sum, these results suggest that children's aggressive behaviors before and after the birth of a sibling may be exacerbated by the stresses and changes in family life surrounding the birth, but many of these changes are short-lived and children are resilient and adapt to stress with the assistance of their parents.

V. DEVELOPMENTAL TRAJECTORIES OF CHILDREN'S ATTENTION PROBLEMS AFTER THE BIRTH OF A SIBLING

Ju-Hyun Song, Wonjung Oh, Richard Gonzalez, Brenda L. Volling, and Tianyi Yu

This article is part of the issue "Developmental Trajectories of Children's Adjustment across the Transition to Siblinghood: Pre-Birth Predictors and Sibling Outcomes at One Year" Volling, Gonzalez, Oh, Song, Yu, Rosenberg, Kuo, Thomason, Beyers-Carlson, Safyer, and Stevenson (Issue Authors). For a full listing of articles in this issue, see: http://onlinelibrary.wiley.com/doi/10.1111/mono.v82.3/issuetoc.

Children show a dramatic change in the ability to sustain and reorient attention between 2 and 5 years of age (Jones, Rothbart, & Posner, 2003; Kopp, 1989). The ability to sustain attention is relevant for children's adjustment during normative transitions such as the transition to siblinghood. As children have increased opportunities to engage with others (e.g., siblings), coordinating behaviors and complying with adults' directions become important across multiple settings (Campbell, 2006), which requires the ability to sustain or redirect attention (Rothbart et al., 2011). Thus, children with attention problems may experience more difficulties meeting social demands in adjusting during the transition.

There may be two possible patterns of attention problems that children experience during the transition to siblinghood: (i) a developmental lag in attentional control or (ii) deviations in temperamental characteristics such as low behavioral inhibition and poor effortful control (Ruff & Rothbart, 1996).

Corresponding author: Correspondence concerning the Family Transitions Study should be addressed to Brenda L. Volling, Center for Human Growth and Development, University of Michigan, 300 N. Ingalls, Ann Arbor, MI 48109-5406. email: volling@umich.edu

For those interested in the statistical code used to analyze these data (including growth mixture models, random forest, and CART procedures), please email Richard Gonzalez, gonzo@umich.edu

DOI: 10.1111/mono.12311

Further, some children may display attention problems as a temporary stress reaction along with tantrums or oppositional behaviors, brought on by stress adjusting to the arrival of an infant sibling (Campbell, 2006; Stewart, 1990). Children may exhibit different trajectories of change in attention problems over this developmental period depending on whether they are exhibiting a developmental lag, a temperamental deviation, or a temporary stress reaction. Despite these possibilities, little research has investigated changes in firstborn children's attention problems during the transition to siblinghood. Although one study found that children's attention span did not change significantly following the birth of the sibling (e.g., Stewart, 1990), more research is needed.

Development of Attention Problems in Early Childhood

From a developmental perspective, attention problems, along with other externalizing behavior problems, are often reported to be transient during the toddlerhood and preschool years (Mesman et al., 2009; Owens & Shaw, 2003), and show a general pattern of linear decline (van Aken, Junger, Verhoeven, van Aken, & Deković, 2008). One possible reason for the average decrease in attention problems is that children show dramatic development in abilities for directing and sustaining attention around 18 months, and these abilities are consolidated around 4 years with increasing skills to inhibit attention to irrelevant tasks (Ruff & Rothbart, 1996; van Aken et al., 2008). Despite this general pattern, there are some children who show stable or increasing patterns of externalizing behavior problems over the preschool years and are more likely to continue to have future problems with attention (Ruff & Rothbart, 1996), as well as socio-emotional and academic difficulties in childhood (Kingston & Prior, 1995).

Individual Differences in Young Children's Attention Problems

Although attention problems decrease during the toddler and preschool years at a group level, studies have found meaningful individual differences in the starting point (i.e., intercept) and the rate of change (i.e., slope) in attention problem trajectories during the preschool years (Mesman et al., 2009; van Aken et al., 2008). For example, van Aken et al. (2008) found that intercepts of attention problems at 17 months were concurrently related to supportive maternal parenting and maternal psychological control, whereas decreases in attention problems from 17 to 54 months were positively related to greater decreases in mothers' physical punishment and negatively related to faster decreases in fathers' supportive parenting. These findings suggest that although young children's attentional problems may be a reaction to distressing circumstances, attentional problems as a form of negative adjustment may be resolved with supportive parenting, or they may persist as more serious behavior problems when there are other family risks (Campbell, 2006).

In this chapter, we aimed to identify different trajectories of children's attention problems during the transition to siblinghood. We expected to identify different groups of children who showed heterogeneous patterns of change in attention problems over the period of the transition before and after the birth of a sibling. Based on the literature on the normative development of attentional control during this age period, the majority of children were expected to show a gradual decrease in attention problems over the transition from the initial prenatal time point (i.e., intercept); although there may be subgroups of children who differ with respect to their starting point with some fairly low on attention problems and others moderate to high on attention problems even before the birth of a sibling. We also expected to find a smaller group of children at greater risk for attention problems that might display a high stable pattern over time.

Risk and Protective Factors in the Prediction of Early Attention Problems

Risk and protective factors that are associated with attention problems can be grouped into characteristics of children, parents, and family situations. Several temperamental child characteristics have been identified as potential risks. Specifically, lower executive attention skills, lower effortful control, higher surgency (extraversion), and higher negative affect predicted mother-rated attention problems in preschool and early childhood (Brown, Weatherhol, & Burns, 2010).

Regarding parental factors, multiple studies have identified attachment security as an important risk factor for the development of attention problems (Fearon & Belsky, 2004). Because mothers of insecurely attached children are more intrusive, less sensitive, and less responsive (Campbell, 2006; De Wolff & van Ijzendoorn, 1997), an insecure attachment most likely reflects an antagonistic dynamic between the parent and child (Kochanska & Kim, 2012) that likely increases interpersonal stress and interferes with children's attentional control (Fearon & Belsky, 2004; Ruff & Rothbart, 1996; Tharner et al., 2012). On the other hand, maternal sensitivity across the first 4.5 years of life predicted children's attentional task performance at age 54 months (NICHD Early Child Care Research Network, 2003). Other dimensions of parenting quality are also reported as important risk and protective factors for the development of attention problems. For example, parental psychological control, physical punishment, and the lack of support positively predicted attention problems, whereas parental sensitivity, positive discipline, and structure (e.g., organized environment, being consistent) negatively predicted attention problems among toddlers and preschoolers (NICHD Early

Child Care Research Network, 2003; van Aken et al., 2008). In addition, mothers' and fathers' emotional instability (van Aken et al., 2008) and high levels of childrearing-related parenting stress have been positively related to preschool children's attention problems (Crnic, Gaze, & Hoffman, 2005; Tharner et al., 2012). In regard to family context factors, high levels of family stress and lower SES predicted the continuation of children's externalizing problems including attention problems from preschool to middle childhood (Campbell, 2002; Moffitt, 1990). For the current analyses examining predictors of children's attention problem trajectories, we expected to find similar relations with children's temperament, parenting interactions, parental stress, and household income as reported in these earlier studies.

Sibling Relationships and Early Attention Problems

Social impairment of children with attention problems has been studied mostly with respect to parent–child and peer relationships. Children with attention problems have a difficult time attending to conversations, following the rules of games, turn-taking, and inhibiting aggression (Whalen & Henker, 1992). What is less studied is how children's early attention problems and their poor self-regulation may be related to sibling relationship quality. A handful of clinical research studies suggest that the sibling relationships of children with ADHD are marked by increased conflict (Mikami & Pfiffner, 2008), presumably due to their lower inhibition (Barkley, 2003) and poor social skills (Wheeler & Carlson, 1994).

The transition to siblinghood may be a challenging developmental period for children with poor regulatory skills as a result of attention problems because the arrival of a sibling may challenge their abilities to cope with both the negative and positive changes co-occurring with the transition, including the jealousy of the new baby, the frustration of caregiver unavailability, and the joy of welcoming a new brother or sister (Dunn & Kendrick, 1980; Volling et al., 2014). Few studies, however, have examined children's emotion regulation and sibling relationship quality. Kolak and Volling (2011) did report that children's jealousy, as indicated by behavioral dysregulation when 16-month-old toddlers observed fathers interacting with their older siblings, predicted more sibling conflict 2.5 years later. Based on the findings that children with attention deficits are more likely to have emotion regulation difficulties (Melnick & Hinshaw, 2000; Walcott & Landau, 2004), the transition period may be particularly challenging for these children.

In the current study, we expected to find associations between children's attention problems over the year following the transition and sibling relationship quality at the end of the year. Specifically, we expected that children with high stable or increasing patterns of attention problems across the transition to siblinghood would also be engaged in more sibling conflict 12 months after the birth when compared to children who were low on attention problems or who declined in attention problems over time.

RESULTS

Individual Differences in Trajectories of Attention Problems

As noted earlier in Chapter III, the unconditional linear model fit the attention problems data better than both the unconditional Adjustment and Adaptation Response and quadratic models, which was then used in our GMM analyses to identify the patterns of attention problems trajectories. The three-class model was considered the best fitting model based on fit indices because the three-class model had lower fit indices, $AIC = 3,055.06$, $BIC = 3,109.99$, $LMR = .01$, than the two-class model, $AIC = 3,066.25$, $BIC = 3,110.89$, and the four-class model, $AIC = 3,053.49$, $BIC = 3,118.73$, $LMR = 0.239$; the three-class model also had higher entropy (0.820) than the four-class model (0.763). Estimates and standard errors for the fixed effects along with the random effects of each of the three classes are presented in Table 6 and the trajectory patterns for the three classes are also displayed in Figure 5.

The first class, representing 75.1% of the sample ($n = 172$), was labeled the *low-decreasing* class, because children in this class were low on attention problems at the prenatal time point with a significant linear decrease throughout the first year postpartum. A second class was denoted as the *mid-decreasing* class, reflecting 22.7% of the sample ($n = 52$). This class had moderate levels of attention problems at the onset and showed a linear decrease over time. The third class was labeled the *high-stable* class, and consisted of only 2.2% of the sample ($n = 5$). Children in this class had high levels of attention problems prenatally, which remained stably high over time. Again, there is more support for linear or stable patterns of adjustment than curvilinear patterns (see Figure 1 in Introduction).

TABLE 6

GROWTH MIXTURE MODEL RESULTS FOR ATTENTION PROBLEMS: PARAMETER ESTIMATES AND STANDARD ERRORS FOR FIXED EFFECTS

Classes Parameters	Low-Decreasing $n = 172$ (75.1%)	Mid-Decreasing $n = 52$ (22.7%)	High-Stable $n = 5$ (2.2%)
Intercept	1.616*** (.084)	3.685*** (.182)	6.403*** (.407)
Linear slope	−.039* (.015)	−.105** (.036)	−.022 (.096)

Note. Standard errors in parentheses. The random effect (variance) of intercept est. $= 0.374$, $SE = .080$, $p < .001$; the random effect of linear slope est. $= .007$, $SE = .004$, $p = .070$.
*$p < .05$, **$p < .01$, ***$p < .001$.

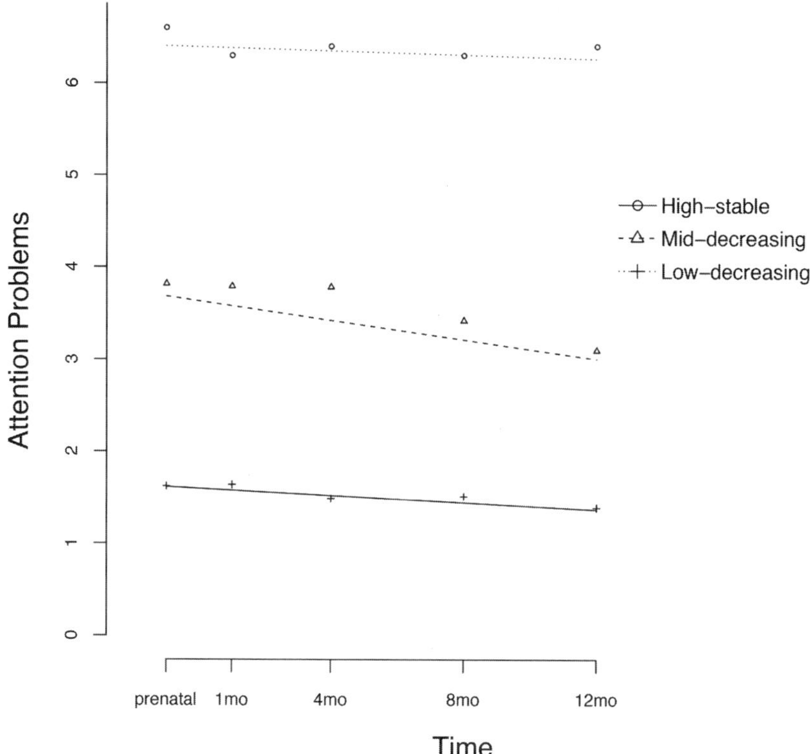

FIGURE 5.—Trajectory classes for attention problems from the Growth Mixture Model ($n = 229$).

We also examined how children in each class fell within the normative (mean), borderline clinical (92.5%), and the clinical cut-off ranges (97%) by examining the spaghetti plots showing the individual trajectories for each child in each class (see Figure S1 in the supporting information online). The intercepts for each class mapped well onto the cut-off ranges, with a majority of children in the low-decreasing class below the normative mean and some slightly above the mean. Most children in the mid-decreasing class fell between the normative mean and the borderline clinical cut-off. Only the five children in the high-stable class were near the clinical cut-off.

Predicting Attention Problem Trajectories

Based on the variable selection procedures, three variables emerged as candidate predictors of the attention problem trajectories: attachment security to mother, fathers' parenting self-efficacy, and mothers' parenting self-efficacy. The multinomial logistic regression model with all possible higher-order interactions in comparison to the model with main effects only was not a significantly better fit, *LR Chisq* (df $= 8$) $= 5.27$, $p = 0.73$, so we report the results from the reduced model with main effects only.

Results for the multinomial logistic regression using the large low-decreasing class as the reference group, are presented in Table 7. The z tests revealed significant main effects of only two variables: attachment security to mother and mothers' parenting self-efficacy. Odds ratios revealed that children's attachment security to the mother significantly predicted the differences between the mid-decreasing class and the low-decreasing reference class, as well as between the high-stable class and the low-decreasing reference class. Children with lower attachment security to mother were more likely to be in the mid-decreasing class or high-stable class relative to the low decreasing reference class. Also, mothers' reports of parenting self-efficacy significantly predicted the difference between the mid-decreasing class and the low-decreasing reference class such that lower levels of mother-reported parenting self-efficacy was associated with a higher probability of being in the mid-decreasing class relative to the low-decreasing reference class. Treating the other two classes as the reference class in separate exploratory analyses yielded an additional significant comparison between the high-stable class and the mid-decreasing class. Specifically, children with lower attachment security to mother were more likely to be in the high-stable class than the mid-decreasing class, $b = -7.202$, $z = -2.012$, $p = .044$, $OR = .001$.

Consequences of Children's Attention Problems for Sibling Relationships at 1 Year

Regression analyses tested whether children's attention problem trajectories predicted the three dimensions of sibling relationship quality

TABLE 7

Results of Multinomial Logistic Regression Analysis Examining Class Differences for Children's Attention Problems With the Low-Decreasing Class As the Reference Class

Predictor	Low-Decreasing vs.	b	SE	z	P	OR
Attachment security to mother	Mid-decreasing	−2.74	1.02	−2.68	0.007	0.06
	High-stable	−9.94	3.61	−2.76	0.006	0.00
Fathers' parenting self-efficacy[a]	Mid-decreasing	1.07	0.54	1.96	n.s.	2.90
	High-stable	1.67	1.60	1.05	n.s.	5.33
Mothers' parenting self-efficacy[a]	Mid-decreasing	1.37	0.56	2.46	0.014	3.94
	High-stable	1.03	1.48	0.69	n.s.	2.79

Note. n.s., nonsignificant; *OR* = odds ratio.
[a]Higher scores indicate lower sense of efficacy as a parent.

78

(i.e., positive engagement, conflict, and avoidance). The results indicated that children in the mid-decreasing class (est. $= 0.194$, $SE = .091$, $p = .036$) and the high-stable class (est. $= 0.498$, $SE = 0.242$, $p = .043$) were more likely to engage in sibling conflict at 12 months relative to children in the low-decreasing reference class.

DISCUSSION OF CHILDREN'S ATTENTION PROBLEM TRAJECTORIES

The current chapter examined heterogeneity in children's attention problem trajectories after the birth of their infant sibling. We identified three trajectory patterns that were roughly consistent with the literature on the development of attention problems in the toddler and preschool period. The largest class of children, approximately 75% of the sample, showed a low-decreasing pattern, implying that they initially showed low levels of attention problems before the birth of the sibling with a further gradual linear decline over the year following the birth, which is in line with current findings showing declines in attention problems over the preschool period. The second largest class of children, nearly 23%, showed a mid-decreasing pattern, in which children had scores on attention problems in the moderate range starting prenatally that were higher than the low-decreasing class, but still well under the clinical level cut-off, and continued to show a decrease in attention problems over the first year of siblinghood. What these two classes have in common is that they both show a linearly decreasing pattern despite the difference in their initial prenatal scores (i.e., intercepts). This overall decreasing pattern for both classes is consistent with the normative decline in attention problems between the ages of 2 and 5 noted in prior studies, coinciding with a dramatic increase in children's abilities to direct and sustain attention (Jones et al., 2003; Rothbart et al., 2011). The smallest class of children, only 2%, showed a high-stable pattern, in which children initially started with significantly high levels of attention problems at the prebirth time point and maintained this level without a noticeable change over time. The proportion of this small group of children resembles the prevalence of ADHD in the preschool years, which is reported to be approximately 3% (Egger & Angold, 2006). Overall, these results suggest that except for a small subgroup of children, children are mostly differentiated by their initial levels of attention problems before the birth of the infant, and most children show linear declines in attention problems over the course of the year after the birth, which is consistent with developmental expectations of a normative linear decline in attention problems over the toddler and preschool years. In sum, the current results provide little evidence that children experience attention problems as a temporary stress reaction while adjusting to the arrival of an infant sibling. Instead, the results support a normative overall decline in attention problems, even though some children may have higher initial levels before the birth than other children.

We identified two important parenting factors at the prenatal timepoint that predicted the different classes and are most likely responsible, in part, for the intercept differences across classes of attention problems. First, children's attachment security to their mothers differentiated all three groups. Children with insecure attachments to their mothers were more likely to be in the mid-decreasing or the high-stable class in comparison to the low-decreasing class. This is consistent with a large body of literature on parenting and children's attention problems showing that poor parenting practices are associated with higher attention problems. For example, negative parent–child interactions and poor parenting characterized by high intrusiveness and low sensitivity predicted children's higher stress levels, which interfered with attentional control (Tharner et al., 2012). Attachment insecurity sets up a caregiving context for antagonistic interactions between the parent and the child (De Wolff & van Ijzendoorn, 1997; Fearon & Belsky, 2004; Kochanska & Kim, 2012), which then interferes with children's attentional focus (NICHD Early Child Care Research Network, 2003). The results of the current study on children's attention problems after the birth of an infant sibling corroborate these earlier reports. Because we measured both parenting and the CBCL attention problems scale at the prenatal time point, we are unable to confirm the direction of causality from the current findings and future research is needed to address this issue further.

Another prebirth predictor for children's attention problems after their sibling's birth was mother-reported parenting self-efficacy, which indicates the level of competence mothers felt as a parent, including how well they believed they could control their children's difficult behaviors. Children whose mothers reported low levels of parenting self-efficacy were more likely to be in the mid-decreasing class as opposed to the low-decreasing class with respect to attention problems. This finding is somewhat consistent with earlier reports finding that high levels of childrearing stress were positively associated with more attention problems (Crnic et al., 2005; Tharner et al., 2012). This relation may be partly mediated by parenting behavior and reflect a bidirectional process in which mothers feeling less efficacious as a parent engage in more coercive and less competent parenting practices with their children, although having to discipline children with attention problems during a stressful transition after the birth of an infant sibling may stress mothers' capacities to effectively parent these children and decrease mothers' sense of parenting efficacy over time.

Besides these two predictors, fathers' parenting self-efficacy also emerged as a potential predictor in our variable selection procedure, but did not pass the more stringent criterion of statistical significance in the multinomial logistic regression by accounting for unique variance above the other predictors. Fathers' self-efficacy in child-rearing may play a role in predicting children's attention problems after the birth of a sibling in ways that we were not able to discern here, and we recommend that future studies examine this possibility further given that earlier research has found that fathers' decrease in supportive parenting was related to a slower decrease in preschool children's attention problems (van Aken et al., 2008).

Unlike earlier studies, child characteristics were not significant predictors for the different trajectory classes of attention problems. Several temperamental characteristics, such as negative affect, high surgency, or low effortful control have been identified as risk factors for attention problems in children from low-income households during the early school years (Brown et al., 2010). One reason why we did not find children's temperamental characteristics as predictors may be due to the low-risk nature of our community-based sample of predominantly middle-income families. It may be the combination of temperamental risk with such family risk factors as low SES and a chaotic home environment that predict attention problems (Brown et al., 2010).

When we considered the sibling relationship outcomes for children in the different classes, we found that children in the mid-decreasing and the high-stable class engaged in significantly more sibling conflict at 12 months compared to children in the low-decreasing class. This is consistent with the finding that the sibling relationships of children with ADHD are characterized by increased disruptive interactions (Mikami & Pfiffner, 2008). Having high levels of conflict is not surprising for children with higher attention problems if one considers that interaction with a sibling requires children to regulate their behavior and emotion (e.g., taking turns, inhibit aggression), and use social skills (e.g., attending to conversation) that children with attention problems often struggle to achieve (Whalen & Henker, 1992). Also, given that young siblings are not yet linguistically sophisticated, children's attention problems may have played a key role in contributing to less positive interactions and more opportunities for disputes. Therefore, although the birth of a sibling did not seem to change the trajectories of children's attention problems, these problems did appear to have consequences for the developing sibling relationship. Given that early sibling interaction during the first year of siblinghood continues to predict sibling relationship quality 3 to 4 years later (Stillwell & Dunn, 1985), our findings suggest that children's difficulties with early attention regulation may play a role in the development of conflictual sibling relationships as early as the first year after the sibling's birth.

Supporting Information

Additional supporting information may be found in the online version of this article at the publisher's website.

VI. DEVELOPMENTAL TRAJECTORIES OF CHILDREN'S ANXIETY AND DEPRESSION AFTER THE BIRTH OF A SIBLING

Elizabeth Thomason, Wonjung Oh, Brenda L. Volling, Richard Gonzalez, and Tianyi Yu

This article is part of the issue "Developmental Trajectories of Children's Adjustment across the Transition to Siblinghood: Pre-Birth Predictors and Sibling Outcomes at One Year" Volling, Gonzalez, Oh, Song, Yu, Rosenberg, Kuo, Thomason, Beyers-Carlson, Safyer, and Stevenson (Issue Authors). For a full listing of articles in this issue, see: http://onlinelibrary.wiley.com/doi/10.1111/mono.v82.3/issuetoc.

Because the depression and anxiety syndrome scale of the CBCL assesses young children's anxiety and fear related to separation from adults (e.g., clings to adults or too dependent) and general nervousness and self-consciousness (e.g., too fearful or anxious), this chapter will focus predominantly on young children's separation anxiety, and increases in attachment behaviors resulting from the potential separation from and loss of attachment figures. Separation anxiety is a normal developmental phase during early childhood in which a young child experiences distress brought on by separation or fear of separation from the primary caregivers (usually the parents). The child displays clinginess to the parent and extreme distress upon separation from the parent and may appear fearful, anxious, or high-strung.

Corresponding author: Correspondence concerning the Family Transitions Study should be addressed to Brenda L. Volling, Center for Human Growth and Development, University of Michigan, 300 N. Ingalls, Ann Arbor, MI, 48109-5406. email: volling@umich.edu

For those interested in the statistical code used to analyze these data (including growth mixture models, random forest, and CART procedures), please email Richard Gonzalez, gonzo@umich.edu

DOI: 10.1111/mono.12312

For some children, the birth of a new baby increases children's anxiety not only because of the stressful nature of the transition, but also because of the significant changes in the mother-firstborn relationship (Volling, 2012). Declines in maternal attention and increases in harsh discipline that accompany the transition may evoke children's fear of separation and loss of the parent to the new baby. Prior research indicates an increase in separation anxiety and attachment behaviors (e.g., clinginess, tearfulness) after the birth of a sibling for many children (Dunn & Kendrick, 1982; Kojima, Irisawa, & Wakita, 2005; Stewart et al., 1987), but these behaviors decrease over the first year following the birth (Kojima et al., 2005; Stewart et al., 1987). Thus, it is possible that children experience an adjustment and adaptation response whereby their feelings of anxiety and attachment behaviors increase soon after the sibling's birth, but decline once the initial period of stress has passed, a family routine has been established, and children feel more secure in their relationships with their parents.

Development of Separation Anxiety in Early Childhood

In typically developing children, signs of separation anxiety (e.g., clinginess, tearfulness) emerge toward the end of the first year of life and extend into toddlerhood. Separation anxiety decreases with age during early childhood (Carter et al., 2010; Kearney, Sims, Pursell, & Tillotson, 2003) and is stable during middle childhood (Broeren, Muris, Diamantopoulou, & Baker, 2013). Through the development of object permanence and the child's increasing sense of independence and exploration, separation anxiety naturally diminishes as children mature and is unlikely to be prolonged unless there is a major life event or stressor. Additionally, separation anxiety may emerge intermittently when the child is in a stressful situation or unfamiliar environment but, even then, it is typically short-lived and a brief reaction to some sort of stressful life event or change (i.e., moving into a new daycare room).

Individual Differences in Young Children's Anxiety

With respect to different pathways, one study reported significant variation in initial levels of separation anxiety symptoms (e.g., becoming distressed when separated from a parent) and found three stable trajectories (low, medium, high) over a 2-year period using growth mixture modeling (Broeren et al., 2013). Following children from ages 4 to 11, the researchers categorized the majority of the community sample as stable-low (63.4%) and normative, whereas a small percentage had consistently high symptoms of separation anxiety (6.3%). Significant individual differences in initial level of separation anxiety symptoms and in rate of change were found in a stratified random sample of children between the ages of 12 and 23 months whose symptoms were measured annually for 3 years (Carter et al., 2010), with a significant decrease in separation anxiety symptoms occurring over time. Two other studies have examined trajectories of anxiety symptoms from 18 months to elementary school-age and reported similar findings with four different trajectory groups: low stable/persistent, low increasing, high decreasing, and high increasing (Battaglia et al., 2016; Feng, Shaw, & Silk, 2008). Similar to Broeren et al. (2013), the low stable/persistent groups were the largest and comprised the majority of the children, whereas the high-increasing groups were the smallest and less than 10% of the sample (Battaglia et al., 2016; Feng, Shaw, & Silk, 2008). Based on these initial studies, we also expected individual differences in children's anxiety after the birth of an infant sibling, with most children in the current community-based sample falling into a large, normative class that would be low and stable over the course of the year following the infant's birth. Although we did anticipate some smaller, riskier trajectory groups where children may have higher initial levels of anxiety and depression than the group of low-stable children, we did not have specific a priori predictions about the rate and direction of change (i.e., decrease or increase) of these group trajectories.

Risk and Protective Factors in the Prediction of Separation Anxiety

Using a developmental ecological systems model can be helpful in examining and understanding the risk and protective factors that contribute to the development of separation anxiety symptoms after the birth of a second child with a focus on child, parent, and family characteristics. Child characteristics include difficult child temperament, which has been operationalized through numerous constructs, such as negative emotionality, withdrawal, and adaptability, and has consistently been associated with increased separation anxiety throughout early and middle childhood. For example, difficult temperament in infancy (i.e., adaptability, intensity) predicted an increase in separation anxiety when children were 2 and 3 years old (Warren & Simmens, 2005). Shaw et al. (1997) reported that negative emotionality at 2 years predicted the development of anxiety and depressive symptoms by the time the children were five.

Other aspects of child temperament, such as increased shyness and behavioral inhibition, are also associated with increased separation anxiety symptoms (Broeren et al., 2013; Carter et al., 2010; Feng et al., 2008; Paulus, Backes, Sander, Weber, & Gontard, 2015). Higher levels of behavioral inhibition predicted increased anxiety symptoms (Feng et al., 2008; Paulus et al., 2015) with children high in separation anxiety more behaviorally inhibited than children low in separation anxiety. Higher levels of behavioral inhibition and internalizing difficulties (e.g., emotional symptoms and peer problems) also predicted membership in the stable-high class relative to the stable-low class of children's anxiety (Broeren et al., 2013). Changes in behavioral inhibition over time were associated with corresponding changes in separation anxiety, such that toddlers and preschoolers with slowly decreasing behavioral inhibition were more likely to experience an increase in separation anxiety symptoms into middle childhood (Carter et al., 2010).

Parent characteristics that have been related to young children's anxiety include the quality of parenting behavior and parental mental health. Maternal depression, in particular, appears to be a risk factor for the development of separation anxiety symptoms in children (Battaglia et al., 2016; Herba et al, 2013; Warren & Simmens, 2005). Higher levels of maternal depression during infancy and toddlerhood predicted higher anxiety and increasing anxiety trajectories into the preschool and early elementary school years (Battaglia, et al., 2016; Herba et al., 2013; Warren & Simmens, 2005).

Family dynamics also predicted increased separation anxiety in young children. Exposure to interparental conflict (Shaw et al., 1997) and family conflict (Kearney et al., 2003) increased 5- to 7-year-old children's anxiety, particularly when children were rated by mothers as high in negative emotionality (Shaw et al., 1997). The mother–child attachment relationship has also been related to separation anxiety symptoms, with insecurely attached children displaying more separation anxiety at 6 years than securely attached children (Dallaire & Weinraub, 2005).

Based on this literature, we predicted that maternal depressive symptoms, children's behavioral inhibition, negative emotionality, insecure maternal-child attachment, and inter-parental conflict would predict separation anxiety trajectories, with children at greater risk of developing anxiety and depression after the transition when mothers were more depressed, children had insecure attachments to their parents, were more behaviorally inhibited and negatively emotional, and parents engaged in marital conflict.

Sibling Relationships and Early Separation Anxiety

We did not propose specific a priori hypotheses about the links between children's separation anxiety after the birth of a sibling and the subsequent development of sibling relations at the end of the first year because of the lack of research in this area. Based on mothers' previous reports that older children displayed increased separation anxiety behavior over this period (Dunn & Kendrick, 1982; Kojima et al., 2005; Richardson, 1983; Stewart et al., 1987) and that children's initial reactions within the first months after birth predicted sibling interactions at 14 months (e.g., initial withdrawal predicted poorer sibling relations), we considered whether there were differences in sibling relationship quality as a result of the different anxiety and depression trajectories, expecting that children higher on anxiety may have less positive and more avoidant sibling relationships than children with lower levels of anxiety and depression.

RESULTS

Individual Differences in Trajectories of Anxiety and Depression

The latent linear growth model was used in the GMM based on earlier findings of the unconditional models in Chapter III. The GMM revealed a three-class model with a linear growth factor was the best-fitting model based on fit indices; the three-class model had a lower BIC, BIC $= 2{,}983.16$, than the two-class, BIC $= 3{,}006.65$, and four-class models, BIC $= 2{,}986.20$. The AIC was lowest for the four-class model, AIC $= 2{,}920.96$, and similar to the three-class model, AIC $= 2{,}928.23$, while the two-class model had the highest AIC, AIC $= 2{,}962.01$. The three-class model also had the highest entropy (0.872) compared to the two (0.799) and four (0.825) class models. Table 8 presents estimates and standard errors for the fixed effects for each of the three classes and Figure 6 shows the different trajectory patterns for the three classes.

Results were consistent with theoretical patterns of linear change and stability (see Figure 1 in the Introduction). The largest class was labeled the *low-decreasing* class and comprised 68.5% of the sample ($n = 157$). This class showed low levels of anxiety symptoms at the prenatal time point, with a moderate linear decrease throughout the 12 months. The second class was labeled the *mid-stable* class and represented 27.5% of the sample ($n = 63$). Children in this class showed moderate levels of anxiety symptoms at the onset (intercept) which remained stable throughout the first year after the birth. Finally, the third, smallest class, 3.9% of the sample ($n = 9$), displayed a *high-increasing* trajectory, and showed the highest levels of anxiety symptoms at the onset with a linear increase throughout the first year after the birth of the sibling.

Once again, we examined the spaghetti plots for each individual trajectory for all children by class membership using the normative mean, borderline clinical range cut-off, and clinical range cut-off for the CBCL anxiety subscale (see Figure S2 in the supporting information online). The low-decreasing class, or majority of the children, fell below the normative mean at all time points, with the exception of a few children who started within the borderline clinical range at the prenatal

TABLE 8

GROWTH MIXTURE MODEL RESULTS FOR ANXIETY AND DEPRESSION: PARAMETER ESTIMATES AND STANDARD ERRORS FOR FIXED EFFECTS

Classes Parameters	Low-Decreasing $n = 157$ (68.5%)	Mid-Stable $n = 63$ (27.5%)	High-Increasing $n = 9$ (3.9%)
Intercept	1.073*** (.080)	2.541*** (.154)	4.268*** (.282)
Linear slope	−.051*** (.014)	.042 (.034)	.203** (.072)

Note. Standard errors in parentheses. The random effect (variance) of intercept est. $= 0.430$, $SE = .093$, $p < .001$; the random effect of linear slope est. $= .008$, $SE = .004$, $p = .050$.
**$p < .01$, ***$p < .001$.

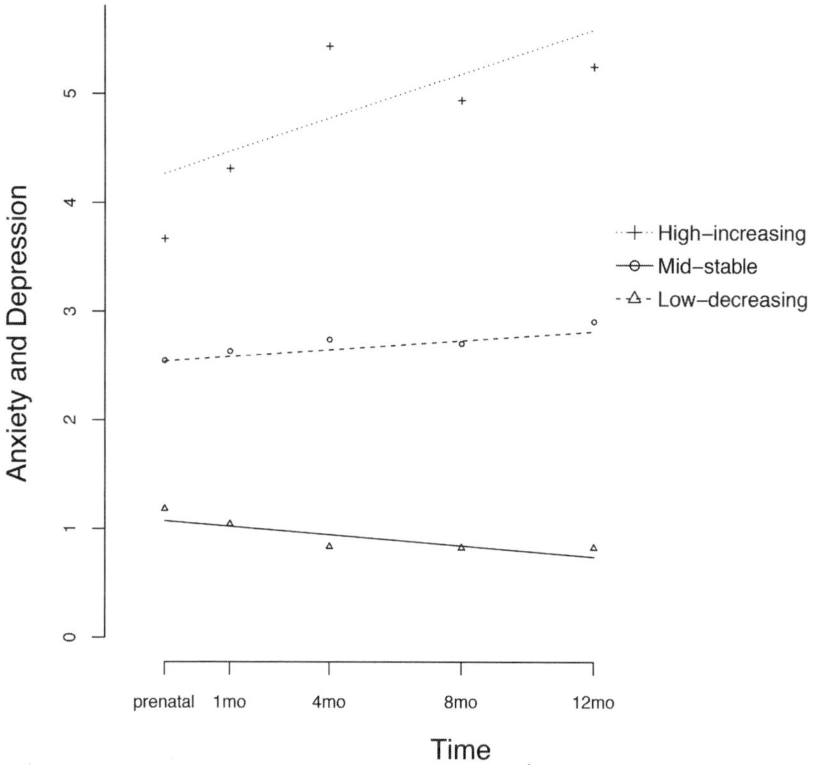

FIGURE 6.—Trajectory classes for anxiety and depression from Growth Mixture Model ($n = 230$).

time point, but were below the normative mean at all other time points. Children in the mid-stable class had trajectories that were higher than the low-decreasing class, but children were either in the normative range or borderline clinical range, with no children in the clinical range at any time point. The smallest class, the high-increasing class, consisted of children who all had trajectories in the borderline clinical range. Once again, the smallest class may have been few in number, but the fact that all children fell within the borderline clinical range indicates that the resulting GMM classes reflected meaningful individual differences.

Predicting Anxiety and Depression Trajectories

Four candidate variables were identified from the variable selection procedure: children's negative emotionality, children's behavioral inhibition, children's age, and parents' reports of negative marital relationship quality. The full multinomial logistic regression model with all interactions was not significantly better than the reduced main effect model, *LR Chisq* $(df = 22) = 32.40$, $p = .071$, thus, the reduced main effect model is used for interpretation of effects.

Results from the multinomial logistic regression using the low-decreasing class as the reference class are presented in Table 9 and reveal significant effects for children's negative emotionality, behavioral inhibition, and age, as well as parents' report of negative marital relationship quality. Children with greater negative emotionality and whose parents reported higher levels of negative marital relationship quality were significantly more likely to be in the mid-stable class or high-increasing class relative to the low-decreasing class. Behaviorally inhibited children were significantly more likely to be in the high-increasing class than the low-decreasing reference class. Older children were more likely to be in the mid-stable class than the low-decreasing reference class.

We also wanted to determine if there were differences between the mid-stable and high-increasing classes, and conducted an additional exploratory multinomial logistic regression with the mid-stable class as the reference class. Negatively emotional children were more likely to be in the high-increasing class than the mid-stable class, $b = 1.994$, $z = 2.287$, $OR = 7.341$, $p = .022$, as were children who were behaviorally inhibited, $b = 2.122$, $z = 2.530$, $OR = 8.351$, $p = .011$, and children whose parents reported higher levels of negative marital quality, $b = 0.881$, $z = 2.141$, $OR = 2.14$, $p = .032$.

Consequences of Anxiety and Depression for Sibling Relationships at 1 Year

Results of the regressions to examine whether sibling relationship quality at 12 months was predicted by separation anxiety trajectory classes revealed no significant differences relative to the low-decreasing reference class.

TABLE 9

RESULTS OF MULTINOMIAL LOGISTIC REGRESSION ANALYSIS EXAMINING CLASS DIFFERENCES FOR ANXIETY AND DEPRESSION WITH THE LOW-DECREASING CLASS AS THE REFERENCE CLASS

Predictor	Low-Decreasing vs.	b	SE	z	p	OR
Child negative emotionality	Mid-stable	0.80	0.29	2.78	0.005	2.23
	High-increasing	2.80	0.88	3.17	0.001	16.43
Child behavioral inhibition	Mid-stable	0.39	0.18	2.14	0.033	1.47
	High-increasing	2.51	0.84	2.97	0.003	12.30
Child age	Mid-stable	0.06	0.02	3.41	<.001	1.06
	High-increasing	<0.01	0.05	0.08	n.s.	1.00
Negative marital relationship quality	Mid-stable	0.27	0.18	1.51	n.s.	1.30
	High-increasing	1.15	0.41	2.78	0.005	3.15

Note. OR = odds ratio; n.s. = nonsignificant.

88

DISCUSSION OF CHILDREN'S ANXIETY AND DEPRESSION TRAJECTORIES

In this chapter, we examined the overall pattern of anxiety and depression in children after the birth of a sibling, as well as subgroups of trajectories that captured individual differences within the overall sample. Additionally, we explored the predictors of these trajectories and tested whether distinct trajectory subtypes were associated with differences in sibling relationship quality when the younger sibling was 1 year of age.

Overall, the unconditional model indicated no overall change in children's anxiety and depression from the prenatal period to 12 months after their sibling's birth, although there was significant variability in the sample, suggesting that children have differing initial levels of anxiety symptoms and patterns of change within the sample. Both of these findings were similar to and support previous research on young children's separation anxiety, finding heterogeneity in initial levels and change in children ages 4 to 11, in addition to children's separation anxiety symptoms remaining stable over time (Broeren et al., 2013).

To further examine heterogeneity within the sample, analyses revealed three trajectories: low-decreasing, mid-stable, and high-increasing. The low-decreasing class was the largest (68.5%), with children displaying low prenatal levels of separation anxiety and attachment behaviors that decreased over the year. The second class, mid-stable (27.5%) consisted of children whose initial separation anxiety was higher than the low-decreasing class and was stable over time. The low-decreasing and mid-stable classes comprised over 95% of the sample and it should be noted that both were below the clinical cut-off for anxiety and depression. It is quite likely that these results reflect the age-normative pattern of decreasing separation anxiety reported by others. The birth of a new infant sibling does not appear to alter this trajectory substantially. Considering the average age of the children (31 months) at the time of the younger sibling's birth, it is not surprising that children had low levels of separation anxiety because separation anxiety emerges in children around 12 months and peaks during the second year of life. With the development of object permanence and an emerging sense of independence, separation anxiety is typically infrequent by the time the child reaches preschool age. Even so, a small percentage of children (4%) did evince high levels of anxiety and depression symptoms that increased after the birth and placed them in the borderline clinical range. These children were already high on anxiety and depression before the birth and continued to increase over the year. Although small in number, these children are probably the children whose families may be most in need of assistance to manage the stresses associated with the transition after the birth of a sibling.

Our results differ in some respects from previous studies that reported an increase in children's anxiety and clinginess following the birth of a sibling (Dunn & Kendrick, 1982; Kojima et al., 2005; Stewart et al., 1987). We found an increase in anxiety symptoms over time for only a small portion of children. Testing for an adjustment and adaptation response in the unconditional model revealed that the unconditional linear model fit the data better, suggesting that for the sample as a whole there was no significant adjustment and adaptation period for children, nor was there any evidence of change over time. Study design differences may account for the differing results across this and earlier studies. We used a longitudinal design incorporating several timepoints that used parents' reports of children's anxiety symptoms on a well-validated measure of children's behavioral and emotional adjustment over time, rather than relying on the mothers' retrospective memory after the birth (Kojima et al., 2005) or collecting information on children's behavior after the birth with no prebirth information for comparison (Stewart, 1990). For instance, Kojima et al. (2005) asked mothers at 6 months postpartum to remember their children's behavior during the last trimester of pregnancy and at 1, 3, and 6 months postpartum. Similarly, Stewart et al. (1987) asked mothers at the 1- and 4-month time points if any behavior problems were new or continued since the prenatal period, but did not ask the mothers about their children's behavior at the prenatal time point. As our findings underscore, differences in children's anxiety across the trajectory classes were already apparent before the birth and not necessarily a result of the birth, further attesting to the need for longitudinal research designs that track changes in children's adjustment over the transition.

Even though most children did not present with clinical levels of anxiety, we should note that the nine children of the high-increasing class did fall in the borderline clinical level even before the birth and continued to increase in their behavior over time. Thus, it is these children and what predicts this group of high-increasing children that becomes of interest when making recommendations for potential intervention. Children in the high-increasing class were more likely to have higher levels of behavioral inhibition and negative emotionality, and had parents reporting higher levels of negative marital relationship quality even before the infant's birth. Behavioral inhibition was operationalized as shyness in relation to new experiences and people, and our findings support previous research that has found that behavioral inhibition differentiates between low and high trajectories of separation anxiety symptoms (Broeren et al., 2013; Feng et al., 2008). There was also more negative marital relationship quality for children with higher anxiety symptoms, highlighting the role of family dynamics in children's emotional adjustment (Shaw et al., 1997). Our results are consistent with earlier studies finding that exposure to inter-parental conflict over child-rearing disagreements was a significant risk factor for the development of preschool children's internalizing disorders, particularly for those children high in negative emotionality (Shaw et al., 1997). Our findings are also in line with the emotional security hypothesis (Davies & Cummings, 1994), which proposes that inter-parental conflict causes children's insecurity and anxiety about family relationships and may help explain why negative marital relationship quality and children's negative emotionality were both predictors of the trajectories of children's anxiety after the birth of a sibling.

The mid-stable class consisted of children who were older, with an average age of just under 3 years old ($M = 34$ months), and were more negatively emotional and had higher behavioral inhibition than those in the low-decreasing class, who were just over two years of age ($M = 28$ months). Almost all of the parents reported some sort of preparation with the older sibling regarding the impending birth in the form of media, books, or discussion (see Table 1), and it is possible that older children were more aware of the impending physical and household changes (e.g., mother's growing stomach, nursery preparation). For the older children, some awareness of the change may have resulted or compounded existing individual characteristics, such as emotional negativity and behavioral inhibition before the birth of the younger sibling than the low-decreasing group, who may not have been able to understand the life transition that was about to occur to the extent that the older children did. It should be noted, however, that children's social-cognitive understanding as assessed with theory-of-mind and emotional understanding tasks did not emerge as a predictor of their anxiety and depressive symptoms so continuing research is needed to clearly elucidate what role children's age plays in the stability and change in children's anxiety across the transition to siblinghood. Because separation anxiety peaks in toddlerhood and many of the children in the current study were older than 2 years of age, this may explain why most children did not experience changes over time. Children's temperament, in the form of both negative emotionality and behavioral inhibition, were, however, significant predictors of the trajectory classes, which is clearly consistent with a body of research finding associations between difficult child temperament and increased anxiety and the development of internalizing problems (Broeren et al., 2013; Feng et al., 2008; Shaw et al., 1997; Warren & Simmens, 2005).

Overall, our findings found support for the role of children's temperament and inter-parental conflict in predicting children's anxiety and depression trajectories after the birth of an infant sibling. Although maternal depression was hypothesized to predict separation anxiety trajectories based on earlier studies, maternal depression did not emerge from our variable selection procedures as a predictor of the trajectory classes. This may be due to the characteristics of our low-risk community-based sample, in which most parents were not depressed. A different situation might exist with samples of clinically depressed parents or mothers at risk for postpartum depression and we must be cautious about concluding that parental depression is not a risk for children's anxiety across the transition to siblinghood and the perinatal period until more studies can address this possibility in more clinically diverse samples. In addition, the sample consisted of two-parent families, so even if a mother was depressed, the support of the father may have buffered the effect of maternal depression and decreased the likelihood that children would experience separation anxiety. Fathers may have taken a more active caregiving role in response to maternal depression and future research is needed to address this possibility further (Mezulis, Hyde, & Clark, 2004). Social mores with respect to father involvement have changed significantly since the publication of the original Dunn and Kendrick (1982) work in which changes in the mother–child relationship were profound and fathers were not as involved and available.

It was also surprising that the children's attachment security to either mother or father was not a significant predictor of trajectory patterns of anxiety given earlier links between insecure attachment and children's separation anxiety (Dallaire & Weinraub, 2005), although others have not found an association between attachment and young children's anxiety (Feng et al., 2008). Differences in results may be due to different methods employed in the Family Transitions Study and the age of children across studies. For instance, we measured attachment security using the Attachment Q-Sort, whereas others have used the strange situation to assess attachment (Dallaire & Weinraub, 2005; Feng et al., 2008).

In conclusion, we found that the majority of children experienced low levels of anxiety over the transition period and that children in the mid-stable group of anxious children tended to be older. These results are in sharp contrast to popular beliefs that children increase in their clinginess and anxiety after the birth of a sibling. Further, we found no evidence that the trajectories predicted differences in sibling relationship quality at the end of the first year. Finally, children high on anxiety and depression before and after the birth were more negatively emotional and behaviorally inhibited prior to the birth of the sibling, which is consistent with a large literature finding links between children's emotional temperament and the development of internalizing problems (Gilliom & Shaw, 2004; Leve et al., 2005; Shaw et al., 1997). Because negative marital relationship quality was also a significant predictor of children with higher anxiety symptoms, a focus on the inter-parental relationship may help decrease the likelihood of anxiety and clinginess throughout the transition period for some families.

Supporting Information

Additional supporting information may be found in the online version of this article at the publisher's website.

VII. DEVELOPMENTAL TRAJECTORIES OF CHILDREN'S EMOTIONAL REACTIVITY AFTER THE BIRTH OF A SIBLING

Patty X. Kuo, Brenda L. Volling, Richard Gonzalez, Wonjung Oh, and Tianyi Yu

This article is part of the issue "Developmental Trajectories of Children's Adjustment across the Transition to Siblinghood: Pre-Birth Predictors and Sibling Outcomes at One Year" Volling, Gonzalez, Oh, Song, Yu, Rosenberg, Kuo, Thomason, Beyers-Carlson, Safyer, and Stevenson (Issue Authors). For a full listing of articles in this issue, see: http://onlinelibrary.wiley.com/doi/10.1111/mono.v82.3/issuetoc.

Emotional reactivity in the current chapter refers to children's moodiness, worrying, emotional instability, and their inability to emotionally cope with new situations (Achenbach & Rescorla, 2000) rather than a temperamental characteristic. Emotionally reactive children often have difficulties adapting to change and are described as moody and anxious. Because the birth of a sibling is considered a significant change within the family, emotionally reactive children may become increasingly emotionally labile after the birth. During the transition to siblinghood, Stewart (1990) reported that children experienced an increase in emotional intensity, a decrease in the range of mood expressions, and an increased tendency to approach rather than withdraw from social interaction in the year following the infant's birth. The likelihood of whether children have problems with emotional reactivity after the sibling's birth was contingent on whether children were described by mothers as emotionally reactive prior to the birth.

Corresponding author: Correspondence concerning the Family Transitions Study should be addressed to Brenda L. Volling, Center for Human Growth and Development, University of Michigan, 300 N. Ingalls, Ann Arbor, MI 48109-5406. email: volling@umich.edu

For those interested in the statistical code used to analyze these data (including growth mixture models, random forest, and CART procedures), please email Richard Gonzalez, gonzo@umich.edu

DOI: 10.1111/mono.12313

Dunn and Kendrick (1982) reported that emotionally reactive children prior to the birth were either emotionally reactive after the birth or actually increased in emotional reactivity in the first 8 months following the sibling's birth. These findings provide support for the accentuation principle, where life stressors accentuate the individual's preexisting psychological traits prior to the life event, in this case, the birth of an infant sibling (Elder & Caspi, 1988; Volling, 2012). Dunn and Kendrick (1982) argued that the change in children's miserable moods and worrying was not simply a matter of age-related developmental change because these behaviors increased only from one month before the birth to 8 months after, and not from 8 to 14 months, when the family had already adjusted to the birth. Thus, there is some evidence to suggest that we might see an adjustment and adaptation response for children's emotional reactivity, with an immediate increase in emotional reactivity that either declines or stabilizes shortly afterward.

Development of Emotional Reactivity in Early Childhood

Emotional reactivity and regulation are key aspects of development in early childhood. Although trajectories of emotional reactivity as a behavior problem have not been widely investigated, developmental components of emotional reactivity (e.g., worrying, moodiness, emotional intensity, instability) have been studied in prior research. For instance, children's emotional instability tends to decrease from 4 to 7 years (Blandon, Calkins, Keane, & O'Brien, 2008), whereas worrying increases with age in young children from 3 to 7 years (Muris, Merckelbach, Gadet, & Moulaert, 2000; Muris, Merckelbach, Meesters, & van den Brand, 2002; Vasey, Crnic, & Carter, 1994) possibly as a result of children's increasing cognitive development (Grist & Field, 2012; Lagattuta, 2007). About half (48.2%) of children aged 3–6 years from a normative, nonclinical sample reported worrying (Muris et al., 2002), and children's top worries included separation from parents, dying or death of others, burglars, and personal harm (Muris et al., 2000). Individual differences in children's moodiness and emotional intensity, however, tend to remain stable between 3 and 4 years (Hinde, Stevenson-Hinde, & Tamplin, 1985). Furthermore, emotional problems during the 0–5 year age range are often considered temporary reactions to stressful life events (such as the transition to siblinghood) rather than enduring emotional disorders (Gardner & Shaw, 2008), once again, underscoring the possibility of a short-lived emotional reaction to the stresses surrounding the birth of an infant sibling.

Individual Differences in Young Children's Emotional Reactivity

Individual differences in emotional reactivity exist among children (Blandon et al., 2008). Different children have varying reactions to new situations that might be stressful and elicit strong emotions. For example, some children may cry and protest during the first day of preschool, whereas other children may be gleeful and energetic. Only one study has examined individual differences in trajectories of emotional reactivity in children from 4 to 7 years (Blandon et al., 2008). Although emotional reactivity decreased, on average, from 4 to 7 years, there was substantial heterogeneity in both the intercept and slope that was predicted by mothers' characteristics (Blandon et al., 2008). Children experienced slower declines in emotional reactivity from 4 to 7 years if their mothers were more depressed and engaged in more negative parenting behavior. The authors reasoned that children's greater emotional reactivity was due, in part, to modeling negative affect from their mothers, indicating a strong role of the family environment on children's emotional reactivity over time. Based on these earlier findings, we also hypothesized there would be individual differences in children's trajectories of emotional reactivity following the birth of a sibling, with children showing either an adjustment and adaptation response indicative of an immediate, but short-lived, stress response to the birth or a decline in emotional reactivity. In any event, we expected children's initial scores before the birth to differ and define individual differences in children's trajectories of emotional reactivity over time.

Risk and Protective Factors in the Prediction of Early Emotional Reactivity

In the context of the transition to siblinghood, difficult temperament plays a key role in the development of emotional reactivity problems after the birth. Children with difficult temperaments at the prenatal timepoint were more likely than non-difficult children to have increased fears, worries, and moodiness 8 months after the birth of their sibling (Dunn & Kendrick, 1982). Several studies have focused on components of emotional reactivity (e.g., moodiness or worry) or internalizing behavior (of which emotional reactivity is a component). In line with the developmental ecological systems framework (Volling, 2005), both personal characteristics of the child and parent characteristics can contribute to emotional reactivity problems during the transition to siblinghood.

Because many mood disorders are heritable, parental psychopathology has been studied as a risk factor for children's internalizing behavior problems. Links between parental depressive symptomology and children's behavioral problems, including internalizing behaviors, are well-established, but effect sizes also tend to be small (see meta-analyses: Connell & Goodman, 2002; Goodman et al., 2011). Mothers' depressive symptomology also appears to be a stronger predictor of children's internalizing problems than fathers' depression (Connell & Goodman, 2002). Parental depression is likely related to children's emotional problems through two pathways: genetic heritability and environmental risk. Parents with depressive symptoms are less likely to provide sensitive care and fewer emotion regulation strategies to their children, which, in turn, could increase children's emotional problems. Therefore, parental depression and associated risks in parental behaviors may create additional risks in the family environment that potentiate changes in children's emotional reactivity during the transition to siblinghood.

Children learn to regulate their emotions through the support of their parents (Calkins, 1994). Sensitive parents tend to use emotionally supportive strategies that help children regulate their emotions (Thompson & Meyer, 2007), thus, managing emotional reactivity and their abilities to cope with emotionally charged situations. But, parenting stress may negatively impact parents' sensitivity to their children. Stressed parents are less likely to provide sensitive and nurturing care to their children, and more likely to be overreactive and harsh with their children. Children, in turn, may either model this negative affect or become dysregulated by it (Blandon et al., 2008; Liu & Wang, 2014). Mothers' parenting stress has been linked to children's greater internalizing behaviors and emotional reactivity problems (Hart & Kelley, 2006; Renk, Roddenberry, Oliveros, & Sieger, 2007; Tharner et al., 2012). For instance, Hart and Kelley (2006) reported that both mothers' and fathers' parenting stress uniquely predicted internalizing behaviors in 1- to 4-year-old children. The transition following the birth of a second child may exacerbate parenting stress for both mothers and fathers as they attempt to balance the care of a newborn infant and an older sibling, which, in turn, may increase children's emotional distress in response to changes in family routines.

In addition to links between children's temperamental characteristics and their emotional reactivity problems (Dunn & Kendrick, 1982), the development of social-emotional understanding appears to be key in the continuity or discontinuity of internalizing problems in childhood. Children's perspective-taking abilities allow them to use others' emotional states to guide their own interpersonal interactions. Children with more advanced emotional understanding and socio-emotional responding may be better at regulating emotional responses, but children's socio-cognitive understanding can operate as a protective factor in some contexts and as a risk factor in other contexts (Keenan & Shaw, 1997). For instance, empathy may lead to feelings of sympathy and prosocial responding in interactions with peers (Eisenberg & Fabes, 2006), but should children become overwhelmed with others' emotions and experience personal distress, they may "over-internalize" both others' and their own emotional problems, and develop internalizing behavior problems as a result (Keenan & Shaw, 1997). Therefore, children with better emotional understanding may be better at understanding the feelings of others, which may help them cope with the emotional changes transpiring across the transition, but they may also become emotionally reactive and increase in their worrying and inability to cope should the stresses become overwhelming during the transition to siblinghood.

Sibling Relationships and Early Emotional Reactivity

Children's emotional reactivity can potentially affect their family relationships (Hinde & Stevenson-Hinde, 1988). Emotionally reactive children who are more sensitive to both the positive and negative emotions of others may be more adept at developing positive and cooperative relationships with siblings, but also have more difficulties managing emotionally salient interactions. On one hand, children with positive emotional intensity may tend to seek interpersonal interaction, but the instability of their emotional reactions could result in frequent positive and negative interactions with other family members (Hinde & Stevenson-Hinde, 1988; Hinde et al., 1985). For example, moody, irritable, sulky children elicited more adult interaction (Hinde et al., 1985), and moody firstborns had frequent hostile and negative interactions with their siblings (Hinde & Stevenson-Hinde, 1988). Moody children controlled their siblings and incurred adult hostility (Hinde & Stevenson-Hinde, 1988; Hinde et al., 1985). Therefore, if firstborns are too emotionally reactive, they may try to control their sibling's behavior and engage in negative interactions, resulting in more sibling conflict and less sibling cooperation 12 months after the sibling's birth. Thus, we hypothesized that children high in emotional reactivity would engage in more conflict and less positive interactions with their siblings 12 months after the sibling's birth.

RESULTS

Individual Differences in Trajectories of Emotional Reactivity

As noted in Chapter III, the unconditional latent linear model fit the emotional reactivity data better than the unconditional Adjustment and Adaptation Response and quadratic models. Although the overall sample exhibited no average change in emotional reactivity over time, there was variability around the growth parameters, supporting the search for individual differences in trajectories. Based on the GMM, we determined that a three-class model best described the different change trajectories because it had lower fit indices, AIC = 3,226.69, BIC = 3,281.63, LMR-LRT = .013, than the two-class model, AIC = 3,241.76, BIC = 3,286.41. Further, there was no significant improvement in the four-class model, AIC = 3,224.31, BIC = 3,289.55, LMR-LRT = 0.689. The three-class model also had higher entropy (0.793) than the four-class model (0.745). Table 10 shows the growth parameters for the three classes, which were used to interpret the trajectory patterns and Figure 7 displays the overall trajectory patterns for each of the three classes.

TABLE 10

GROWTH MIXTURE MODEL RESULTS FOR EMOTIONAL REACTIVITY: PARAMETER ESTIMATES AND
STANDARD ERRORS FOR FIXED EFFECTS

Classes Parameters	Low-Stable $n = 167$ (73%)	Mid-Increasing $n = 58$ (25%)	High-Stable $n = 4$ (2%)
Intercept	1.704*** (.112)	2.902*** (.227)	6.914*** (.686)
Linear slope	−.034 (.018)	.117** (.043)	−.197 (.103)

Note. Standard errors in parentheses. The random effect (variance) of intercept est. = .718, *SE* = .126, $p < .001$; the random effect of linear slope est. = .007, *SE* = .004, $p = .098$.
**$p < .01$, ***$p \leq .001$.

Most children fell into a *low-stable* class, 73% of the sample ($n = 167$). The low-stable class had relatively low levels of emotional reactivity at the onset and showed stability over time consistent with the hypothesized stable trajectories

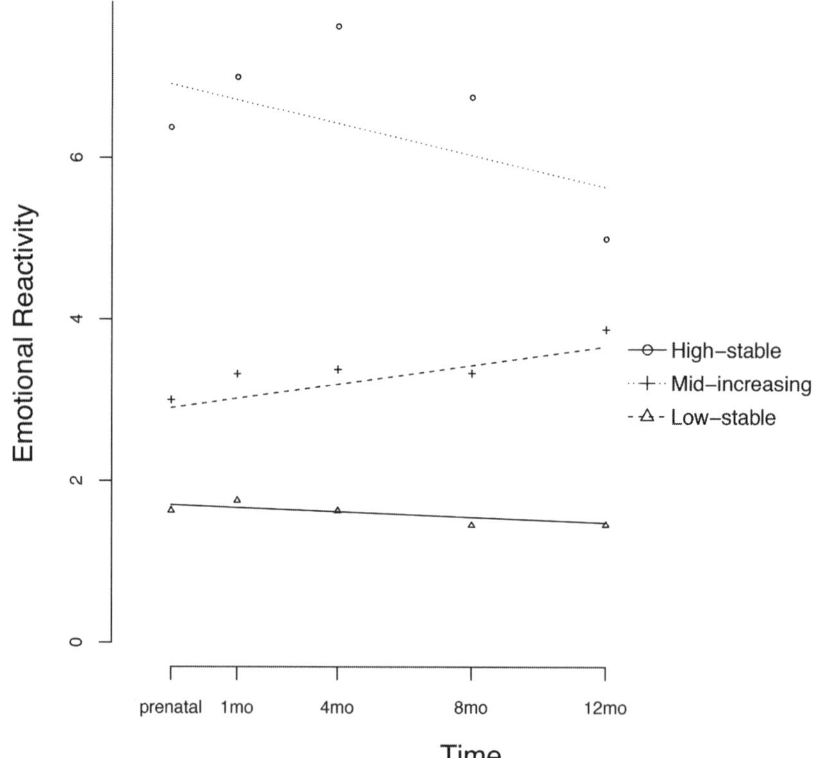

FIGURE 7.—Trajectory classes for emotional reactivity from Growth Mixture Model ($N = 230$).

in Figure 1 of the Introduction. The second class comprised 25% of children ($n = 58$) and was labeled the *mid-increasing* class because children had moderate levels of emotional reactivity at the prenatal timepoint and increased over time. The third, much smaller class (2%, $n = 4$) displayed a *high-stable* pattern of emotional reactivity, with higher scores than other children that remained stable over time. Although smaller in comparison to the other classes, these children fell squarely in the borderline clinical range cutoff across the entire year substantiating the uniqueness of this small group of children (spaghetti plots can be found in Figure S3 of the supporting information online). These plots also revealed that all children in the low-stable class fell below the mean on the emotional reactivity scale. Children in the mid-increasing class had scores above the normative mean, with some children close to the borderline clinical cut-off (92.5%), but none of these children hit the clinical range cut-off (97%) and most children in the mid-increasing class were below the borderline clinical range cut-off.

Predicting Emotional Reactivity Trajectories

Five variables (mothers' parenting stress, children's negative emotionality, children's emotion understanding, children's behavioral inhibition, and fathers' attitudes about physical punishment) emerged as candidate predictors of the emotional reactivity trajectories from the variable selection and data mining analyses. The reduced multinomial logistic regression model

TABLE 11

RESULTS OF MULTINOMIAL LOGISTIC REGRESSION ANALYSIS EXAMINING CLASS DIFFERENCES FOR CHILDREN'S EMOTIONAL REACTIVITY PROBLEMS WITH THE LOW-STABLE CLASS AS THE REFERENCE CLASS

Predictor	Low-Stable vs.	b	SE	z	p	OR
Children's negative emotionality	Mid-increasing	0.52	0.30	1.74	n.s.	1.68
	High-stable	4.58	1.75	2.62	0.009	97.57
Children's behavioral inhibition	Mid-increasing	−0.05	0.18	−0.30	n.s.	0.95
	High-stable	0.40	0.71	0.57	n.s.	1.50
Children's emotion understanding	Mid-increasing	0.12	0.06	2.17	0.03	1.13
	High-stable	0.22	0.21	1.02	n.s.	1.24
Mother-reported parenting stress	Mid-increasing	1.04	.37	2.82	0.005	2.82
	High-stable	−0.16	1.40	−0.12	n.s.	0.85
Fathers' physical punishment	Mid-increasing	−0.22	0.12	−1.81	n.s.	0.80
	High-stable	−0.54	0.50	−1.09	n.s.	0.58

Note. n.s. = nonsignificant; OR = odds ratio.

with additive main effects using the low-stable class as the reference group was used to interpret findings because the multinomial logistic regression that included all possible higher-order interactions between the predictors did not significantly predict the classes better than the reduced model with only main effects, *LR Chisq* (52) $= 47.56$, $p = 0.65$.

Table 11 presents the results of the multinomial logistic regression showing that mothers' parenting stress, children's emotion understanding, and children's negative emotionality were unique predictors of class membership. As mothers' parenting stress and children's emotion understanding increased, there was an increased likelihood of children being in the mid-increasing group compared to the low-stable group. As children's negative emotionality increased, there was an increased likelihood of the child being in the high-stable group relative to the low-stable group. Using the mid-increasing group as the reference group in an exploratory analysis yielded additional insights. As children's negative emotionality increased, the more likely they were to be in the high-stable group relative to the mid-increasing group, $b = 4.06$, $z = 2.32$, $p = .02$.

Consequences of Children's Emotional Reactivity for Sibling Relationships at 1 Year

We conducted regression analyses to test whether children's emotional reactivity trajectories predicted siblings' positive involvement, conflict, or avoidance 12 months after the infant was born. Membership in the high-stable class relative to the low-stable class predicted more conflict with the infant sibling at 12 months, $b = 0.56$, $SE = 0.27$, $p = .039$. Emotional reactivity trajectories did not predict positive involvement or avoidance of the infant sibling at 1 year.

DISCUSSION OF CHILDREN'S EMOTIONAL REACTIVITY TRAJECTORIES

Findings revealed that although there was no evidence of change, on average, for the entire sample, there was heterogeneity among children's emotional reactivity trajectories after the birth of their sibling. We identified three trajectory patterns. The largest class, consisting of 73% of the sample, had low emotional reactivity during the prenatal period, which continued to be stable across the year following the infant's birth. The second class with 25% of children had moderate levels of emotional reactivity prior to the birth of the infant that subsequently increased during the year. The smallest class, only 2%, had the highest levels placing them in the borderline clinical cut-off range for emotional reactivity during the prenatal period that continued over time. Overall, however, there was no evidence of a sudden, persistent change pattern in children's emotional reactivity problems during the transition to siblinghood that would indicate maladaptation and also no evidence of an adjustment and adaptation response, suggesting a short-term stress reaction to the changes of the transition.

Our results are partially consistent with previous findings on changes in children's miserable moods and worrying during the transition to siblinghood (Dunn & Kendrick, 1982) and consistent with previous work that found stability in children's moodiness and emotional intensity between 3 and 4 years of age (Hinde et al., 1985). Because there are no age-related changes in emotional reactivity within the early preschool years, any exhibited changes are most likely in response to stressful life events (Gardner & Shaw, 2008), such as the transition to siblinghood.

Whereas previous research found that children's intensity of emotional expression increased after the birth of a sibling if they were emotionally intense beforehand (Dunn & Kendrick, 1982), we found that children's emotional reactivity increased after the transition if they had moderate levels of emotional reactivity before the infant's birth, whereas children who were in the borderline clinical range and high on emotional reactivity prior to the birth remained high over time. Differences between our results and previous findings may be due to measurement differences across facets of emotional reactivity or to sample size differences across the studies. Previous research examined intensity of emotional expression separately from other indicators of worrying and moodiness (Dunn & Kendrick, 1982), whereas we examined behaviors that combined moodiness, worrying, emotional instability, and ability to emotionally cope with new situations as facets of emotional reactivity.

Children's emotional reactivity trajectories were uniquely predicted by mother and child characteristics. We found that children with greater emotional understanding and whose mothers reported more parenting stress prenatally were more likely to be classified into the mid-increasing class relative to the low-stable class. Further, negatively emotional children were more likely to be classified into the high-stable class compared to the mid-increasing and low-stable classes. Consistent with previous work linking children's difficult temperament and emotional reactivity during the transition to siblinghood (Dunn & Kendrick, 1982), we also found that children high on negative emotionality were also more likely to evince problems with emotional reactivity during the transition to siblinghood, as their scores placed them in the borderline clinical range of emotional reactivity problems (i.e., high-stable class).

Children with greater emotional understanding may be more aware of the changes that come with the infant sibling's birth. Children in the mid-increasing emotional reactivity group had higher emotion understanding than children in the low-stable group. According to developmental social-information-processing models, emotionality and emotion regulation are central to creating children's social schemas and social behaviors (Crick &

Dodge, 1994; Lemerise & Arsenio, 2000). Thus, children with greater emotion understanding may also have stronger emotional reactions and act accordingly. These children may be more cognitively aware of the social changes within the family and become more emotionally reactive (within normative levels) as the transition to siblinghood progresses. Although children in the mid-increasing class had greater emotional understanding, being part of the mid-increasing class was not predictive of sibling outcomes. It may be that children's other family relationships are impacted during the transition to siblinghood. For example, Teti, Sakin, Kucera, Corns, and Eiden (1996) found that older children (2–5 years old) experienced declines in security of mother-child attachment, but younger children (under 24 months) did not. Teti et al. hypothesized that age-related changes in mother-child attachment were a result of older children having advanced social-cognitive skills compared to younger children. They further hypothesized that children's advanced emotional understanding enabled children to feel threatened and displaced by a new baby. Thus, children's emotional understanding may predispose them to be more emotionally reactive as family interactions increasingly involve the developing infant sibling.

Mothers' parenting stress may also contribute to these children's increases in emotional reactivity over time, as children in the mid-increasing group had mothers with greater parenting stress. Mothers reporting more parenting stress may engage in more hostile or overreactive parenting, which may place their children at risk for the development of problems with emotional reactivity either through modeling of mother's negative affect or from emotional dysregulation resulting from less emotionally supportive parenting during times of stress (Liu & Wang, 2014). Mothers were already reporting feeling hassled on a regular basis with the children during the prenatal timepoint, and these hassled and stressed mothers may have responded to their children differently before and after the birth than mothers who were less stressed. Hassled and stressed mothers may be more critical, irritable, and harsher toward their children, which, in turn, decreases their children's abilities to emotionally cope with the changes occurring during the transition and as a result, increases their children's worry and moodiness. A mother-child relationship characterized by harshness and parental overreactivity may create a dynamic that increases children's emotional reactivity before and after the birth of an infant sibling.

Although previous meta-analyses have established links between maternal and paternal depression with children's internalizing problems (Connell & Goodman, 2002; Goodman, et al. 2011), maternal depression did not increase the risk of children's emotional reactivity in the current study, which may be due to a few different factors. First, our sample was a low-risk community sample and few parents had depression scores in the clinical range. The limited variability in parental depression may be one reason depression did not exert a significant impact on children's emotional reactivity problems after the birth of a sibling. Second, because depression is also associated with maladaptive parenting in both mothers and fathers (Lovejoy, Graczyk, O'Hare, & Neuman, 2000; Wilson & Durbin, 2010), parenting stress and parenting behaviors may mediate the link between maternal depression and children's emotional reactivity during the transition. Because young children experience parenting behaviors directly and are indirectly influenced by their parents' depression via parenting, maladaptive parenting (e.g., parenting stress, physical punishment) likely overshadowed any potential effects of depression on children's emotional reactivity in this study.

Although fathers have been theorized to play a role in children's adjustment after the birth of a sibling (Stewart, 1990), we did not find that fathers' characteristics were uniquely predictive of children's emotional reactivity in the current research. It should be noted, however, that fathers' endorsement of physical punishment emerged as a candidate predictor of children's emotional reactivity in the variable selection procedures but was not a unique predictor of children's emotional reactivity above and beyond the other variables in the more conservative multinomial logistic regression analysis. Thus, fathers' physical punishment may play some role in explaining individual differences in children's emotional reactivity after the birth of a sibling, but more research is needed to address this possibility. Given that parents' use of corporal punishment is linked with detrimental child outcomes, including more internalizing problems (Gershoff & Grogan-Kaylor, 2016), fathers who spank their children may be exacerbating child difficulties across the transition, especially when in conjunction with greater maternal parenting stress and harsh parenting. Children who experience harsh parenting and physical punishment from both parents may be especially vulnerable to behavioral and emotional difficulties during the transition.

Children's emotional reactivity trajectories predicted sibling conflict, but not avoidance or positive involvement with the infant sibling at 1 year. Specifically, children classified in the high-stable class were more conflictual with their siblings by the end of the first year after their sibling's birth than children classified in the low-stable class. These results can be interpreted as a function of the negative components of emotional reactivity (i.e., emotional instability, difficulty adapting to new situations). Children in the high-stable class were more emotionally reactive and may be more easily provoked in conflict situations, making it difficult for them to disengage or avoid their infant siblings. Note that the different emotional reactivity trajectories did not differ on positive sibling relations, suggesting that they are as likely to engage in cooperative and friendly interactions with their siblings as children in the low-stable and mid-increasing groups, but these positive exchanges are occurring within the context of high levels of sibling antagonism. Put another way, these children have sibling interactions that are marked by ambivalence (Dunn, 1983), with both positive and negative interactions with their siblings. By the end of the first year, these children have developed a sibling relationship with higher levels of sibling antagonism in addition to positive sibling interaction, which may give rise to sibling collusion processes over time (Oh et al., 2015). These results on sibling conflict, however, should be interpreted cautiously because they involve comparisons with the small high-stable class, which included only four participants.

In sum, the trajectories of children's emotional reactivity revealed that there are relatively stable patterns of behavior over the transition and that children high on emotional reactivity prior to the birth of a sibling were also relatively high afterwards. The vast majority of children fell into a low-stable class well within a normative, nonclinical range of behavior, suggesting that most children have few to no emotional reactivity difficulties in response to the impending birth of their infant sibling. Children, whose mothers were more stressed and hassled about parenting responsibilities prenatally, were more emotionally reactive and actually increased in their emotional reactivity after the birth of a sibling. These findings underscore the fact that parenting stresses (with the firstborn) experienced by mothers during the pregnancy with the secondborn may set in motion a family dynamic that gives rise to increased emotional reactivity before and after the birth. It is also possible that emotionally reactive children create additional burdens and stresses for parents. No doubt the process is probably bi-directional, with emotionally reactive children creating more parenting stress, which, in turn, contributes to children's feelings of emotional insecurity, worrying, and reactivity over time, and future work would be well advised to consider investigating these developmental processes.

Children with better emotional understanding before the birth were also more likely to be emotionally reactive and increase in their emotional reactivity over time (i.e., mid-increasing) than children in the low-stable class. Because children with better emotional understanding are more prone to emotional problems through an over-internalization of others' and one's own distress (Keenan & Shaw, 1997), perhaps children with better emotional understanding are more attuned to the emotional climate of the family and are better able to comprehend the impending changes that accompany the birth of a sibling. Finally, children in the high-stable class of emotional reactivity were not only characterized by greater negative emotionality, but were also at-risk for developing conflictual interactions with their siblings 1 year after the birth, which is not surprising given prior research finding that children high in negative emotionality are more involved in sibling conflict and have higher internalizing and externalizing behavior problems (Dirks et al., 2015). Given the predictive utility of early sibling conflict for later sibling conflict (Dunn et al., 1994), and the links between sibling conflict and other negative developmental outcomes for children and adolescents (e.g., externalizing and internalizing problems; Buist et al., 2013), these highly emotionally reactive children, although few in number, may be potentially at-risk for later developmental difficulties.

Supporting Information

Additional supporting information may be found in the online version of this article at the publisher's website.

VIII. DEVELOPMENTAL TRAJECTORIES OF CHILDREN'S WITHDRAWAL AFTER THE BIRTH OF A SIBLING

Wonjung Oh, Ju-Hyun Song, Richard Gonzalez, Brenda L. Volling, and Tianyi Yu

This article is part of the issue "Developmental Trajectories of Children's Adjustment across the Transition to Siblinghood: Pre-Birth Predictors and Sibling Outcomes at One Year" Volling, Gonzalez, Oh, Song, Yu, Rosenberg, Kuo, Thomason, Beyers-Carlson, Safyer, and Stevenson (Issue Authors). For a full listing of articles in this issue, see: http://onlinelibrary.wiley.com/doi/10.1111/mono.v82.3/issuetoc.

Dunn and Kendrick (1982) reported that some children became withdrawn after the birth of their infant sibling and Nadelman and Begun (1982) also reported an increase in children's lying around from before to 1 month after the transition. What is important to note is that it was the withdrawn children who would later go on to develop poor sibling relationships at 14 months after the birth, not the children who acted out and expressed their frustration and anger (Dunn & Kendrick, 1982). Therefore, understanding socially withdrawn behavior after the transition to siblinghood is an important focus for the current study given its predictive significance for subsequent sibling relationship quality.

Development of Withdrawal in Early Childhood

Social withdrawal is the behavioral tendency to isolate oneself from others and it is moderately stable from early childhood through adolescence

Corresponding author: Correspondence concerning the Family Transitions Study should be addressed to Brenda L. Volling, Center for Human Growth and Development, University of Michigan, 300 N. Ingalls, Ann Arbor, MI. 48109-5406. email: volling@umich.edu
For those interested in the statistical code used to analyze these data (including growth mixture models, random forest, and CART procedures), please email Richard Gonzalez, gonzo@umich.edu
DOI: 10.1111/mono.12314

106

(Caspi et al., 2003; Degnan, Henderson, Fox, & Rubin, 2008; Rubin, Coplan, & Bowker, 2009). Withdrawn children spend most of their time playing alone and on the periphery of the social scene, often due to anxiety or distress provoked in those contexts. Behavioral inhibition, an early precursor and manifestation of social withdrawal, is biologically based wariness (Fox, Henderson, Marshall, Nichols, & Ghera, 2005; Rubin et al., 2009), is found in approximately 15–20% of infants (Kagan, 1997), and is predictive of social withdrawal in early childhood (Rubin et al., 2009). Inhibited infants and toddlers display socially wary, withdrawn behaviors when they encounter novel situations and they are unlikely to show spontaneous positive social initiation in unfamiliar peer groups (Rubin, Hastings, Stewart, Henderson, & Chen, 1997). For example, behavioral inhibition among 2-year-old toddlers was a significant predictor of withdrawal at four years (e.g., Kagan, Reznick, & Snidman, 1988; Rubin, Burgess, & Hastings, 2002) and high levels of behavioral inhibition and withdrawal were stable across infancy and early childhood (Fox, Henderson, Rubin, Calkins, & Schmidt, 2001). Rubin, Chen, McDougall, Bowker, and McKinnon (1995) found that approximately two-thirds of children identified as extremely withdrawn at 5 years remained withdrawn through 11 years of age. Further, social withdrawal in childhood is a significant risk factor for internalizing problems such as anxiety and depression in childhood and adolescence (Lane & Song, 2015).

Individual Differences in Young Children's Withdrawal

A growing body of research has demonstrated heterogeneity in the longitudinal progression of withdrawal (Booth-LaForce & Oxford, 2008; Eggum et al., 2009; Oh et al., 2008). Although extant literature on withdrawal has shown moderate stability and continuity in childhood (Fox et al., 2001; Kagan, Reznick, & Snidman, 1987; Rubin et al., 1995), not all inhibited infants and toddlers are withdrawn and socially anxious later in life (Degnan & Fox, 2007). Some children display withdrawn behavior as a sign of distress in response to stressful life events (e.g., a move, birth of a sibling), but they are often short-lived and transient (Campbell, 2006). For example, Mathiesen and Sanson (2000) examined behavior problems among young Norwegian children from 18 to 30 months and found that shy and fearful children had short-lived transitory patterns of adjustment problems (e.g., eating, sleeping, dependency and attention seeking, mood, worries, and fears), whereas children who were aggressive and overactive-inattentive had more stable adjustment problems over time.

The transition to siblinghood may be especially stressful for young, socially wary, and behaviorally inhibited children because the arrival of the infant sibling may exacerbate family stress and challenge these children's abilities to cope with the stress. To date, there is no study examining change patterns of social withdrawal across the year following the birth for young children undergoing the transition to siblinghood. Dunn and Kendrick (1982) found that children who initially showed no interest and affection toward the baby at 1 month after the birth were more likely to be socially withdrawn and to interact less with the infant sibling at 14 months after the birth. They argued that withdrawn children may have a difficult time accepting the arrival of the sibling and adjusting to their infant sibling's birth. In fact, children's withdrawal after the arrival of a sibling was concurrently associated with an unfriendly attitude toward the sibling shortly after the infant's birth, and was longitudinally predictive of poor sibling relationship quality 14 months after the birth.

Risk and Protective Factors in the Prediction of Early Withdrawal

Literature on the etiology of social withdrawal suggests that both child characteristics and parenting contribute to developmental patterns of social withdrawal. For example, some studies have reported links between children's temperament, the quality of parent–child relationships, and the development of social withdrawal (see Rubin et al., 2009 for a review). Based on the developmental ecological systems perspective (Volling, 2005), we discuss child, parent, and family contextual variables as risk and protective factors of social withdrawal across the transition to siblinghood.

Children's temperament has been implicated as important for understanding their behavioral difficulties after the birth of a sibling. For instance, Dunn and Kendrick (1982) reported that children with negative emotionality showed an increase in withdrawal after the birth. In general, children's temperamental reactivity, including physiological and behavioral responses to stimulation, was a significant predictor of shyness (Lane & Song, 2015) and socially reticent behavior in infancy and early childhood (Kagan, 1997; Rothbart, Sheese, Rueda, & Posner, 2011). Four-month-old infants with reactive temperaments were more distressed, and showed fear and withdrawn behavior when they encountered novel objects or unfamiliar events at 1 and 2 years of age than less reactive infants (Kagan, 1997; Kagan & Snidman, 1991). Relatedly, Fox et al. (2005) suggested that shy, anxious and fearful temperamental dispositions resulted in the expression of social withdrawal later in development.

Both individual parent characteristics, such as depression and parenting behaviors have been associated with children's maladaptive social behavior. Children of depressed mothers were more likely to develop internalizing behavior problems (i.e., low activity, unresponsiveness, and elevated shy-sensitivity) compared to children of non-depressed mothers (Campbell, Matestic, von Stauffenberg, Mohan, & Kirchner, 2007; Cummings & Davies, 1994; Field, 1992; Mathiesen & Sanson, 2000). Mothers' and fathers' parental self-efficacy at 1 month after the infant's birth predicted the older sibling's antagonistic behavior as well as avoidance of the infant sibling later in the year following the birth (Oh et al., 2015), suggesting that when parents did not feel competent in their abilities to respond to their children's misbehavior shortly after the birth, children were more socially withdrawn and aggressive toward their sibling later in the year.

Parenting behavior has also been related to children's social withdrawal. Parents of socially withdrawn children are often overprotective and intrusive due, in part, to parents' perceptions that their withdrawn children are socially vulnerable and in need of protection; thus, they use overly solicitous and protective or intrusive parenting (Rubin et al., 1995; Coplan, Hughes, Bosacki, & Rose-Krasnor, 2011). Overprotective and intrusive parenting reduces opportunities for children to develop coping skills and problem-solving strategies in social situations, which can be especially detrimental for withdrawn children. For example, overprotective parenting predicted inhibited children's negative adjustment outcomes (e.g., peer difficulties, internalizing problems) among kindergarteners (Hastings et al., 2011; Rubin et al., 2009). Mothers' overprotective parenting and fathers' controlling parenting predicted preschoolers' internalizing problems, including withdrawal, and anxious behavior (McShane & Hastings, 2009). These findings suggest that fathers' and mothers' intrusive or controlling parenting may increase children's social withdrawal after the transition to siblinghood. In contrast, responsive and sensitive caregiving mitigates social withdrawal by empowering the development of social competence (Degnan & Fox, 2007). In addition, a growing body of research suggests that coparenting, the interplay of mothers' and fathers' childrearing, plays an important role in children's adjustment beyond individual parenting. Studies have shown links between coparenting and children's internalizing problems. For example, the lack of cooperative coparenting when children were 2 years old was significantly associated with 3-year-old boys' behavioral inhibition (Belsky et al., 1996). Jacobvitz, Hazen, Curran, and Hitchens (2004) also found that triangulated coparenting when children were 2 years old was significantly and positively associated with internalizing symptoms 5 years later. A recent meta-analysis by Teubert and Pinquart (2010) reported significant positive associations between coparenting conflict, triangulated coparenting, and children's internalizing problems, as well as significant negative associations between coparenting cooperation and children's internalizing problems.

The quality of the mother–child attachment relationship has also been linked to children's social withdrawal in early childhood. For instance, children with an insecure-resistant attachment with their mothers in infancy were more inhibited and withdrawn in early childhood (Calkins & Fox, 1992; Stevenson-Hinde, Shouldice, & Chicot, 2011) and engaged in more social withdrawal in the preschool period (Hastings, Nuselovici, Rubin, & Cheah, 2010). Marital relationship quality and children's withdrawal are also associated. Johnston, Gonzalez, and Campbell (1987) found that poor marital relationship quality predicted 4- to 12-year-old children's withdrawal and aggression 2 years later. Yet, little is known regarding the extent to which marital relationship quality is associated with the longitudinal changes in children's social withdrawal after the birth of a sibling. For the current analyses looking at predictors of children's withdrawal trajectories, we also expected to find associations with children's shy and reactive temperament, intrusive and negative parenting behaviors, the quality of interparental relations, and children's social withdrawal.

Sibling Relationships and Early Social Withdrawal

Although few studies have examined withdrawn children's sibling relationships, shy children are more likely to have less positive social relationships with parents (Coplan, Arbeau, & Armer, 2007), teachers (Rydell, Bohlin, & Thorell, 2005), and peers (Gazelle & Ladd, 2003), so they may also have less positive sibling relationships. Shy children talk and smile much less than their peers in the preschool years (Kagan, 1997) and withdrawn children are more likely than sociable children to be disliked and bullied by peers during the formal school years (Rubin et al., 2009). Thus, withdrawn children may be more likely to form negative relationships with their siblings, although Graham and Coplan (2012) recently found no significant association between shyness and sibling relationship quality in preschool-age children. Given that the arrival of a sibling creates an unfamiliar and novel social context for firstborn children, withdrawn children may also be socially wary and avoidant of their infant sibling and build less friendly relationships with the infant (Dunn & Kendrick, 1982; Dunn et al., 1981). Alternatively, children who are withdrawn and uncomfortable in social situations outside of the family may feel safer in the family. In that case, the presence of a sibling may help these children develop better social skills that alleviate withdrawn behaviors in other social situations.

We hypothesized there would be meaningful links between changes in children's withdrawal over the year following the sibling's birth and sibling relationship quality at the end of the first year. Specifically, we hypothesized that socially withdrawn children, either those stably high over time or those increasing in social withdrawal over the transition, would have more avoidant, and possibly more conflicted, sibling interactions at 12 months compared to children low on social withdrawal.

RESULTS

Individual Differences in Trajectories of Withdrawal

The initial modeling of latent trajectories provided support for the use of the unconditional quadratic model in the GMM analyses when uncovering individual differences in the withdrawal trajectories. We determined the four-class nonlinear quadratic model solution with the fixed effects (i.e., intercept, linear slope, and quadratic slope) and the random effects (i.e., intercept, linear slope) of growth parameters was considered the best fitting model because the four-class model had lower fit indices, AIC = 2,681.71, BIC = 2,760.78, LMR-LRT = 0.14, than both the three-class, AIC = 2,701.46, BIC = 2,766.79, LMR-LRT = 0.51, and five-class, AIC = 2,675.08, BIC = 2,767.91, LMR-LRT = 0.76, models, and higher entropy (0.843) than the five class model (0.797). Table 12 presents estimates and standard errors for the fixed effects for each of the four classes and Figure 8 shows the different trajectory patterns for the four classes.

The largest class, the *low-stable* class (76.1% of the sample, $n = 175$) showed the lowest level of withdrawal at the prenatal timepoint that remained low over time. A second class was labeled the *mid-stable* class, comprising 13.5% of the sample ($n = 31$). This class showed moderate levels of withdrawal at the prenatal timepoint that remained stable over time. A third class was labeled the *mid-curvilinear* class (8.7% of the sample, $n = 20$) and showed moderate

TABLE 12

GROWTH MIXTURE MODEL RESULTS FOR WITHDRAWAL: PARAMETER ESTIMATES AND STANDARD ERRORS FOR FIXED EFFECTS

Classes Parameters	Low-Stable $n = 175$ (76.1%)	Mid-Stable $n = 31$ (13.5%)	Mid-Curvilinear $n = 20$ (8.7%)	High-Decreasing $n = 4$ (1.7%)
Intercept	.821*** (.069)	1.306*** (.235)	2.459*** (.525)	4.711*** (.689)
Linear slope	.088 (.047)	.166 (.280)	.763*** (.237)	−1.232* (.624)
Quadratic	−.009 (.007)	.016 (.040)	−.113*** (.029)	.137 (.085)

Note. Standard errors in parentheses. The random effect (variance) of intercept est. = 0.209, *SE* = .057, $p < .001$; the random effect of linear slope est. $< .001$, *SE* = .005, $p > .05$; Quadratic random variance was constrained to be 0.
*$p < .05$, ***$p = .001$.

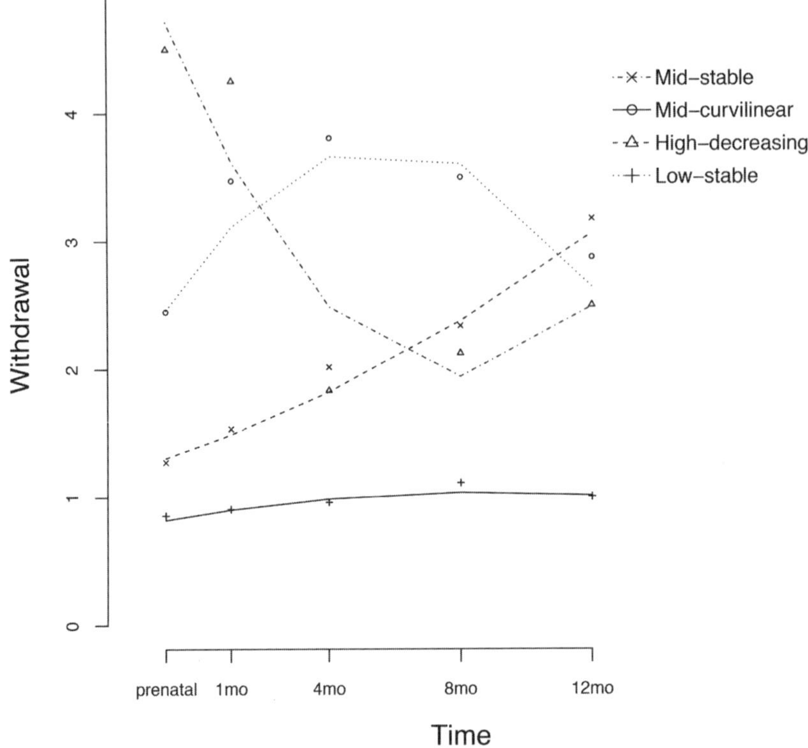

FIGURE 8.— Trajectory classes for withdrawal from Growth Mixture Model ($n = 230$).

levels of withdrawal problems at the prenatal timepoint with a moderate linear increase and decelerating rate of growth over time. The last class was labeled the *high-decreasing* class and accounted for only 1.7% of the sample ($n = 4$). Children in this class showed the highest level of withdrawal at the prenatal timepoint with a significant linear decrease over time. Here, we have for the first time, some evidence of a curvilinear pattern of growth, but it does not support any of the potential patterns hypothesized in Figure 2 of the Introduction, including the sudden persistent maladaptive pattern, the delayed impact, or the growth and maturity pattern.

As with previous scales, we examined the individual trajectories by class membership using spaghetti plots to determine whether the class membership was meaningful in relation to the CBCL borderline and clinical cut-offs (see Figure S4 in the supporting information online). The spaghetti plots clearly demonstrated that the four classes fit within these cut-off ranges, indicating that the majority of children were well within the normative range for withdrawal, and relatively few children fell in the clinical cut-off range. For

112

instance, all children within the low-stable class were well below the normative mean, whereas most children in the high-decreasing class and the eight children in the mid-curvilinear class fit within the borderline clinical range. Thus, the identified trajectory classes of social withdrawal fall within the normative and borderline ranges established for the CBCL; even the small class of four in the high-decreasing group is a meaningful class indicative of borderline levels of withdrawal behaviors.

Predicting Withdrawal Trajectories

The combined recursive partitioning and random forest variable selection procedure identified five candidate predictors from our candidate pool: children's behavioral inhibition, children's negative emotionality, observed undermining coparenting during the prenatal home visit, observed negative marital interaction at the prenatal home visit, and spouses' reports of positive marital relationship quality. Using the low-stable class as the reference class, the full model with all possible higher-order interactions was not significantly better than the reduced model with main effects, *LR Chisq* ($df = 78$) $= 89.432$, $p = 0.18$, so we used the reduced model for interpretation of predictors.

As seen in Table 13, the z tests show that children's behavioral inhibition is a significant predictor of differences between each of the three classes and the low-stable group (all four $zs > 1.96$, $ps < .05$); there is a decreasing likelihood of being in the low-stable class for children higher in behavioral inhibition. Positive marital relationship quality also significantly differentiated the mid-stable class from the low-stable class, showing that the children whose parents reported positive marital relationships had a greater probability of being in the low-stable class than in the mid-stable class.

Using the mid-stable class as the reference class in an exploratory analysis, we found that children's behavioral inhibition significantly predicted class membership in the mid-curvilinear class, and that observed undermining coparenting significantly predicted the mid-stable class compared to the high-decreasing class. Specifically, children who were more behaviorally inhibited were more likely to be in the mid-curvilinear class, $b = 0.743$, $z = 2.071$, $p = .038$, $OR = 2.102$, than children in the mid-stable class; and children whose parents used undermining coparenting were more likely to be in the mid-stable class than in the high-decreasing class, $b = -1.143$, $z = -2.015$, $p = .044$, $OR = 0.319$.

Consequences of Children's Withdrawal for Sibling Relationships at 1 Year

We used regressions denoting the low-stable class as the reference group, to test whether children's withdrawal trajectories predicted the quality of the

TABLE 13

RESULTS OF MULTINOMIAL LOGISTIC REGRESSION ANALYSIS EXAMINING CLASS DIFFERENCES FOR WITHDRAWAL WITH THE LOW-STABLE CLASS AS THE REFERENCE CLASS

Predictor	Low-Stable vs.	b	SE	z	p	OR
Children's behavioral inhibition	Mid-stable	0.46	0.23	2.01	0.044	1.59
	Mid-curvilinear	1.21	0.31	3.83	<0.001	3.34
	High-decreasing	6.56	3.24	2.02	0.043	703.78
Children's negative emotionality	Mid-stable	−0.31	0.33	−0.93	n.s.	0.74
	Mid-curvilinear	0.24	0.43	0.56	n.s.	1.27
	High-decreasing	−1.32	2.62	−0.50	n.s.	0.27
Observed undermining coparenting	Mid-stable	0.07	0.12	0.56	n.s.	1.07
	Mid-curvilinear	−0.23	0.19	−1.23	n.s.	0.80
	High-decreasing	−1.08	0.56	−1.92	n.s.	0.34
Observed negative marital interaction	Mid-stable	0.15	0.08	1.91	n.s.	1.16
	Mid-curvilinear	−0.18	0.20	−0.93	n.s.	0.83
	High-decreasing	0.46	0.42	1.09	n.s.	1.58
Positive marital relationship quality	Mid-stable	−0.49	0.24	−2.02	0.043	0.61
	Mid-curvilinear	−0.04	0.33	−0.10	n.s.	0.97
	High-decreasing	6.72	3.81	1.76	n.s.	832.47

Note. n.s. = nonsignificant; *OR* = odds ratio.

sibling relationship (positive engagement, conflict, and avoidance) at 12 months. Results showed that parents of children in the mid-curvilinear class reported less positive sibling involvement at 12 months than the low-stable class, $b = -0.250$, $SE = 0.126$, $p = .052$, but this difference just missed our statistical significance criterion.

DISCUSSION OF CHILDREN'S WITHDRAWAL TRAJECTORIES

This chapter explored the overall pattern of children's social withdrawal after the birth of an infant sibling, as well as heterogeneity in children's developmental trajectories of social withdrawal. In addition, we examined the risk and protective factors that predicted children's social withdrawal trajectories and the consequences of different patterns of social withdrawal for the children's developing sibling relationship.

Our initial findings revealed a nonlinear, quadratic model of change best characterized the overall pattern of social withdrawal for the sample across the transition with a gradual increase in withdrawal from prenatal to 4 months and subsequent decrease from 4 to 12 months. The analyses also revealed that there were four different trajectory patterns uncovered that were relatively consistent with the literature on social withdrawal in young children. The largest class

(76% of children) displayed a low-stable pattern of withdrawal following the transition, with the remaining 24% of children showing either moderate to high levels of social withdrawal or a curvilinear pattern of gradual increase with a gradual decline over time. These findings are fairly consistent with the literature on the prevalence of social withdrawal in childhood (Rubin et al., 2009) and behavioral inhibition, and the early manifestation of withdrawal in infancy (Kagan, 1997), in which approximately 15–20% of children are inhibited and withdrawn. Most children who displayed considerable withdrawal captured in the mid-stable, mid-curvilinear, and high-decreasing classes were high on behavioral inhibition, showing a temperamental predisposition of inhibited behavior even before the birth of their infant sibling. Because temperamental characteristics of shyness, behavioral inhibition, and negative emotional responses (e.g., wariness, anxiety) when encountering novel social situations predicted social withdrawal in early childhood (Chen, Wang, & Cao, 2011; Rubin, Burgess, Kennedy, & Stewart, 2003), the transition surrounding the birth of an infant sibling may be especially stressful for children with these behavioral propensities.

Among those children (24% of the sample) who were considerably withdrawn, the mid-stable class (13.5% of children) displayed moderately high levels of withdrawal at the prenatal timepoint and remained so over time. Children in the mid-stable class were moderately high on behavioral inhibition and had mothers and fathers with less positive marital relationships prenatally, relative to the low-stable class. Their parents also engaged in more undermining coparenting during observations of triadic interaction at the prenatal home visit, relative to the high-decreasing class. These findings are consistent with the literature in which a behaviorally inhibited or shy temperament contributed to sustained withdrawal over time (Kagan, 1997; Kagan & Snidman, 1991) and that negative marital relationship quality and marital conflict predicted children's internalizing problems (Davies & Cummings, 1994). In particular, interparental disagreement may have set the stage for greater emotional unavailability of parents across the transition (Campbell et al., 2007; Mathiesen & Sanson, 2000), which, in turn, created more emotional insecurity for behaviorally inhibited children (Davies & Cummings, 1994). Thus, undermining coparenting and negative marital quality coupled with children's temperamental predisposition toward behavioral inhibition may have further exacerbated children's withdrawal during the transition period.

Unlike the two stable classes noted above, both the mid-curvilinear and high-decreasing classes showed somewhat distinct nonlinear or linear patterns of longitudinal change in withdrawal. The mid-curvilinear class displayed moderately high levels of withdrawal before the birth of an infant sibling, with a significant increase after the birth and decelerating rate of growth over time. The high-decreasing class, consisting of only four children, was very high on social withdrawal, within the borderline cut-off range, and showed a linear decrease in social withdrawal over the transition. Further analyses revealed several child and parent factors that predicted these classes. For example, children in the mid-curvilinear class showed higher levels of behavioral inhibition, relative to the low- and mid-stable classes. In addition, the children in the mid-curvilinear class were less positive in their engagement with the younger sibling at 12 months, although this was not statistically significant ($p = .05$). Thus, stress surrounding the transition may actually exacerbate children's withdrawal after the transition (birth through 4 months) for temperamentally inhibited children. These findings illuminate the importance of temperamental predispositions that predict children's reactivity to disruptions and changes in the environment during the transition surrounding the birth of an infant sibling.

In contrast, the high-decreasing class showed the highest level of withdrawal and scored in the borderline clinical range prenatally, with a significant decrease over time. Although it was the smallest class with four participants, children in the high-decreasing class were more behaviorally inhibited before the birth and had mothers and fathers who used less undermining coparenting during observed interactions at the prenatal timepoint, relative to the mid-curvilinear class. This may reflect mothers' and fathers' willingness and commitment to coparenting, which ultimately may have protected children displaying the highest level of withdrawal (near the clinical cut-off range) before the birth of their infant sibling, and who became significantly less withdrawn over time.

The fact that marital relationship quality and observed coparenting proved to be significant family predictors in addition to children's behavioral inhibition highlights the potential buffering role of fathers for children's adjustment across the transition to siblinghood. Others have suggested that highly committed fathers to both their wives and children may be more involved in their families during the transition and play a critical role in their children's adjustment (Kreppner et al., 1982; Stewart, 1990). When fathers were engaged in supportive marital relationships and less undermining coparenting, behaviorally inhibited children appeared to benefit and become less withdrawn over time. These findings are certainly consistent with prior literature finding relations between marital relationship quality, father–child relationships, and children's emotional adjustment (Davies et al., 2009; Schacht et al., 2009).

Although small in size, the identification of the above mentioned two classes (the mid-curvilinear and high-decreasing classes) is particularly notable because a growing body of research suggests there is heterogeneity in the longitudinal patterns of withdrawal in childhood due to different underlying behavioral mechanisms and relationship processes (e.g., Booth-LaForce & Oxford, 2008; Eggum et al., 2009; Oh et al., 2008). There were also

116

signs that children's withdrawal after the birth had repercussions for the developing sibling relationship by the end of the year. Children in the mid-curvilinear class were less positively engaged with their infant sibling at 12 months compared to children in the low-stable class. Children in the mid-curvilinear class initially showed moderate levels of withdrawal problems that were mostly between the average and the borderline-clinical cutoff at prebirth, with a significant increase in withdrawal problems until 4 months, which was followed by a gradual decline. Our result is consistent with Dunn et al.'s findings (Dunn et al., 1981; Kendrick & Dunn, 1982) that children who were initially withdrawn at 1 month postpartum were less likely to engage in friendly interactions with their sibling at 14 months. It is also in line with the literature on withdrawn children's general relationship quality, which has shown that withdrawn children are less likely to establish positive social relationships (e.g., smile or talk less) with others in the family and school contexts (Coplan et al., 2007; Gazelle & Ladd, 2003), although they may not be prone to engage in negative social interactions (e.g., conflicts). Given that this trajectory pattern reflected an increase in problems followed by a gradual decline over the year after the birth, these children may be experiencing the arrival of a sibling as troublesome, and having difficulties adjusting to the arrival of their sibling and changes ongoing in the family. Eventually, these children do appear to return to prebirth levels of withdrawal, but they remain higher on social withdrawal even at the end of the year than children in the low-stable class. These results, combined with our earlier finding that children who were approach-avoidant in response to mother–infant interaction at 1 month had higher levels of externalizing and internalizing behavior problems at 4 months than other children (Volling et al., 2014), lends further support that children who are initially withdrawn require attention by parents after the arrival of an infant sibling (Dunn & Kendrick, 1982) and where intervention efforts may need to focus to prevent sibling relationship and behavioral difficulties later in the year. Our results also attest to the important role of fathers as coparents in helping withdrawn children adjust to the transition to siblinghood.

Supporting Information

Additional supporting information may be found in the online version of this article at the publisher's website.

IX. DEVELOPMENTAL TRAJECTORIES OF CHILDREN'S SOMATIC COMPLAINTS AFTER THE BIRTH OF A SIBLING

Emma Beyers-Carlson, Matthew M. Stevenson, Richard Gonzalez, Wonjung Oh, Brenda L. Volling, and Tianyi Yu

This article is part of the issue "Developmental Trajectories of Children's Adjustment across the Transition to Siblinghood: Pre-Birth Predictors and Sibling Outcomes at One Year" Volling, Gonzalez, Oh, Song, Yu, Rosenberg, Kuo, Thomason, Beyers-Carlson, Safyer, and Stevenson (Issue Authors). For a full listing of articles in this issue, see: http://onlinelibrary.wiley.com/doi/10.1111/mono.v82.3/issuetoc.

The transition to siblinghood is a time of adjustment and change for some children (Dunn et al., 1981). Given the substantial empirical research that links stress with somatic complaints in children (Eminson, 2007), it seems likely that children experiencing the birth of a younger sibling might develop somatic complaints in response to this stressful change in family composition. Although several studies have documented somatic complaints during early childhood as a stress response (see review in Eminson, 2007), research that directly examines somatic complaints in children as a response to the birth of a sibling is lacking. We address this gap by examining trajectories of change in children's somatic complaints during the immediate transition to siblinghood and throughout the first year after the birth of the sibling.

Corresponding author: Correspondence concerning the Family Transitions Study should be addressed to Brenda L. Volling, Ph.D., University of Michigan, Center for Human Growth and Development, 300 N. Ingalls, Ann Arbor, MI, 48109-5406, email: volling@umich.edu. For those interested in the statistical code used to analyze these data (including growth mixture models, random forest, and CART procedures), please email Richard Gonzalez, gonzo@umich.edu.

DOI: 10.1111/mono.12315

Development of Somatic Complaints in Early Childhood

Young children with somatic complaints may manifest their distress in different ways. Recurrent abdominal pain without organic causes, headaches, and limb pain are the most common forms of somatic complaints for very young children (Campo & Fritsch, 1994; Egger, Costello, Erkanli, & Angold, 1999; Galli et al., 2007), with stomachaches more common among children ages 3–5 years old (Borge, Nordhagen, Moe, Botten, & Bakketeig, 1994; Domènech-Llaberia et al., 2004; Eminson, 2007). The prevalence of somatic complaints is generally low in early childhood (Beck, 2008), with 8–9% of preschoolers having recurrent abdominal pain and only 2–3% of preschoolers having persistent headaches (Domènech-Llaberia et al., 2004; Zuckerman, Stevenson, & Bailey, 1987).

Somatic complaints can also manifest as disruptions in eating behavior, nausea, aches, diarrhea, musculoskeletal pains, dizziness, fatigue, or constipation (Achenbach & Rescorla, 2000; Egger et al., 1999). For many children, somatic complaints in early childhood appear to be an adjustment reaction to a stressor or disruption in children's normal routines (Eminson, 2007). The lack of empirical work that directly examines children's somatic complaints in the context of the transition to siblinghood makes strong conclusions difficult; however, results from a single study suggest two intriguing findings that help to conceptually guide the present study. Children over the age of 4 did not show many complaints around toileting or eating disruptions (e.g., regression to less age-appropriate eating behaviors) after the birth of a sibling, yet younger 2- to 3-year-olds in the sample manifested problems with toilet training and normal eating habits in the year following the birth (Stewart, 1990; Stewart et al., 1987). Younger children may not behave this way intentionally, but the increased problems with eating and toileting may be a direct result of anxiety after the birth. By 4 months after the birth, Stewart (1990) found that difficulties with toileting were greatly reduced and disruptions in eating habits were reduced in the 2- to 3-year-olds. This finding suggests that by 4 months, children adjusted to the new family structure and no longer exhibited toileting issues or eating disruptions (Stewart, 1990). High levels of anxiety, however, were still present at 4 months after the birth, so it may manifest in other behaviors. Given the paucity of research on children's adjustment to the birth of a sibling, however, any broad conclusions remain speculative.

Several studies have assessed the prevalence of somatic complaints during the period of early childhood, without specific attention to the transition to siblinghood, and found that children often experience somatic complaints in two ways: as a short-term distress reaction (Eminson, 2007; Wolff et al., 2009) or long-term functional somatic symptoms, defined as physical symptoms of unknown pathology (Beck, 2008; Dhossche, Ferdinand, van der Ende, &

Verhulst, 2001; Steinhausen, 2006). Somatic complaints are common as an adjustment reaction to stress in young children and indeed make up the largest and most recognizable group in a pediatric or primary care setting (Eminson, 2007). In contrast to some of the other maladaptive behavior problems in this monograph, somatic complaints are often short-lived, present as a single complaint or a small number of complaints, usually do not cause functional impairment, and do not typically reach clinical levels (Eminson, 2007). Thus, somatic complaints of this type appear to be more transitory than persistent across development in response to stress. Given that somatic complaints in early childhood are considered normative only if the complaints are short-lived, the longitudinal trajectories for children whose complaints do not subside are of great interest. We would expect based on the current literature that it would be far more common for children to manifest an adjustment and adaptation response with an immediate increase from prenatal to 1 month and a subsequent decline by 4 months than a pattern of sudden and persistent maladjustment after the birth of their infant sibling.

In contrast, long-term functional somatic symptoms are associated with comorbid psychiatric symptoms, such as anxiety and depression, as well as a high degree of functional impairment (Beck, 2008; Garber, Zeman, & Walker, 1990; Walker & Greene, 1989). Wolff et al. (2010) reported that somatic complaints in toddlers were associated with increased internalizing and externalizing behavior problems in adolescence. Thus, although somatic complaints generally present as a short-term adjustment reaction, it appears that early somatic complaints that do not subside may predispose children for salient problems later in life.

Individual Differences in Young Children's Somatic Complaints

Though few studies have examined individual differences in somatic complaints across children, Mulvaney, Lambert, Garber, and Walker (2006) found that individual differences in somatic complaints do exist. In their 5-year longitudinal study of somatic complaints, three different trajectories for somatic complaints were identified, particularly recurrent abdominal pain in children (ages 6–18): a low-risk group (70%), a short-term risk group (16%), and a long-term risk group (14%). The majority of children fell within the low-risk group and initially showed low levels of impairment, improved within 2 months, and maintained their improvement 1 and 5 years later. The short-term risk group initially had the highest level of symptoms but improved considerably during the following months and maintained that improvement at year 5. The final group, the long-term risk group, displayed high levels of somatic complaints across time that did not improve. Additionally, the long-term risk group displayed significantly lower self-worth, more depression and anxiety, and more negative life events. Such results indicate that even though the majority of children with somatic complaints had low-level symptoms and improved over time, the

120

children with high levels of somatic complaints who did not improve over time warrant further attention, due to their vulnerability to both somatic complaints and other mental health outcomes, though it is unclear if similar results would be evident for very young children after the birth of a sibling.

Risk and Protective Factors in the Prediction of Early Somatic Complaints

Utilizing the developmental ecological systems perspective (Volling, 2005), risk, and protective factors for the development of somatic complaints in young children are grouped according to child characteristics, parental characteristics, and environmental factors. Children's temperament has been strongly associated with the development of somatic complaints in young children. Fearful temperament and temperamental falling reactivity, which refers to the rate of recovery from peak frustration or distress, have been found to increase the likelihood of children's somatic complaints at 18 months of age (Wolff et al., 2010). Rocha and Prkachin (2007) also found that children's negative mood, withdrawal, and adaptability at age 5 were related to increased somatic complaints at age 12. Children at 18 months who reacted fearfully to new people were more prone to develop somatic symptoms than nonfearful children (Wolff et al., 2009).

Parenting characteristics represent another set of key risk factors for the development of somatic symptoms in children. Maternal somatic symptoms and depression or anxiety have been associated with higher reported somatization in their children (Domènech-Llaberia et al., 2004; Galli et al., 2007; Wolff et al., 2010). Walker, Garber, and Greene (1993) found that boys in families with a high incidence of negative life events (e.g., negative changes in family relationships, health, employment) and whose mothers expressed high levels of somatic complaints had higher levels of somatic complaints themselves, which indicated that children may learn by modeling maternal anxious behavior and mood, or attending to internal physiological symptoms and sensations.

Additionally, parenting stress (Wolff et al., 2010) and maternal insensitivity to child cues have been associated with the development of children's somatic complaints (Grunau, Ruth, Whitfield, Petrie, & Fryer, 1993). These results are consistent with the family systems approach, which maintains that somatic complaints may function as a communication attempt or a "cry for help" by the child (Campo & Fritsch, 1994). According to this perspective, this communication attempt may be particularly evident in families that have poor parent–child communication and/or poor parent–child and coparental relationships (Aro, 1989; Aro, Paronen, & Aro, 1987). Because mother–child relationships change across the transition to siblinghood with increases in harsh and punitive discipline and decreases in joint attention and play (Volling, 2012), these changes may manifest as somatic complaints in the child.

Family risk factors are also associated with the development of somatic complaints in early childhood. Marital tension and conflict, as well as general family tension, have been associated with somatic complaints in children (Grunau, Ruth et al., 1993; Terre & Ghiselli, 1997; Wolff et al., 2009). Consistent with emotional security theory, repeated exposure to interparental conflict over time may result in greater child emotional reactivity (Davies, Sturge-Apple, Winter, Cummings, & Farrell, 2006). Indeed, rather than acclimate to exposure to marital conflict with less reactivity, children are often sensitized to marital conflict and demonstrate increased emotional and physiological reactivity with repeated exposure (Goeke-Morey, Papp, & Cummings, 2013; Zemp, Bodenmann, & Mark Cummings, 2014), which may manifest as somatic complaints. Other family stressors, such as occupational changes or work-family stress for an immediate family member were also significant risk factors for somatic complaints in children (Boey & Goh, 2001). Therefore, it appears that early exposure to stressful environments, family stressors, and/or negative life events, increased the risk of somatic complaints in both clinical and community samples of young children (Beck, 2008). As such, we would expect some children to manifest somatic complaints after the birth of a sibling, particularly in families with increased levels of parenting stress, marital conflict, and work-family stressors.

Sibling Relationships and Early Somatic Complaints

No empirical research currently exists that has examined the relation between somatic complaints and the emerging sibling relationship, and it is not clear whether such a link should exist. It seems unlikely that symptoms of somatic complaints would affect the sibling relationship given how highly individualized somatic complaints are in response to stress.

The current study aims to elucidate further knowledge on somatic complaints during the transition to siblinghood by examining children's trajectories of somatic complaints across the year following the birth of a sibling, and investigating predictors of the identified trajectories. We hypothesized that most children with few difficulties with somatic complaints before the birth of a sibling would maintain that trajectory after the birth. We also hypothesized, however, that some children with few difficulties prior to the birth might manifest somatic complaints after the birth as an adjustment reaction to the possibly stressful event of the birth of a sibling. With respect to sibling relationships, our analyses were exploratory given lack of any prior empirical evidence.

RESULTS

Individual Differences in Trajectories of Somatic Complaints

Having ascertained in Chapter III that the unconditional linear model best fit the somatic complaints data, we used growth mixture modeling (GMM) to estimate linear patterns of somatic complaints trajectories across the five timepoints. The GMM analysis indicated a three-class model with a linear growth factor best described the different change trajectories within the sample because it had better fit indices, AIC$=3,2140.7$, BIC$=3,195.79$, LMR-LRT$=0.116$, than the two-class model, AIC $=3,163.86$, BIC$=3,214.55$, LMR-LRT$=.014$, and the four-class model, AIC$=3,125.61$, BIC 3,190.93, LMR-LRT$=0.168$; the three-class model had higher entropy (0.864) than the four-class model (0.829). Table 14 presents the fixed effects of each class and Figure 9 shows the different trajectory patterns for the three classes.

The largest class was denoted as the *low-stable* class and represented 60% of the sample ($n=138$). Children in this class showed the lowest level of somatic complaints at the prenatal timepoint that remained low throughout the following year. All children in the low-stable class fell below the normative mean (bottom line) on the somatic complaints scale (see spaghetti plots in Figure S5 of the supporting information online). A second class was labeled as the *mid-decreasing* class, accounting for 35.2% of the sample ($n=81$), and showed moderate levels of problems at the prenatal timepoint with a gradual linear decrease throughout the 12 months after the birth of the sibling. The spaghetti plots of individual trajectories showed that the majority of children in the mid-decreasing group had scores above the normative mean, but below the borderline cut off range (92.5%). The final class, the *high-stable* class, comprised only 4.8% of the sample ($n=11$), but showed the highest levels of somatic complaints at the prenatal timepoint and remained high throughout the year, with most children falling within the borderline clinical range (92.5%) and some exceeding the clinical cutoff (97%; plots can be seen in Figure S5 of the

TABLE 14

GROWTH MIXTURE MODEL RESULTS FOR SOMATIC COMPLAINTS: PARAMETER ESTIMATES AND STANDARD ERRORS FOR FIXED EFFECTS

Classes Parameters	Low-Stable $n=138$ (60%)	Mid-Decreasing $n=81$ (35.2%)	High-Stable $n=11$ (4.8%)
Intercept	.837*** (.079)	2.58*** (.120)	4.976*** (.331)
Linear slope	−.016 (.016)	−.087** (.030)	−.078 (.088)

Note. Standard errors in parentheses. The random effect (variance) of intercept est. $= .053$, $SE = .081$, $p > .05$; the random effect of linear slope est. $= .008$, $SE = .004$, $p = .060$.
**$p < .01$, ***$p < .001$.

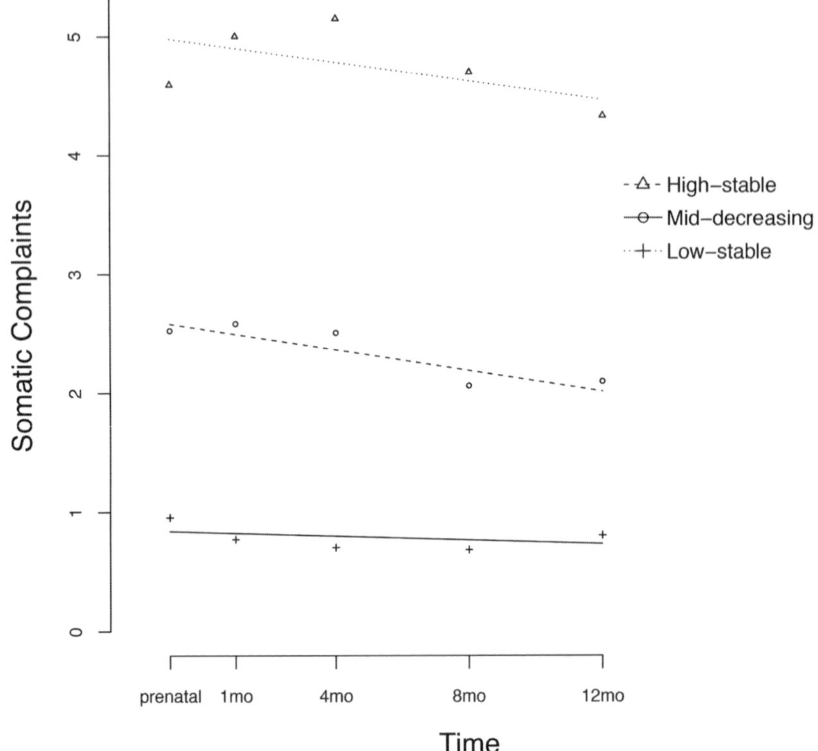

FIGURE 9.—Trajectory classes for somatic complaints from Growth Mixture Model ($n = 230$).

supporting information online). Trajectory patterns were also consistent with the linear and stable patterns denoted initially in Figure 1 in the Introduction.

Predicting Somatic Complaint Trajectories

Based on the variable selection methods, four variables emerged as candidate predictors of the three classes: children's negative emotionality, positive marital relationship quality, children's attachment security to the father, and the mothers' parental efficacy. The full multinomial logistic regression model using the low-stable class as the reference class with all higher-order interactions had significantly better fit than the reduced model with main effects, *LR Chisq* ($df = 22$) $= 39.16$, $p = .014$, so we report the results of the main effects using the main effects only model and the two-way interactions using the full interaction model.

Odds ratios and z tests in Table 15 indicate that child's negative emotionality significantly predicted differences between the high- and the

124

TABLE 15

Results of Multinomial Logistic Regression Analysis Examining Class Differences for Children's Somatic Complaints With the Low-Stable Class As the Reference Class

Predictor	Low-Stable vs.	b	SE	z	p	OR
Main effect model						
Child negative emotionality	Mid-decreasing	0.91	0.28	3.19	0.001	2.48
	High-stable	1.69	0.77	2.19	0.029	5.44
Positive marital relationship quality	Mid-decreasing	−0.59	0.20	−2.96	0.003	0.55
	High-stable	−0.45	0.41	−1.11	n.s	0.64
Attachment security to father	Mid-decreasing	0.26	0.77	0.33	n.s.	1.29
	High-stable	−2.90	1.64	−1.78	n.s.	0.05
Mothers' parental efficacy[a]	Mid-decreasing	−0.62	0.43	−1.43	n.s.	0.54
	High-stable	2.60	1.07	2.44	0.015	13.42
Full interaction model						
Child negative emotionality × attachment security to father	Mid-decreasing	−6.39	1.93	−3.30	0.001	0.002
	High-stable	4.18	7.08	0.59	n.s.	65.30
Child negative emotionality × attachment security to father × positive marital relationship quality	Mid-decreasing	−5.38	2.18	−2.47	0.013	0.005
	High-stable	1.43	6.86	0.21	n.s.	4.16
Child negative emotionality × attachment security to father × mothers' parental efficacy[a]	Mid-decreasing	−15.13	5.74	−2.63	0.008	<.001
	High-stable	−28.85	15.76	−1.83	n.s.	<.001

Note. n.s. = nonsignificant; *OR* = odds ratio.
[a]Higher scores indicate lower sense of efficacy as a parent.

low-stable class, and between the mid-decreasing class and the low-stable class. Children with higher negative emotionality were more likely to be in the mid-decreasing or high-stable class relative to the low-stable reference class. Positive marital relationship quality significantly predicted a higher probability of being in the low-stable class relative to the mid-decreasing class. Additionally, mother's reports of feeling less efficacious as a parent were associated with a greater probability of being in the high-stable class relative to the low-stable reference class.

Interaction Effects

In addition to the main effects, there was one two-way interaction and two three-way interactions that emerged from the full logistic model that predicted class membership with the low-stable class as the reference class.

The z tests, odds ratios, coefficients, and standard errors for the three interactions of the multinomial logistic regression analyses using the low-stable class as the reference class are presented in Table 15. Due to the complexity of the three-way interactions and the likelihood of spurious findings due to our sample size, we will only interpret the two-way interaction.

Children's negative emotionality × attachment security to father predicted decreased chances of being in the mid-decreasing class relative to the low-stable reference class. Children with low negative emotionality and low levels of attachment security to fathers were more likely to be in the mid-decreasing class. Children with high levels of negative emotionality and high levels of attachment security to fathers were more likely to fall in the low-stable class. At moderate levels of negative emotionality and high levels of attachment security to fathers, children were more likely to be in the mid-decreasing class relative to the low-stable class.

We also conducted exploratory multinomial logistic regressions using other classes as the reference class, due to our interest in assessing differences between classes that reflect different levels of clinical significance. Using the mid-decreasing class as the reference class, mother's reports of feeling less efficacious as a parent predicted an increased probability of being in the high-stable class relative to the mid-decreasing class, $b = 3.22$, $z = 2.97$, $OR = 25.02$. Utilizing the high-stable class as the reference class did not reveal any additional significant results.

Consequences of Children's Somatic Complaints for Sibling Relationships at 1 Year

Results of the regression analyses using the trajectory classes to predict siblings' positive involvement, conflict, or avoidance at 12 months were all nonsignificant relative to the reference class (low-stable).

DISCUSSION OF CHILDREN'S SOMATIC COMPLAINTS TRAJECTORIES

In this chapter, we assessed the overall pattern of children's somatic complaints after the birth of a new sibling, and the subgroups that captured individual differences in somatic complaints. We also examined the predictors of these trajectories and tested whether distinct trajectory subtypes were associated with differences in sibling relationship outcomes when the second child was 1 year of age.

In contrast to our original prediction that children experiencing the birth of a younger sibling might develop somatic complaints in response to this stressful change in family composition, children in the current study showed an overall linear decrease in somatic complaints over the year rather than an adjustment and adaptation response or a pattern of sudden and persistent change indicative of maladjustment. Although previous work indicated that somatic complaints are often seen as a short-term stress response (Eminson, 2007), our work indicates that young children do not appear to evince an increase in somatic complaints in response to the transition to siblinghood, at least based on parental reports using the CBCL. Instead, we found that 66% of the sample (low-stable) were low and remained low in somatic complaints over the transition and the year following the sibling's birth. An additional 35% of children fell into a mid-decreasing class where they had moderate levels of somatic complaints before the birth, but actually declined after the birth. Finally, only 5 % of children were in the high-stable class where their somatic complaints were high and remained high over time. Our results strongly suggest, as is the case with other problem behaviors examined in this monograph, that children's postbirth behavior is often a direct result of their prebirth behavior. Children high on somatic complaints after the birth are the same children high on somatic complaints before the birth. It is possible that the transition to siblinghood is less stressful for children than popular notions lead us to believe, or that children's prebirth scores are already a reflection of stress building in the family before the arrival of their infant sibling. We would need more assessment points before the third trimester of the pregnancy to be able to determine whether this was the case, but our current findings do not find strong evidence of change in children's somatic complaints from the last trimester of their mother's pregnancy to a year after the birth.

Consistent, however, with evidence in the literature that children's negative mood and difficult temperament were related to higher somatic complaints in young children (Rocha & Prkachin, 2007), children's temperament, particularly their negative emotionality, played a significant role in the prediction of the different trajectories of somatic complaints in children experiencing the transition to siblinghood. Children high on negative emotionality prior to the birth of the infant sibling were more likely to be in the mid-decreasing and high-stable classes relative to the low-stable class.

Children's negative emotionality was also a significant moderator of family risk as demonstrated in the significant two-way interaction between children's temperament and attachment security to the father. Emotional security theory suggests that the family environment, specifically the inter-parental relationship, influences how secure a child feels within the home, which, in turn, influences children's emotionality, emotion regulation, and the development of psychopathology (Davies et al., 2006). The results from our study indicate support for emotional security theory as well as potentially more complex family systems processes. With respect to the negative emotionality and attachment security to father interaction, attachment security to fathers appeared to play a relevant role in reducing children's somatic complaints after the transition to siblinghood. Children high in negative emotionality with greater attachment security to their fathers were more likely to be in the low-stable class compared to the mid-decreasing class, whereas children with lower attachment security with their fathers and moderate negative emotionality were more likely to be in the mid-decreasing class. These results suggest attachment insecurity to the father, even when negative emotionality is low, may increase children's anxiety, which is a known predictor for somatic complaints (Wolff et al., 2010).

Previous research on adolescents and adults supports this anxiety hypothesis. Ciechanowski et al. (2002) found that adult attachment style was significantly associated with somatic symptom reporting in women with preoccupied or fearful attachment. Stuart and Noyes (1999) explained that somatization may be a maladaptive strategy learned by children with insecure attachments as a way to satisfy their attachment needs, and a similar explanation may account for the current results linking attachment security between fathers and children with somatic complaints after the birth, particularly for negatively emotional children. Given that mothers may be more occupied with the care of the infant in the early months, some children may rely more on the emotional support of their fathers after the birth of their infant sibling, which may explain why the attachment security to father, and not to the mother, was more important in predicting children's somatic complaints. More research is needed to test these interpretations directly.

Our findings regarding marital relationship quality and parental efficacy also provide support for emotional security theory. High positive marital quality may act as a protective factor for children (e.g., increased emotional security), as children with parents who reported more positive marital relationships were likely to be in the low-stable class of somatic complaints. Such results suggest that when mothers and fathers are engaged with their marriages and put forth effort into sustaining the quality of marital communication and constructive problem-solving (Cummings & Davies, 2002), children may feel more emotionally secure in times of stressful change such as the transition after the birth of a sibling, thereby avoiding the development of somatic complaints.

In addition to the marital relationship, children also fared better when their mothers felt more confident in their parental efficacy. Children with mothers who felt less efficacious in parenting the older sibling and responding to their misbehavior were more likely to belong to the high-stable class rather than the low-stable or mid-decreasing classes. Given the link between lower parental efficacy and poor parenting practices and discipline (Sanders & Woolley, 2005), it is possible that mothers with a greater sense of parental efficacy were better at providing consistent discipline and helping their child to self-regulate at an early age, and, in turn, decrease rates of somatic complaints. It is also possible that mothers were unable to influence the high-stable children's somatic issues and felt less efficacious as a result.

Finally, with respect to the relation between somatic complaints and sibling outcomes, we found no significant results based on children's trajectory classes, which is not surprising as it is not entirely clear why children's physical symptoms and somatic complaints would affect their interactions with an infant sibling, other than perhaps to limit their involvement.

In summary, the potential stress or adjustment period associated with the infant sibling's birth did not appear to act as a catalyst for increased somatic complaints in children. Indeed, there were overall decreases in somatic complaints, which may reflect the decline in somatic symptoms that occurs over the early period of childhood. Although there was individual variability in children's somatic complaints in the current community-based sample, most children, as expected, fell into the low-stable class with far fewer children falling in the mid-decreasing and high-stable class. Both child and family characteristics predicted children's somatic complaint trajectories following the birth of a sibling. In this regard, children's negative emotionality was a prominent predictor of class membership, particularly in combination with attachment security to father. Although the scarcity of previous literature that directly examines the development or prevalence of children's somatic complaints during the transition to siblinghood makes robust conclusions challenging, it appears that the development of somatic complaints in this time period is not an immediate reaction to the birth of the sibling, but may be due instead to complex interactions between both individual characteristics of the children and the changing family context.

Supporting Information

Additional supporting information may be found in the online version of this article at the publisher's website.

X. DEVELOPMENTAL TRAJECTORIES OF CHILDREN'S SLEEP PROBLEMS AFTER THE BIRTH OF A SIBLING

Paige Safyer, Matthew M. Stevenson, Richard Gonzalez, Brenda L. Volling, Wonjung Oh, and Tianyi Yu

> This article is part of the issue "Developmental Trajectories of Children's Adjustment across the Transition to Siblinghood: Pre-Birth Predictors and Sibling Outcomes at One Year" Volling, Gonzalez, Oh, Song, Yu, Rosenberg, Kuo, Thomason, Beyers-Carlson, Safyer, and Stevenson (Issue Authors). For a full listing of articles in this issue, see: http://onlinelibrary.wiley.com/doi/10.1111/mono.v82.3/issuetoc.

One of the most important developmental milestones in infancy is the ability to sleep, uninterrupted, throughout the night. From the time the infant is brought home from the hospital, sleep is a major concern for parents and is discussed frequently at visits with health care professionals (Jenni & Carskadon, 2007). The ability to sleep through the night not only provides a respite from intensive childcare for parents, it also represents the normative maturation of children's regulatory processes and the capacity to self-soothe. Fragmented sleep patterns in early childhood have been linked to poorer neurobehavioral functioning and behavior problems (Sadeh, Raviv, & Gruber, 2000).

The transition to siblinghood may be an especially disruptive time for children's sleep, as changes in the family system, less focused parental attention, and irregular infant sleep patterns are factors likely to disturb the quality of the

Corresponding author: Correspondence concerning the Family Transitions Study should be addressed to Brenda L. Volling, Center for Human Growth and Development, University of Michigan, 300 N. Ingalls, Ann Arbor, MI. 48109-5406; e-mail: volling@umich.edu

For those interested in the statistical code used to analyze these data (including growth mixture models, random forest, and CART procedures), please email Richard Gonzalez, gonzo@umich.edu.

DOI: 10.1111/mono.12316

130

older sibling's sleep, leading to increased night awakenings as well as remaining awake for prolonged periods (Dunn & Kendrick, 1982; Trause et al., 1981). Field and Reite (1984) found that following the transition to siblinghood, older children experienced increases in night awakenings, the time it took to fall asleep, the amount of time slept, and bouts of crying during the night, providing evidence that a new infant may galvanize or increase older sibling's sleep problems.

Development of Sleep Problems in Early Childhood

Although we know the development of sleep regularity is important for normative functioning, few empirical studies exist examining sleep trajectories longitudinally from infancy throughout childhood (Acebo et al., 2005). Jenni and Carskadon (2007) caution against the pursuit of a universal sleep framework, stating that there is much variability in children's sleep across cultures and that sleep patterns should be viewed within a biopsychosocial framework. In other words, what constitutes normative sleep is malleable and is often dependent on extrinsic circumstances.

Studies suggest that infants begin to develop consolidated sleep patterns by 6–9 months of age (Anders & Keener, 1985; Jenni, Achermann, & Carskadon, 2005; Löhr & Siegmund, 1999). Once the infant begins to sleep through the night, total sleep hours remain fairly consistent throughout the first year. From ages 3 to 5, children tend to nap less and go to bed later in the evening (Sadeh, Mindell, Luedtke, & Wiegand, 2009). Although sleep patterns are more consistent during this period, toddlers and preschoolers still awaken frequently during the night (Jenni & Carskadon, 2007). Fragmented sleep from ages 3 to 5 is thought to be related to several major developmental processes converging—newfound cognitive abilities producing nightmares, attachment issues generating separation anxiety, and the need to assert independence exercised through bedtime resistance (Jenni & Carskadon, 2007; Jenni, Fuhrer, Iglowstein, Molinari, & Largo, 2005).

Several large-scale studies investigating children's sleep have found comparable trajectories of nighttime sleep consolidation during the first year, with decreases in daytime napping beginning at age 3. Sadeh, Mindell, Luedtke, and Wiegand (2009) sampled North American parents of 5,006 children from birth to 36 months regarding children's sleep patterns, the sleep environment, bedtime routines, and sleep positions. Findings suggested sleep duration does decrease with age, yet there is a wide range of individual variability when it comes to the total amount of hours slept. A cross-cultural study of the sleep patterns of 29,287 infants and toddlers in 17 different countries found that the amount of daytime sleep decreased with age, and nighttime sleep duration was primarily influenced by parental behaviors at bedtime, such as holding, rocking, rubbing/patting, or feeding, as well as how long parents waited to respond (Mindell, Sadeh, Kohyama, & How, 2010).

These studies demonstrated that even though there is large individual and cross-cultural variability among children's sleep patterns, predictable overall trends have been found, with decreases in daytime sleep and increases in nighttime sleep as children reach toddlerhood.

Individual Differences in Young Children's Sleep Problems

In a further examination of sleep pattern variability, Weinraub et al. (2012) identified two distinct sleep trajectories present over the first 3 years of life. Although two-thirds of children followed the normative pattern of increases in night sleep from 6 to 36 months, the remaining group awoke six to seven nights per week at 6 months, and three nights per week at 15 months. The children following this atypical trajectory were described as having a difficult temperament, were from a larger family, and their mothers were significantly more likely to be depressed. Despite early sleep difficulties, these children were sleeping through the night by age 2. Kataria, Swanson, and Trevathan (1987) identified a group of 60 children ranging in age from 15 to 48 months with documented sleep difficulties, and then followed these same children 3 years later. Eighty-four percent of children who suffered from sleep problems at 15 to 48 months continued to demonstrate these issues 3 years later. A more recent study by Lam, Hiscock, and Wake (2003) examined 114 mothers of 3- and 4-year-olds who had sleep difficulties in infancy, with 12% reporting their children's sleep problems had persisted, and 19% stating that their sleep issues had recurred. These children, for whom sleep remained an issue, had higher mean scores on the Child Behavior Checklist subscales for aggressive behavior and somatic complaints. These studies demonstrated that for a minority of children, sleep problems that persist into the preschool years may be indicative of an abnormal sleep trajectory that endures throughout childhood.

Risk and Protective Factors in the Prediction of Early Sleep Problems

Research on the development of sleep patterns in early childhood notes variability in children's sleep trajectories, and the role of both the child as well as the environment in the development of the sleep/wake system. Using the developmental ecological systems theory as a guiding organizational framework, factors internal to the child, parental variables, and family processes have been found to affect developing sleep patterns.

Temperament is often implicated as a major factor in children diagnosed with sleep problems. Toddlers with sleep difficulties have been described by their parents as being more difficult, having higher levels of reactivity, being distractible, more demanding, and less adaptive (Sadeh, Lavie, & Scher, 1994). Children diagnosed with sleep problems also display more negative emotionality and disruptive behavior during the day (Owens-Stively et al., 1997), indicating that these children may be having difficulties with emotion regulation.

The presence or absence of bedtime routines is also frequently implicated in the development and persistence of sleep problems throughout childhood (Staples, Bates, & Petersen, 2015). Adherence to a bedtime routine reflects a more organized parenting style, and is often conceptualized as consistency of parental responsiveness at three critical moments: sleep onset, episodes of sleep difficulty, and nocturnal awakening. Parents are very likely to facilitate children's development of self-soothing behaviors during these episodes through rubbing/patting, holding, rocking, or feeding. Early bedtimes, reliable routines, and scaffolding of self-regulation skills are all factors important in the development of sleep consolidation (Mindell et al., 2010).

Paradoxically, more attention and responsiveness to children with sleep difficulties may exacerbate the problem rather than improve children's sleep. For example, the more distressed and anxious mothers believed their infants were during night awakenings, the more likely they were to respond to infants' cries by attempting to soothe their children. Repeated involvement by mothers led to poorer infant sleep outcomes over the first 12 months of life (Tikotzky & Sadeh, 2009). As children age, interventions teaching self-soothing behaviors and providing verbal comfort during a nocturnal awakening were more effective at reducing sleep problems than holding or feeding the child during night awakenings (Sadeh et al., 2009).

The findings of these studies, and others, suggest that parents who are overly involved at bedtime may be stymying the development of important self-soothing abilities, resulting in a cycle leading to increased sleep problems (Touchette et al., 2005). Parents who respond appropriately, take into account the developmental abilities of the child (Weinraub et al., 2012). Sensitive parents are able to put the needs of their children before their own, providing the scaffolding necessary for children to learn healthy self-regulation abilities, whereas insensitive parents either respond inappropriately or neglect their children's needs altogether. In this sense, the qualities of the parent can be a risk or protective factor in children's sleep difficulties (Bélanger, Bernier, Simard, Bordeleau, & Carrier, 2015).

Family functioning has also been found to contribute to sleep problems during childhood (El-Sheikh & Sadeh, 2015). Researchers have identified detrimental family dynamics that are often associated with childhood sleep difficulties. Family stress is thought to play an important role in the development of sleep problems (Gregory, Eley, O'Connor, Rijsdijk, & Plomin, 2005; Klackenberg, 1982; Sadeh et al., 2000; Tobia, Wolfson, & Gallagher, 1995). Further, children with sleep problems often have poorer relationships with their parents and have parents with higher rates of marital dissatisfaction (Quine, 1992). In fact, marital conflict has been found to be a key variable affecting children's sleep (El-Sheikh, Hinnant, & Erath, 2015). Interparental conflict may contribute to sleep problems in multiple ways—parents under the stress of constant disagreement are likely to be dysregulated, lacking the ability to model healthy emotion regulation skills for their children. Additionally, children who are exposed to conflict are more anxious, aggressive, and hypervigilant—physiological arousal and dysregulation that prevent the child from settling (El-Sheikh, Buckhalt, Cummings, & Keller, 2007; Hall, Zubrick, Silburn, Parsons, & Kurinczuk, 2007).

Maternal sleep quality postpartum and maternal depression have also been linked to children's long-term sleep difficulties (Seifer, Sameroff, Dickstein, & Hayden, 1996; Zuckerman et al., 1987). Paternal involvement, however, may mitigate the influence of these factors on children's sleep patterns. Increased involvement of fathers and more equitable sharing of caregiving responsibilities during the postpartum period predicted greater quality maternal sleep which, in turn, predicted increased consolidation of infant sleep patterns (Tikotzky et al., 2015). It has been hypothesized that the relationship between sleep problems and family functioning are by-products of family stress and parenting deficiencies, which also contribute more broadly to the development of childhood behavioral problems (Deater-Deckard, Dodge, Bates, & Pettit, 1998). This is one reason why the ability of the parents to support one another and work together during this period of transition may be so important.

Sibling Relationships and Early Sleep Problems

Though few studies have focused specifically on sleep problems during the transition to siblinghood, this time period is often viewed as a stressful period and a time of adjustment for the entire family. How the family responds throughout this normative transition may influence the firstborn's adaptation and behavior (Volling, 2012). Of the studies that have examined sleep problems across the transition to siblinghood, Field and Reite (1984) found an increase in overall sleep time, nocturnal awakenings, night crying, and duration of deep sleep from 10 days before birth to 2 days after the mother was hospitalized. Ten days after the mother returned home, these behaviors decreased. This suggests that sleep problems in children may have been a result of separation issues rather than the transition to siblinghood itself. Trause et al. (1981) also found increased sleep problems during the transition to siblinghood, but the study only extended to the mother's discharge from the hospital, making it difficult to ascertain whether sleep problems were permanent, transitory, or simply a reaction to parental separation. No study has examined directly whether children's sleep problems are related to the developing sibling relationship, but it is possible that the nocturnal awakenings of an infant sibling in the months after the birth may affect children's sleep patterns. It is less clear whether such disruptions in sleep would affect sibling relations so we advanced no specific hypotheses in this regard.

RESULTS

Individual Differences in Trajectories of Sleep Problems

The unconditional latent linear model which revealed no significant change in sleep problems for the sample overall was chosen as the final model to be used in the GMM analyses (see Chapter III). Results of the GMM indicated that the four-class model with a linear growth factor was considered the best fitting model for the sleep problems subscale based on fit indices. The four-class model had better fit indices, AIC = 4,056.387, BIC = 4,121.710, LMR = 0.321, than the three-class model, AIC = 4,066.814, BIC = 4,121.823, and no major improvement in fit from the five-class model, AIC = 4,053.389, BIC = 4,129.035, LMR-LRT = 0.177; the four-class model also had higher entropy (0.839) than the five-class model (0.824). Estimates and standard errors for the fixed effects of each class are presented in Table 16 and the different trajectory patterns for the four classes are displayed in Figure 10; all of which are consistent with projected linear patterns of change and stability shown in Figure 1 in the Introduction.

The largest class representing 55.6% of the sample ($n = 128$) was denoted the *low-stable* class; these children showed low levels of sleep problems at the prenatal timepoint that remained low throughout the first year. The second class, and 37.8% of the sample ($n = 87$), represented a *mid-decreasing* trajectory. These children had moderate levels of sleep problems at the

TABLE 16

GROWTH MIXTURE MODEL RESULTS FOR SLEEP PROBLEMS: PARAMETER ESTIMATES AND STANDARD ERRORS FOR FIXED EFFECTS

Classes Parameters	Low-Stable $n = 128$ (55.6%)	Mid-Decreasing $n = 87$ (37.8%)	High-Stable $n = 13$ (5.6%)	Extreme-High-Stable $n = 2$ (1%)
Intercept	1.431*** (.216)	4.328*** (.291)	7.788*** (.671)	12.140*** (.888)
Linear slope	.053 (.036)	−.093** (.039)	−.216 (.181)	−.075 (.071)

Note. Standard errors in parentheses. The random effect (variance) of intercept est. = 0.449, $SE = 0.308$, $p = 0.145$; the random effect of linear slope est. = .035, $SE = .013$, $p = .008$.
**$p < .01$, ***$p < .001$.

135

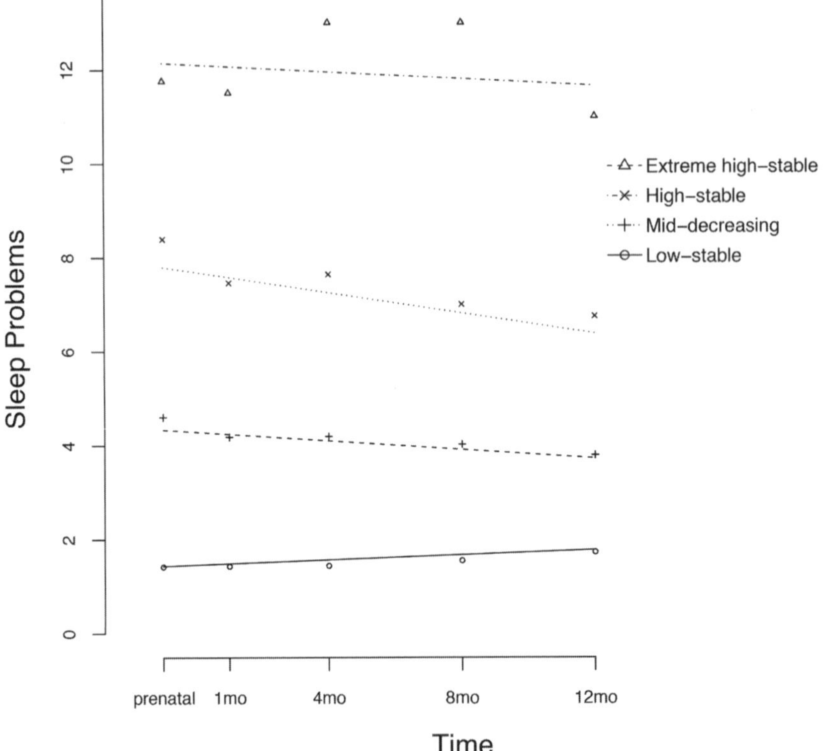

FIGURE 10.—Trajectory classes for sleep problems from Growth Mixture Model ($n = 230$).

onset and their symptoms showed a linear decrease over time. A third class and 5.6% of the sample ($n = 13$) denoted the *high-stable* class, showed high levels of sleep problems at the prenatal timepoint that were stable over time. The fourth class and 1% of the sample ($n = 2$) was labeled the *extreme-high-stable* class, and the children in this class showed the highest levels of sleep problems at the prenatal timepoint, which remained high over time.

When examining the spaghetti plots of the individual trajectories for each class, we found, as with prior CBCL subscales, that the intercepts of the various classes mapped well onto the cut-off ranges (see Figure S6 in the supporting information online). That is, children in the low-stable class were below the normative mean with a few children above the mean. Most children in the mid-decreasing class were between the normative mean and the borderline clinical cut-off. This was similar to the high-stable group, where the children fell between the normative mean and the clinical range cut-off, with a few children presenting with symptoms above the clinical cut-off. Of the two

136

children who were in the extreme-high-stable class, both showed symptoms above the clinical cut-off. Thus, our results showed that the identified classes represented meaningful distinctions between children falling within the normative, borderline, and clinical ranges on sleep problems, even though several of the riskier classes were quite small.

Predicting Sleep Problem Trajectories

Five variables emerged from the data mining procedures as candidate prenatal predictors for children's sleep trajectories: children's negative emotionality, parents' reports of coparenting conflict, mothers' age, observed marital negative interaction, and mothers' parental self-efficacy. The multinomial logistic regression analyses revealed that the model testing higher-order interactions among the five candidate predictors was not a significantly better fit than the reduced model with direct effects, $LR\ Chisq$ $(df = 78) = 75.13$, $p = 0.57$; therefore, the results of the reduced model with additive, centered main effects are presented in Table 17.

Using the low-stable class as a reference, children's negative emotionality and coparenting conflict had significant effects (z's > 1.96).

TABLE 17

RESULTS OF MULTINOMIAL LOGISTIC REGRESSION ANALYSIS EXAMINING CLASS DIFFERENCES FOR SLEEP PROBLEMS WITH THE LOW-STABLE CLASS AS THE REFERENCE CLASS

Predictor	Low-Stable vs.	b	SE	z	p	OR
Mothers' age	Mid-decreasing	−0.04	0.04	−1.18	n.s.	0.96
	High-stable	0.003	0.09	0.03	n.s.	1.00
	Extreme-high	−0.13	0.17	−0.73	n.s.	0.88
Children's negative emotionality	Mid-decreasing	0.57	0.28	2.07	0.038	1.77
	High-stable	1.92	0.63	3.03	0.002	6.80
	Extreme-high	−0.46	1.30	−0.35	n.s.	0.63
Mothers' parental efficacy[a]	Mid-decreasing	−0.03	0.44	−0.08	n.s.	0.97
	High-stable	1.01	0.95	1.06	n.s.	2.74
	Extreme-high	0.16	2.27	0.07	n.s.	1.18
Coparenting conflict	Mid-decreasing	1.33	0.39	3.41	<0.001	3.77
	High-stable	0.69	0.83	0.84	n.s.	2.00
	Extreme-high	1.51	1.86	0.81	n.s.	4.54
Observed negative marital interaction	Mid-decreasing	−0.07	0.07	−0.96	n.s.	0.93
	High-stable	0.32	0.15	0.21	n.s.	1.03
	Extreme-high	−0.27	0.49	−0.55	n.s	0.76

Note. n.s. = nonsignificant; OR = odds ratio.
[a]Higher scores indicate lower sense of efficacy as a parent.

As children's negative emotionality increased, there was an increased likelihood of children being in the mid-decreasing class relative to the low-stable reference class and an increased likelihood of being in the high-stable class relative to the low-stable reference class. In addition, increased coparenting conflict predicted increased chances of membership in the mid-decreasing class relative to the low-stable class.

Because of our interest in discerning differences between classes hitting different levels of clinical significance, we also conducted exploratory multinomial logistic regressions using several of the other classes as the reference class. Using the mid-decreasing class as the reference class, we found that children's negative emotionality significantly predicted membership in the high-stable class. Specifically, children with increased negative emotionality were significantly more likely to be in the high-stable class, $b=1.34$, $z=2.13$, $OR=3.8$, versus the mid-decreasing class. Other results using the mid-decreasing and then high-stable class as the reference did not differ from the results reported above.

Consequences of Sleep Problems for Sibling Relationships at 1 Year

We conducted regression analyses using the low-stable class as the reference class to test whether children's sleep problem trajectories predicted siblings' positive involvement, conflict, or avoidance 12 months after the infant was born. Results were nonsignificant indicating no mean differences for sibling relationship quality.

DISCUSSION OF CHILDREN'S SLEEP PROBLEM TRAJECTORIES

Results indicated the best fitting model describing children's sleep problems across the transition to siblinghood was a linear latent growth model that indicated no change in children's sleep problems, on average, following the birth of a sibling. This is inconsistent with previous literature examining the transition to siblinghood, which found that the presence of the infant might create or exacerbate children's sleep disturbances (Dunn & Kendrick, 1982). When examining individual differences within the sample, however, children's sleep trajectories revealed four different patterns following the birth of their sibling. The first class (55.6% of the sample) showed low levels of sleep problems before and after the birth of their sibling. The second class, accounting for 38% of children, exhibited moderate levels of sleep problems initially that waned over time, a typical trajectory often found by sleep researchers and reflects the normative development of regulatory systems (Weinraub et al., 2012). The third smaller class of only 6% of children (high-stable) suffered from a number of sleep issues both before and after their sibling's birth with little change across timepoints. The two children in the extreme-high-stable class (1%) also did not evidence changes in their sleep problems over time indicating that the transition was not responsible for these children's clinically significant levels of sleep difficulties before and after the birth of their infant sibling.

When examining the predictors of these different trajectory patterns, our findings suggest that child characteristics and family processes may be more responsible for individual differences in children's sleep problems before and after the birth than the birth of the infant sibling, as most patterns revealed low, modest, or high problems before the birth that remained stable or actually decreased over the transition period. Indeed, the multinomial logistic regressions indicated children's temperament (i.e., negative emotionality), as well as coparenting conflict before the birth, distinguished children in the mid-decreasing class from the low-stable class. Thus, it appears that both temperamental characteristics of children and family relationship functioning were important predictors of children's sleep patterns after the birth. Although our results were found in a community-based sample of low-risk parents, the findings were consistent with many prior studies finding children's difficult temperament and parenting conflict as predictors of children's sleep problems (DeLeon & Karraker, 2007; Weinraub et al., 2012).

Numerous studies have emphasized the importance of temperament in the development of sleep difficulties (Owens-Stively et al., 1997; Sadeh et al., 1994; Schaefer, 1990). Children who are temperamentally reactive may have a harder time developing the self-regulation skills necessary for sleeping throughout the night (Bates, Pettit, Dodge, & Ridge, 1998; Belsky, Hsieh, & Crnic, 1998; Rothbart & Bates, 2006). Additionally, difficult child temperament influences the quality of care children often receive, which may also play a role in the parental strategies used to put children to sleep, as well as respond to night awakenings.

Research has emphasized the bidirectional relationship between parental behaviors and children's sleep and the importance of viewing children's sleep difficulties within an ecological family systems model (Scher & Asher, 2004). Coparenting conflict can increase stress and deplete the resources needed for mothers and fathers to parent sensitively and effectively. At the same time, children living in a family with a high amount of interparental conflict experience a multitude of negative emotions and become dysregulated, making it harder for children to calm down at night (El-Sheikh & Sadeh, 2015). According to a neurobehavioral perspective, sleep and vigilance are opposing processes—sleep requires a lack of awareness and monitoring of the external environment, whereas vigilance requires heightened monitoring of the external environment for threats (Dahl & El-Sheikh, 2007). From an evolutionary perspective, social bonds, family, and specifically safety and security provided by caregivers enable greater safety for periods of sleep. Thus, it makes sense that when a core component of safety provided by parents is threatened, children respond with vigilant biobehavioral processes, and therefore, decreased sleep.

Family systems theory underscores that family members have bidirectional influences on one another (Cox & Paley, 2003). Therefore, interparental conflict and children's sleep can be viewed as a bidirectional relation—conflict between parents can lead to a dysregulated child who is harder to soothe, and parents are less sensitive and responsive due to the stress of their own discord. Indeed, infant crying at night during the first few months has a negative impact on parents own sleep quality, marital quality, stress, mood, and general fatigue (Meijer & van den Wittenboer, 2007; Meltzer & Mindell, 2007), all of which are key determinants of parenting (Belsky, 1984). Sensitive parents are more likely to be able to respond to their children's nighttime distress while also respecting the growing need for autonomy and the scaffolding of self-soothing skills (El-Sheikh & Sadeh, 2015). Sleep processes represent some of the earliest interactions between innate variables, such as temperament and family functioning, and further studies examining sleep across the transition to siblinghood may elucidate these dynamics.

Relations were not found between children's sleep problems and sibling relationships at 12 months, which is not surprising as it is not clear why disturbed sleep would translate directly into behaviors directed to an infant sibling. Further research, however, may need to take a more nuanced look at family and sleep processes than we were able to capture here with the CBCL syndrome scale to articulate whether a crying infant that may be responsible for disruptions in children's sleep may eventually be the recipient of the older sibling's hostile and reactive behaviors.

In sum, findings from this relatively low-risk, community-based sample of children experiencing the birth of an infant sibling demonstrated that a majority of parents reported their children had no sleep problems over the course of the year following the birth. Of those with borderline or even clinical elevations in sleep problems, there was no evidence of a drastic change in their sleep problems once the infant was born and brought home, which is somewhat surprising given the significant number of night awakenings and feedings a newborn infant requires and the sleep disturbances and fatigue that parents often experience during the early postpartum months. These levels of children's sleep problems already existed before the birth of the sibling. We must acknowledge, however, that parent reports, particularly during a time when they, themselves, are busy attending to a newborn at night, may not reliably capture the true extent of children's sleep difficulties over the transition. For example, Field and Reite (1984), using time-lapse video footage, found that the quality of the older children's sleep quality did decrease in the 10 days after the mother returned home from the hospital with the infant sibling. Thus, the use of these assessments to track children's actual sleep patterns may indicate levels of sleep difficulties for these children that we were unable to uncover here and we would recommend future studies move beyond parent report in order to address such a possibility. Dunn and Kendrick (1982) also reported disruptions in older children's sleep patterns after the birth of the sibling. Their sample, however, consisted of working class families in Cambridge, England, and it is likely that many of the siblings were sharing a room, or living in small houses where a crying infant could cause disruption, or parents were experiencing greater stress due to financial difficulties. Previous research has linked low SES to sleep problems in children (Sheridan et al., 2013). Our study consisted of middle- to high-SES families so it is possible that sample differences with respect to SES and financial stress accounted for our lack of findings in contrast to those of Dunn and Kendrick (1982).

Supporting Information

Additional supporting information may be found in the online version of this article at the publisher's website.

XI. GENERAL DISCUSSION: CHILDREN'S ADJUSTMENT AND ADAPTATION FOLLOWING THE BIRTH OF A SIBLING

Brenda L. Volling

This article is part of the issue "Developmental Trajectories of Children's Adjustment across the Transition to Siblinghood: Pre-Birth Predictors and Sibling Outcomes at One Year" Volling, Gonzalez, Oh, Song, Yu, Rosenberg, Kuo, Thomason, Beyers-Carlson, Safyer, and Stevenson (Issue Authors). For a full listing of articles in this issue, see: http://onlinelibrary.wiley.com/doi/10.1111/mono.v82.3/issuetoc.

There were three major aims to the work presented here. First, we examined individual differences in children's adjustment after the birth of an infant sibling. By using information obtained from the Family Transitions Study, a longitudinal investigation with five time points (prenatal, 1, 4, 8, and 12 months), we explored the underlying trajectory patterns of change in children's behavior problems over the course of a year. We expected distinct patterns of change in how children reacted to the birth. Second, because we wanted findings from this research to generate evidence-based recommendations for future intervention efforts or prebirth education classes, we utilized a series of data mining and confirmatory testing strategies that together took advantage of predictive validity and traditional hypothesis testing criteria to pinpoint prebirth predictors of the different trajectory patterns. We also analyzed each of the seven behavioral syndromes of the CBCL—aggression, attention problems, anxious-depressed, emotional reactivity, withdrawal, somatic complaints, and sleep problems—separately because Dunn et al. (1981) claimed that a single assessment could not

---

Corresponding author: Brenda L. Volling, Center for Human Growth and Development, University of Michigan, 300 N. Ingalls, Ann Arbor, MI 48109-5406, e-mail: volling@umich.edu
DOI: 10.1111/mono.12317

capture the variability in children's problematic reactions seen after the birth of a sibling. As a result, we now have a better understanding of the risk and protective factors that predicted the severity of children's emotional and behavioral problems and can discuss where to target interventions for the future. Finally, we examined whether children's adjustment trajectories had repercussions for the developing sibling relationship at the end of the first year, knowing that there is considerable stability in the quality of children's sibling relationships through childhood and adolescence. Making sure this relationship gets off to a good start not only alleviates parenting stress in the year after the birth, but has long-term developmental benefits for children (e.g., Buist & Vermande, 2014; Dunn et al., 1994).

THE SEARCH FOR INDIVIDUAL DIFFERENCES

In a recent review of children's adjustment after the birth of a sibling, Volling (2012) concluded that there was far more support for individual differences in children's reactions to the transition to siblinghood (i.e., disruption, growth, and no change) than psychological maladjustment. Yet, there are few studies that have examined this important developmental transition in young children's lives and many are fraught with significant methodological and design limitations (e.g., very small samples, only two time points). Further, there is an overarching belief even today that the transition after the birth of a second child is going to be a difficult one for children and their parents, and they best be prepared for the jealousy and rivalry that will ensue. Take the following description, for instance, from a website designed to help parents prepare for the second child:

> You're pregnant and thrilled. Junior, less so. After all, from his perspective, the little interloper's already taking your time and energy. Nothing you can do will guarantee sibling bliss, but there are steps you can take to reassure your little one and minimize resentment …. If, despite your best efforts, your child begins acting out [address] her underlying concerns rather than the behavior itself. The new arrival is going to change her world as well as yours; it may take time, but one day she'll agree it was for the better. (Boyd, 2009)

Such accounts with a focus on resentment and rivalry suggest there is some underlying psychosocial trauma that is responsible for children's difficult behavior when the infant is born and is part of the psychodynamic legacy underscoring the difficulties children will face with the arrival of an infant sibling (Adler, 1928; Levy, 1934; Petty, 1953; Winnicott, 1978). This emphasis on the dethronement of the child, the building resentment and frustration of losing parental attention, and the belief that children suffer severe maladjustment is in stark contrast to a developmental psychopathology perspective that situates the child within a family context so as to understand how child characteristics interact with family circumstances to determine behavioral and psychopathological outcomes (Volling, 2005), and is also inconsistent with the findings emerging from the present investigation.

The Family Transitions Study was designed to take a developmental psychopathology perspective to search for individual differences in children's reactions with a focus on operationalizing different patterns of change that would reflect maladjustment indicative of a psychosocial crisis model (i.e., sudden, persistent change), as well as adjustment and adaptation, using a longitudinal design with five time points over the course of a year in a community sample. Given the number of children with siblings (80%) and the fact that the birth of a second child is a frequent occurrence, we recruited a community-based, low-risk sample to determine whether children's problem behavior changed over the transition to siblinghood and if there were any signs of disturbance. We collected information on children's behavior problems using the Child Behavior Checklist for the 1.5–5 year age group, which is a widely used and validated measure of children's problem behavior with identifiable clinical cut-offs (Ivanova et al., 2010). Across all problem areas examined, there was no evidence of a pattern of long-term maladjustment after the birth of a sibling that would indicate sudden increases in problem behavior immediately following the birth that persisted over time. In fact, for most of the behaviors examined the vast majority of children were low on problem behaviors before the birth and remained low over the course of the year following the birth with little to no noticeable change. In some cases, children's behavioral and emotional problems actually declined, which may reflect the gradual maturation and growth in social and cognitive functioning over the toddler years. The one exception was for aggressive behavior in which we found an adjustment and adaptation response, a sudden increase from prenatal to 1 month with a subsequent decline to prebirth levels by 4 months. Thus, there is little evidence from the Family Transitions Study to suggest children have a maladaptive response to the transition to siblinghood and even when sudden change is apparent, it is short-lived, providing more evidence of children's resilience in the face of change than long-term problems of psychological maladjustment.

Even though most children did not experience significant change in behavior immediately following the birth, in all instances, there was evidence of different groups of children based on the growth mixture modeling. Many of these classes of children showed increases or decreases in behavior over time, but the most striking similarity across all the subscales examined were the intercept differences (i.e., where children started prenatally), attesting to the stability in individual differences over time and the fact that children having behavioral difficulties after the birth were often the same children

144

having difficulties before the birth. The other remarkable finding was that each of the classes identified by the GMM often fell within the specified range for nonclinical, borderline-clinical, and clinical cut-offs, which provided further confirmation that the classes of children identified were meaningful, and not just statistical anomalies or outliers. In this community-based, low-risk sample, we would not expect large numbers of children in the clinical range cut-off unless the transition to siblinghood was a traumatic developmental crisis resulting in significant psychological turmoil or pathology (which it is not). The small classes with few children were always those at the extreme high end of the clinical or borderline-clinical range, never just a few children at the low-end or mid-range, and they were already at this point before the birth, suggesting that whatever was responsible for these children's extreme scores, it was already in place before the infant was born.

It is possible the prenatal scores of children's behavior problems were already elevated due to changes occurring during the mother's pregnancy, but additional prenatal time points before the last trimester would be needed to rule out this possibility and to provide a further test of whether linear increases in children's emotional and behavioral problems were already underway before the infant was born. Such changes may not have been adequately captured in the current analyses with a single prenatal time point. Observant children are keenly aware of the physical changes of their mother's pregnancy and mothers have reported that changes in their relationships with the firstborn are already evident during the pregnancy (Richardson, 1983). Further, all women in the current study had singleton births with no known birth complications to our knowledge. The entire transition and months leading up to the birth may be more stressful if the pregnancy was difficult, mothers were on bed rest, or there were labor and birth complications (Affonso, Mayberry, & Sheptak, 1988). Such complications no doubt increase family stress and children's anxiety even before the infant is born and additional research is needed to address these issues directly.

One of the unique aspects of the current report is the search for individual differences in trajectories of children's adjustment across the transition to siblinghood based on multiple CBCL subscales of emotional and behavioral problems. Our decision, however, to examine each subscale separately may have meant we were missing the "whole child" and whether our high-risk groups were identifying the same troublesome group of children. In order to address this possibility further, we conducted a post hoc analysis using cross-tabulations across the CBCL subscales looking specifically at whether children in the high-risk groups were the same children. For these analyses, we utilized the same pairings as we have throughout, looking at relations within the externalizing (aggression attention), internalizing (emotional reactivity, withdrawal, anxiety-depression), and physical (somatic complaints, sleep) symptoms domains.

For aggression and attention problems, we defined the mid-AAR-decreasing and high-decreasing classes as risk groups for the aggressive children because both fell within or reached the clinical cut-off either at prenatal or 1 month, and focused on the high-stable class as high risk for attention problems. Four of the five high-stable children on attention problems (80%) did fall within the mid-AAR (2 of 18) and high-decreasing classes (2 of 8), Fisher's exact test $p < .001$. Yet, one of the high-stable children for attention problems fell in the low-increasing group of aggressive children. It should be noted, however, that there was much more dispersion across other classes. For instance, for the 52 mid-decreasing (i.e., moderate risk) group of children on attention problems, 5 fell in the low-increasing, 14 in the low-AAR, 23 in the mid-stable, and 5 in the mid-AAR. Of the 172 children in the low-decreasing group of children with attention problems, most ($n = 86$ or 50%) fell in the low-increasing class for aggression, 54 in the low-AAR, 21 in mid-stable, and 11 in mid-AAR revealing far more dispersion across the attention problems and aggression groups at low and moderate risk. Thus, even though the few children at very high-risk for attention problems were more likely to be in the two high-risk aggressive groups, there was less association between attention problems and aggression with the more abundant numbers of children in the low and moderate risk groups.

For the three internalizing scales of emotional reactivity, withdrawal, and anxiety-depression, the picture is even more complicated. Of the nine children in the high-increasing anxiety-depression group, zero were in the high-decreasing group of withdrawn children, although four (44.4%) were in the moderate-increasing group, three in the low-stable, and two in the mid-curvilinear class. Of the four high-risk children in the high-decreasing withdrawal group, none were in the high-risk high-increasing group of anxiety-depression, with three in the low-decreasing, and one in the mid-stable. Finally, of the eight children in the high-risk group of high-increasing anxiety-depressed children, two were in the low-stable, four in the mid-increasing, and two in the high-decreasing group of emotionally reactive children; 75% of high-risk children were in the moderate to high-risk groups, Fisher's exact test, $p < .001$. Two of the four high-risk children in the high-decreasing emotional reactivity group were also in the high-increasing anxiety-depression group (50%), although one was also in the low-decreasing and one in the mid-stable groups. Although there appears to be some association across internalizing scales, there is clearly not a one-to-one correspondence between those children at high-risk on one internalizing scale and those children high on another.

Finally, a comparison of children across the sleep problems and somatic complaints scales found little association. For instance, the two children in the extreme high-stable group on sleep problems actually fell in the low-stable group on somatic complaints. Of the 13 high-stable children on sleep problems, 2 were in the low-stable, 7 in the mid-decreasing, and 4 in the high-stable groups of somatic complaints.

In sum, although there is some correspondence across the CBCL subscales in the higher-risk classes, as might be expected given that many preschoolers have comorbid behavioral and emotional disorders (Gardner & Shaw, 2008), enough of the children were dispersed across the different classes to suggest that for children making the transition to siblinghood, Dunn and Kendrick (1982) were correct in admonishing the use of single broadband measures of adjustment to capture the variability in children's adjustment following the birth of a sibling.

EXPLAINING EARLIER ACCOUNTS OF CHILDREN'S MALADJUSTMENT AFTER THE BIRTH OF A SIBLING

Given the resounding evidence from the current study that children did not undergo a developmental crisis or maladjustment response after the birth of a sibling, one is left wondering about earlier accounts of children's maladaptive responses. Much of the earlier research on the transition to siblinghood was conducted before developmental science and the study of normative developmental changes were introduced to the field of childhood psychopathology (Cicchetti, 1984). Further, early sibling rivalry studies were clearly entrenched in psychoanalytic thinking and a search for childhood disturbance (Levy, 1937; Winnicott, 1978). One of the most influential developmental theories in the last century is Bowlby's (1969) ethological theory of attachment. Attachment theory focuses on the intensely emotional nature of the young child's attachment to a primary caregiver, in most cases, the mother. Young children express attachment behaviors such as smiling, crying, and clinging in their efforts to seek proximity to and maintain contact with the attachment figure, and also experience considerable distress and upset when separated from the primary caregiver for even brief periods of time.

The effects of maternal separation on the mother–child attachment relationship are well-accepted and understood today, but this was not always the case. Indeed, the earliest documentation of the distress of young children to separation from the mother for brief and extended periods of time took advantage of a natural experiment by observing children's reactions to maternal separation when mothers entered the hospital to *give birth to a second child* and children were left either in foster care or a residential nursery (e.g., Heinicke & Westheimer, 1966; Robertson & Robertson, 1971). For instance, Heinicke and Westheimer (1966) in their study of 2-year-olds separated anywhere from 2 to 20 weeks while their mother gave birth to another child, noted that within the first 3 days after separation, children were seen crying and fretting for the parent, having difficulty sleeping during the night, refusing to partake in daily routines such as eating, dressing, and toileting, showing an increase in sucking a bottle or thumb, having more toileting accidents, attempting to establish some sort of positive relationship with alternate caregivers in the nursery, and as the separation continued, an increase in hostility. "The studies of other investigators as well as our own work had left no doubt that the normal 2-year-old child, being placed into a residential nursery, even if only temporarily, is very likely to be experienced as a traumatic event" (p. 4).

Today, there would be no question that these children's behaviors and emotional upset were due to the extended separations from caregivers and the placement in a strange and unfamiliar setting, but one must ask whether these lengthy separations from the mother at a time before attachment theory took prominence in our understanding of young children's emotional well-being seriously confounded the effects of the transition to siblinghood and the birth of an infant sibling, with the consequences of attachment, separation, and loss. Further, hospital practices in terms of the length of a stay after a birth and allowing children visitation have changed considerably over the years. Because of the active involvement these days of fathers in caregiving, it is also unlikely that children are being left in the care of unfamiliar others while their mothers give birth to an infant sibling. Due to both theoretical and social changes over the decades, it is our contention that findings from some of the earliest studies of the transition to siblinghood reflect disturbances coinciding with disruptions in attachment, extended maternal separations, and feelings of loss due to the mother's lengthy hospitalization, and not to the actual arrival of an interloper (i.e., the infant sibling).

UNCOVERING THE BEST PREDICTORS OF BEHAVIOR PROBLEM TRAJECTORIES FOR INTERVENTION EFFORTS

The second overarching goal of this research program was to identify targets for intervention by identifying those prenatal indicators of child, parent, and family functioning that would best predict individual differences in our adjustment trajectories. To do so, we relied on a series of data mining analyses combined with statistical confirmation to pinpoint the best predictors of children's adjustment following the birth of their infant sibling, which are highlighted here.

Children's Temperament

Characteristics of the child, namely, temperamental predispositions of negative emotionality and behavioral inhibition, were some of the most consistent predictors of children's problem behavior across the seven CBCL

148

syndrome scales. In every case, one or both aspects of temperament predicted children's class membership, usually with children higher in negative emotionality and behavioral inhibition falling into the riskier classes (i.e., higher intercepts). Children high in negative emotionality were more likely to be in classes high in problem behavior for aggression, anxiety-depression, emotional reactivity, withdrawal, and somatic complaints, whereas children, who parents described as high in behavioral inhibition, were more likely to be classified as high on anxiety-depression and withdrawal before the birth regardless of the pattern of change after the transition. These findings are not all that surprising given the influential role of children's temperament, particularly negative reactivity and behavioral inhibition, in predicting children's externalizing and internalizing behavior problems across ages (Chen, Deater-Deckard, & Bell, 2014; Crawford, Schrock, & Woodruff-Borden, 2010). In an earlier report, we also found that children with difficult temperaments (high negative emotionality, low in soothability) were more likely to increase in externalizing behavior from prenatal to 1 month after the birth, particularly when coparenting between mothers and fathers was low in support and high in undermining during prenatal home observations (Kolak & Volling, 2013).

These results are also amazingly similar to those reported by Dunn and Kendrick (1982) in their study of 41 British children in the 1970s and 1980s. Children described by their mothers as high in negative mood before the sibling was born increased in withdrawal, clinging, and sleep problems after the birth. Further, children high in negative mood and intensity of emotion also had increases in fears, worrying, and ritualistic behaviors by 8 months after the birth, behaviors comprising the emotional reactivity syndrome scale of the current study. These same children were also more likely to protest mother–infant interaction at 14 months, or watched mother–infant interaction, sucking their thumbs and holding comfort objects, signs of anxiety, and self-comforting behaviors. In line with recent theories positing that some children, particularly those high in negative reactivity, appear to be more sensitive to environmental changes (Belsky & Pluess, 2009), children high on negative emotionality and behavioral inhibition in the current study were more inclined to have behavioral and emotional difficulties before and after the birth of their infant sibling.

Attachment Security to Mother and Father

The results of our work also provide support that attachment security to parents, and particularly the mother, played a role in children's externalizing behavior problems across the transition to siblinghood. In two instances, aggression and attention problems, the two subscales that comprise externalizing behaviors, children in the riskier classes (e.g., high-decreasing for aggression and high-stable and mid-decreasing for attention problems), were more insecurely attached to their mothers even before the birth of their infant sibling. Teti et al. (1996) reported overall decreases in attachment security to mothers after the birth of the secondborn, and numerous studies report significant change in the mother–child relationship after the birth of an infant sibling (see Volling, 2012), including increases in mothers' use of harsh and punitive discipline, more confrontations and prohibitions, and decreases in joint attention and play (Baydar et al., 1997; Dunn & Kendrick, 1982). It is plausible that the differences enumerated across the different classes of aggression and attention problems reported here may be due to changes in the mother–child attachment relationship once the infant was born, but it is also of interest that attachment security to mother differed across classes even before the birth. Changes in the attachment between mother and child could elicit feelings of jealousy, as jealousy is elicited when children believe their attachment relationship to their beloved parents is threatened by a rival, in this case, an infant sibling (Volling, McElwain, & Miller, 2002). Thus, children may well be reacting to changes in the mother–child relationship even before the birth and parents should be attuned to the emotional and behavioral changes taking place and make special time for their elder child.

All families in the current study were two-parent, consisting of a mother and a father, so one possible means of buffering the drastic changes in the mother–child relationship is having the emotional and physical support of the father. Indeed, we recruited two-parent families for the Family Transitions Study to test whether the children's relationship with their fathers would buffer children from emotional difficulties that might result from changes in the mother–child relationship. In only one instance did attachment security to father emerge as an important predictor of children's somatic complaints, particularly for children high in negative emotionality. Children high in negative emotionality were more likely to be in the low-stable as opposed to the mid-decreasing class if they had higher attachment security to their fathers, underscoring the buffering role of a close father–child relationship in decreasing somatic complaints.

In some preliminary analyses, Volling, Oh, and Gonzalez (2012) reported that children with more secure attachments to their fathers than their mothers over the course of the transition had fathers who felt more efficacious in their parenting role than did mothers, and children were more likely to be engaged in positive interaction with their infant sibling later in the year after the birth. In contrast, children whose attachment security with both mothers and fathers was low before the birth and continued to deteriorate over the transition, not only had parents who felt ineffective in their parental role, but children also engaged in more antagonistic sibling interactions. Dunn and Kendrick (1982) also asked mothers to describe how close and affectionate the father–child relationship was before the infant's birth. In those families where mothers reported the father–child relationship was exceptionally close, there was less escalation in mother–child conflict and confrontations, and less of a decrease in joint play between mother and child, after the birth. In the current study, we collected information directly from fathers rather than relying on maternal reports of father involvement, and also found that children's relationships with their fathers may serve a protective role in adjusting to the transition to siblinghood. Further research is clearly needed to help delineate how children's attachment security to their fathers may help support and protect them over this developmental transition.

Fathers' Sense of Parenting Efficacy

One possibility may lie in fathering behavior itself. We did find, for instance, that fathers' confidence in their parental role was important in preventing their children's problem behaviors in many instances. Paternal self-efficacy, particularly how confident a father felt about his ability to discipline the firstborn's misbehavior, was critically important in distinguishing the different classes of aggression. When fathers were confident, their children were far more likely to be in the low-increasing class and less likely to be in the riskier classes (e.g., mid-stable or high-decreasing) when they were not. This suggests that fathers' abilities to manage their children's behaviors and confidence in their fathering role proved important for their children's aggression after the infant's birth, a time when mothers may be busy with the newborn. From these results, we would recommend that fathers learn effective discipline practices for handling children's aggressive misbehavior, in addition to providing emotional support to the child during a potentially stressful transition. Assisting fathers with these skills and informing them of their important role in supporting their children's emotional needs can be incorporated into prebirth education classes that will help fathers feel more effective as parents, help children manage their behavior and feel supported, and help mothers by providing child-rearing support during the postpartum period after the birth of a newborn infant.

Maternal Depression

Postpartum maternal depression is a cause for concern given the deleterious effects on infants, children, and families (Letourneau et al., 2012). More attention is now directed to maternal depression during pregnancy because of the potential effects on early fetal brain development via the hypothalamic–pituitary–adrenal axis (HPA) and stability in maternal depression over the perinatal period (Thomason et al., 2014). Few parents in the current study were clinically depressed, which may explain why neither maternal nor paternal depressive symptoms before the infant's birth predicted children's behavioral or emotional adjustment across the transition. These findings are in contrast to those reported by Dunn et al. (1981) who found that when mothers reported they were extremely tired or depressed 3 weeks after the birth, their children were more likely to be withdrawn. Given the significant associations between maternal and paternal depression in the perinatal period and children's adjustment difficulties, we do not want to conclude that parental mental health is unimportant for children's adjustment across the transition to siblinghood at this time and strongly advise that future research is needed to address how parental moods, depression, and anxiety symptoms influence children's adjustment after the birth of a sibling (Gottlieb & Mendelson, 1995).

Family Dynamics

It is possible that the effects of maternal and paternal depression were affecting children's adjustment indirectly through parenting stress, parental efficacy, and inter-parental relationship functioning, as each of these are correlates of depressed mood for mothers and fathers. In several instances, marital and coparenting dynamics predicted internalizing behaviors such as children's anxiety-depression and withdrawal, and sleep problems. When parents were engaged in more inter-parental conflict and reported less positive marital relations, children were more likely to feel anxious and withdrawn, and experience sleep problems. Thus, intervention efforts that focus on improving marital problem-solving skills may help couples adjust to the transition from one child to two, and, in turn, their children (Shapiro & Gottman, 2005).

Given the sheer number of predictors available for inclusion in our analysis, it is noteworthy that the same variables emerged as the "candidate" predictors of children's problem behavior time and again: children's temperament, attachment security to parents, fathers' sense of parental efficacy, and inter-parental relationship functioning. The analyses did not prioritize one set of child, parent, or family contextual variables as more important than any other, but went through systematically to test and check each one for its relevance in predicting the trajectory classes of children's outcomes. So it is noteworthy to mention those that did not emerge consistently in our analyses, including the age and gender of the children. Only in the case of anxiety-depression did the child's age predict class membership, with older children in the mid-stable class compared to the low-decreasing class. In her review of changes in children's adjustment across the transition, Volling (2012) found that younger children across studies did appear to have more behavioral difficulties than older children so it is not entirely clear why age of the child did not emerge in the current analyses as consistently as other child and family factors.

152

One possibility may reflect the family processes that coincide with children's age. Younger children at the time of their sibling's birth are closer in age to the infant sibling so the birth interval between children is shorter. Having two young children closer in age no doubt creates different family dynamics that may be influential for determining how children will fare. Parenting stress may be greater when trying to care for two young children, both in diapers and requiring more direct supervision and child care than an older child. Younger children at around 18–24 months are still in need of their attachment figures for a sense of felt security whereas older children of 4 or 5 years of age are more autonomous, have more advanced social understanding, and a greater ability to entertain and occupy themselves in play activities. The age of the older children was relatively large in this sample, as is typical of age differences between older and younger siblings, so restriction of range cannot account for the lack of age effects.

Gender did not emerge as a candidate predictor for any of the syndrome scales examined, nor was the gender composition of the sibling dyad related to any of the classes uncovered, which was somewhat surprising given how many sibling studies, in general, examine gender differences and make claims about the gender constellation and whether the transition is easier for boys or girls. Again, this emphasis on whether or not it makes a difference if the child is an older or younger brother or sister is a remnant of the individual psychology of Alfred Adler and the theory of birth order differences (Adler, 1928). The effects of gender, however, are not consistent across studies examining the transition to siblinghood (Volling, 2012). For instance, Nadelman and Begun (1982) reported boys were more withdrawn than girls, whereas Baydar et al. (1997) reported girls had more anxiety and depressive symptoms than boys after the birth of a sibling. These inconsistencies and others in the literature (see Volling, 2012) may be why gender and gender constellation did not emerge here as significant predictors of any of the syndrome scales.

It may be that once other candidate predictor variables enter the predictive model (whether the data mining techniques or the multinomial logistic regressions) there was no additional unique variance for age and gender to explain. Whatever the possible family processes involved, our results strongly suggest that family and child characteristics reflecting children's temperamental predispositions and family functioning are more predictive of children's behavioral adjustment after the birth of a sibling than are the age and gender of the child. As a result, intervention efforts and supports to families anticipating the birth of their second child that target these areas of family and child functioning may be far more helpful to parents than focusing on immutable characteristics such as the child's age or gender at the time of the birth that parents are unable to change. Assisting parents to learn how to manage children's disruptive behavior, to identify early signs of anxiety and withdrawal, and to work together as coparents may be particularly promising for parents of the most challenging children who are feeling less efficacious in their abilities to manage disruptive or anxious behaviors.

Other family variables that were not significant in predicting class membership included work-family stress, which Stewart (1990) claimed was particularly important for many fathers as they increased their work hours after the infant's birth. The division of household and childcare labor, and social support from family and friends were also not consistent predictors of the different trajectories of behavior problems. It is quite possible that these variables are more predictive of children's adjustment at different time points after the birth, for instance, to explain concurrent behavior from child and family functioning at the same point in time (e.g., 1-month parenting stress predicts sleep problems at 1 month). The fact that these other family-level variables did not emerge as prenatal predictors from this analysis does not mean they are unimportant or do not contribute to family functioning over time and, in turn, children's behavioral and emotional difficulties. What it does mean is that if we wish to assist children and families having difficulties on the seven constructs assessed by the CBCL over the course of the year following the transition and need a quick means of identifying what discriminated those children having difficulties from those children who did not in order to maximize the effects of intervention before the birth, we would recommend focusing on more proximal family processes that involve the child's relationships with parents and the parents' relationship with one another than on other extra-familial supports.

EARLY SIBLING INTERACTIONS: FRIENDS OR FOES?

Because the earliest reactions to the arrival of the infant sibling predicted the quality of early sibling relationships (Dunn & Kendrick, 1982), and there is continuity in sibling relationship quality throughout childhood and adolescence (Dunn et al., 1994), we were also interested in whether or not children's behavioral adjustment in the year following the birth might have ramifications for the relationship developing between the siblings at 12 months. Our results suggested that sometimes it did and other times it did not. The CBCL trajectories of aggression, attention problems, and emotional reactivity significantly predicted children's interactions with their 12-month-old sibling with more conflict and less positive sibling involvement with children higher on these problems. Not surprisingly, the syndrome scales most reflective of psychosomatic or physical symptoms (e.g., somatic complaints, sleep) did not predict children's interactions with their younger sibling. These findings are in contrast to the earlier results of Dunn and Kendrick (1982), who reported that children's early withdrawal after the birth

154

predicted problematic sibling relationships nearly a year later. Instead, we found it was the externalizing scales of aggression and attention problems that were related to sibling relationship quality at 12 months. We do not want to rush to conclude, however, that children's initial anxiety and withdrawal are not relevant to subsequent sibling relations. Based on observations of children's initial reactions to their parents' interactions with their infant siblings at 1 month, Volling et al. (2014) found that children who were approach-avoidant (i.e., withdrew and avoided interaction) had higher scores on all of the CBCL syndrome scales at 4 months after birth than children who were willing to join positively and play nearby. Further, children's trajectories of the internalizing dimension of emotional reactivity in the current analyses were also significantly related to sibling relations at 1 year providing evidence that understanding how children react to the transition to siblinghood and knowing how to prevent children's behavioral and emotional difficulties will provide parents with the knowledge needed to scaffold their children's relationship with their younger sibling and put the relationship on firm ground for future success.

LIMITATIONS AND CAVEATS

Despite the many strengths of the Family Transitions study, there are several limitations that needed to be noted. First, families were predominantly middle- to upper-middle class, two-parent, and relatively low-risk with respect to adversity and family background. We must also acknowledge the low response rate for participation of the eligible families and the fact that families of more difficult children and those undergoing more family stress may have declined participation, leaving us with a less representative and better functioning sample. The use of a community-based, low-risk sample that was not screened for childhood externalizing or internalizing disorders could, however, be seen as a strength as it means the results from the current research are more generalizable to the broader population of families, at least those with similar demographics, undergoing the transition from one child to two. Given the overarching focus on psychosocial trauma and disordered behavior prominent in this area of research, examining low-risk, community-based samples would seem to be a good starting point when addressing the adjustment outcomes for children undergoing one of the most significant developmental transitions of early childhood. Nearly 80% of families in the United States have two or more children, so living with a sibling and going through the transition to siblinghood is a frequent occurrence for many families, many of whom are middle-class. Cowan and Cowan (2000) also noted that families do not have to be from high-risk backgrounds and undergoing significant adversity to experience difficulties across a normative transition and, as a result, be deserving of assistance. In fact, the problems faced by second-time parents may often be overlooked or minimized because of the inherent belief that they know all there is to know about raising an infant, having done so once before (Mercer, 1979). Yet, second-time mothers often have different concerns, generally focused on their relationship with the older child, how this relationship will change, whether they can love two children the same, and feeling guilty about destroying the first child's life (Jordan, 1989; Mercer, 1979). Regardless, future research is still needed to replicate our findings both in community-based samples and higher risk families from different backgrounds.

One of the strengths of the current study was the longitudinal nature of the research with five time points across the transition and for a year after the birth, including a prebirth assessment point. Many prior studies often relied on mothers' reports after the birth asking them to recount what had changed since the infant was born, which can be particularly problematic during a stressful transition where changes in the mother–child relationship are many (e.g., increased confrontations, prohibitions, decreased attention) and parents are adapting to their new roles caring for two children. Even though we had longitudinal data spanning the time from before to a year after the birth, and used prenatal variables to predict our change trajectories, we are not able to determine the direction of effects because the initial assessment of the CBCL trajectories and the predictors were both obtained at the prenatal time point. It is possible that parenting and family characteristics in place before the birth were responsible for children's problematic behaviors, but it is also possible that more difficult children create more parenting stress and family conflict. We acknowledge the correlational nature of our design and the constraints it imposes on the interpretation of our results. We hope our findings spark additional interest and research in this important, but under-studied, aspect of young children's development. The current analyses were designed specifically to examine prenatal predictors with the goal of offering recommendations for prebirth intervention, but future analyses are needed that can follow the transactional relations between child behavior, parenting, and family context in order to uncover developmental processes that unfold over time.

We believe the analysis strategies we employed in the current report were appropriate for the questions we addressed: (i) to identify different developmental trajectories of children's behavior (growth mixture modeling fixing the classes); (ii) to examine the prenatal antecedents that predict these trajectories (data mining using random forest and CART variable selection with standard hypothesis testing criteria in a multinomial logistic regression); and (iii) to determine whether there are consequences for the developing sibling relationship by the end of the first year (restricted maximum likelihood regression). These analytic strategies, although relevant for our goals, are exploratory and the results must be replicated in other samples. Because the literature base for the transition to siblinghood is both scarce and quite dated, and because this is the first large-scale ($n = 241$) longitudinal study to include mothers' and fathers' reports on an established measure of children's problem behaviors to address changes in children's adjustment from a developmental psychopathology framework, we had little information from which to generate hypotheses. We believe the results from our exploratory analyses provide some of the first systematic evidence of individual differences in developmental trajectories across the transition to siblinghood and we invite future investigators to use the information provided here to formulate and test additional hypotheses about children's adjustment after the birth of a sibling.

Finally, we utilized multiple methods in the current study when available, including observations of parent–child, coparenting, and marital interaction during the prenatal home visits, Attachment Q-sorts obtained from mothers and fathers, assessments of children's socio-cognitive understanding, and both mothers' and fathers' self-reports of child, parent, and family functioning. Yet, our primary measurement of children's adjustment, although a widely used and validated measure of emotional and behavioral disorders in young children (Achenbach & Rescorla, 2000), was based on parental reports and not actual home observations of children's behaviors. We aggregated across parents in order to increase construct validity and to reduce the possibility of a single-reporter bias, at a time when parents and children are having to adjust to the stresses and changes surrounding the birth of a new infant. Further, given the nature of some of the problem behaviors examined, it is unlikely that home observations could be conducted that would be lengthy enough to observe the occurrence of low-frequency events or provide access to periods of the day to observe some behaviors (e.g., sleep problems). This is often why researchers rely on parental reports for such information. Still, we must acknowledge that our results may have differed had we used observed or other measures (e.g., actigraphy, sleep diaries) rather than parent-reported measures of problem behaviors.

OVERALL CONCLUSION

Individual differences in developmental trajectories of children's behavioral and emotional adjustment were evident after the birth of an infant sibling for all problem areas examined—aggression, attention problems, anxiety/depression, emotional reactivity, withdrawal, somatic complaints, and sleep problems. The inclusion of a prebirth assessment clearly showed that many children were similarly low or high on emotional and behavioral difficulties before the birth and with the exception of aggressive behavior, there was little evidence that children showed an abrupt change in their behavior with the birth of the infant sibling. These behavioral trajectories of different problematic behaviors were predicted by a common set of child and family variables (e.g., temperament, attachment security, father's parental efficacy, marital, and coparental relationship functioning) that are potential targets for intervention before the transition to siblinghood. Finally, the different trajectories of aggression, attention problems, and emotional reactivity predicted how well children related to their younger sibling at the end of the first year. Findings suggest that early patterns of behavior problems after the birth have implications for the developing sibling relationship, which can be predicted already by child, parent, and family factors prior to the birth. The birth of an infant sibling may exacerbate problems already apparent in the family system consistent with a family systems and developmental psychopathology perspective, but there is little evidence to suggest that most children experience clinically significant levels of psychopathology as a result of the sibling's birth or that children's behaviors are a result of psychological conflicts brought on by feelings of resentment, dethronement, or displacement. Indeed, most children experience little to no disruption after the birth of their infant sibling, and when immediate changes were apparent, as was the case with aggression, it only characterized children from riskier family situations, was short-lived, and was resolved by 4 months after the birth, providing more support for childhood resilience than childhood disturbance after the birth of an infant sibling.

REFERENCES

This article is part of the issue "Developmental Trajectories of Children's Adjustment across the Transition to Siblinghood: Pre-Birth Predictors and Sibling Outcomes at One Year" Volling, Gonzalez, Oh, Song, Yu, Rosenberg, Kuo, Thomason, Beyers-Carlson, Safyer, and Stevenson (Issue Authors). For a full listing of articles in this issue, see: http://onlinelibrary.wiley.com/doi/10.1111/mono.v82.3/issuetoc.

Acebo, C., Sadeh, A., Seifer, R., Tzischinsky, O., Hafer, A., & Carskadon, M. A. (2005). Sleep/wake patterns derived from activity monitoring and maternal report for healthy 1- to 5-year-old children. *Sleep-New York Then Westchester*, **28**(12), 1568.

Achenbach, T. M., & Rescorla, L. (2000). *Manual for the ASEBA preschool forms & profiles*. Burlington: University of Vermont, Research Center for Children, Youth & Families.

Adler, A. (1928). Characteristics of the first, second and third child. *Children*, **3**(5), 14.

Affonso, D. D., Mayberry, L. J., & Sheptak, S. (1988). Multiparity and stressful events. *Journal of Perinatology*, **8**, 312–317.

Ainsworth, M. D. S., Blehar, M. C., Waters, E., & Wall, S. (1978). *Patterns of attachment: A psychological study of the strange situation*. Hillsdale, NJ: Erlbaum.

Akaike, H. (1987). Factor analysis and AIC. *Psychometrika*, **52**(3), 317–332. https://doi.org/10.1007/BF02294359

Alink, L. R. A., Mesman, J., Van Zeijl, J., Stolk, M. N., Juffer, F., Koot, H. M., et al. (2006). The early childhood aggression curve: Development of physical aggression in 10- to 50-month-old children. *Child Development*, **77**(4), 954–966. https://doi.org/10.1111/j.1467-8624.2006.00912.x

Amato, P. R., & Cheadle, J. E. (2008). Parental divorce, marital conflict and children's behavior problems: A comparison of adopted and biological children. *Social Forces*, **86**(3), 1139–1161. https://doi.org/10.1353/sof.0.0025

Anders, T. F., & Keener, M. A. (1985). Developmental course of nighttime sleep-wake patterns in full-term and premature infants during the first year of life: I. *Sleep: Journal of Sleep Research & Sleep Medicine*, **8**(3), 173–192.

DOI: 10.1111/mono.12318

Aro, H. (1989). Stress, development and psychosomatic symptoms in adolescence: A comparison of the sexes. *Psychiatria Fennica*, **20**, 101–109.

Aro, H., Paronen, O., & Aro, S. (1987). Psychosomatic symptoms among 14- to 16-year-old Finnish adolescents. *Social Psychiatry*, **22**(3), 171–176. https://doi.org/10.1007/BF00583852

Barkley, R. A. (2003). Assessment of teens with ADHD. *The ADHD Report*, **11**(4), 1–7. https://doi.org/10.1521/adhd.11.4.1.23485

Baruch, G. K., & Barnett, R. C. (1986). Fathers participation in family work and children's sex-role attitudes. *Child Development*, **57**(5), 1210–1223. https://doi: 10.2307/1130444

Bates, J. E., Maslin, C. A., & Frankel, K. A. (1985). Attachment security, mother-child interaction, and temperament as predictors of behavior problem ratings at age three years. *Monographs of the Society for Research in Child Development*, **50**(1/2), 167–193. http://doi.org/10.2307/3333832

Bates, J. E., Pettit, G. S., Dodge, K. A., & Ridge, B. (1998). Interaction of temperamental resistance to control and restrictive parenting in the development of externalizing behavior. *Developmental Psychology*, **34**(5), 982–995. https://doi.org/10.1037/0012-1649.34.5.982

Battaglia, M., Touchette, É., Garon-Carrier, G., Dionne, G., Côté, S. M., Vitaro, F., et al. (2016). Distinct trajectories of separation anxiety in the preschool years: Persistence at school entry and early-life associated factors. *Journal of Child Psychology and Psychiatry*, **57**(1), 39–46. https://doi.org/10.1111/jcpp.12424

Baydar, N., Hyle, P., & Brooks-Gunn, J. (1997). A longitudinal study of the effects of the birth of a sibling during preschool and early grade school years. *Journal of Marriage and Family*, **59**(4), 957–965. https://doi.org/10.2307/353795

Beck, A. T., Steer, R. A., & Carbin, M. G. (1988). Psychometric properties of the Beck Depression Inventory: Twenty-five years of evaluation. *Clinical Psychology Review*, **8**(1), 77–100. https://doi.org/10.1016/0272-7358(88)90050-5

Beck, A. T., Ward, C. H., Mendelson, M., Mock, J., & Erbaugh, J. (1961). An inventory for measuring depression. *Archives of General Psychiatry*, **4**(6), 561–571. https://doi.org/10.1001/archpsyc.1961.01710120031004

Beck, J. E. (2008). A developmental perspective on functional somatic symptoms. *Journal of Pediatric Psychology*, **33**(5), 547–562. https://doi.org/10.1093/jpepsy/jsm113

Bedford, V. H., & Volling, B. L. (2003). A dynamic ecological systems perspective on emotion regulation development within the sibling relationship context. In F. R. Lang & K. L. Fingerman (Eds.), *Growing together: Personal relationships across the lifespan* (pp. 76–102). New York, NY: Cambridge University Press.

Bélanger, M.-È., Bernier, A., Simard, V., Bordeleau, S., & Carrier, J. (2015). Chapter VIII. Attachment and sleep among toddlers: Disentangling attachment security and dependency. *Monographs of the Society for Research in Child Development*, **80**(1), 125–140. https://doi.org/10.1111/mono.12148

Belsky, J. (1984). The determinants of parenting: A process model. *Child Development*, **55**, 83–96. https://doi.org/10.2307/1129836

Belsky, J., Hsieh, K.-H., & Crnic, K. (1998). Mothering, fathering, and infant negativity as antecedents of boys' externalizing problems and inhibition at age 3 years: Differential susceptibility to rearing experience? *Development and Psychopathology*, **10**(02), 301–319.

Belsky, J., & Pluess, M. (2009). Beyond diathesis stress: Differential susceptibility to environmental influences. *Psychological Bulletin*, **135**(6), 885–908. https://doi.org/10.1037/a0017376

Belsky, J., Spanier, G. B., & Rovine, M. (1983). Stability and change in marriage across the transition to parenthood. *Journal of Marriage and Family*, **45**(3), 567–577. https://doi.org/10.2307/351661

Belsky, J., Woodworth, S., & Crnic, K. (1996). Trouble in the second year: Three questions about family interaction. *Child Development*, **67**(2), 556–578. https://doi.org/10.1111/j.1467-8624.1996.tb01751.x

Blandon, A. Y., Calkins, S. D., Keane, S. P., & O'Brien, M. (2008). Individual differences in trajectories of emotion regulation processes: The effects of maternal depressive symptomatology and children's physiological regulation. *Developmental Psychology*, **44**(4), 1110–1123. http://doi.org/10.1037/0012-1649.44.4.1110

Boey, C. C. M., & Goh, K. L. (2001). The significance of life-events as contributing factors in childhood recurrent abdominal pain in an urban community in Malaysia. *Journal of Psychosomatic Research*, **51**(4), 559–562. https://doi.org/10.1016/S0022-3999(01)00232-X

Boldt, L. J., Kochanska, G., Yoon, J. E., & Koenig Nordling, J. (2014). Children's attachment to both parents from toddler age to middle childhood: Links to adaptive and maladaptive outcomes. *Attachment & Human Development*, **16**(3), 211–229. https://doi.org/10.1080/14616734.2014.889181

Bonds, D. D., Gondoli, D. M., Sturge-Apple, M. L., & Salem, L. N. (2002). Parenting stress as a mediator of the relation between parenting support and optimal parenting. *Parenting*, **2**(4), 409–435. https://doi.org/10.1207/S15327922PAR0204_04

Booth, A., & Amato, P. R. (1994). Parental marital quality, parental divorce, and relations with parents. *Journal of Marriage and Family*, **56**(1), 21–34. https://doi.org/10.2307/352698

Booth-LaForce, C., & Oxford, M. L. (2008). Trajectories of social withdrawal from grades 1 to 6: Prediction from early parenting, attachment, and temperament. *Developmental Psychology*, **44**(5), 1298–1313. https://doi.org/10.1037/a0012954

Borge, A., Nordhagen, R., Moe, B., Botten, G., & Bakketeig, L. (1994). Prevalence and persistence of stomach ache and headache among children. Follow-up of a cohort of Norwegian children from 4 to 10 years of age. *Acta Pædiatrica*, **83**(4), 433–437. https://doi.org/10.1111/j.1651-2227.1994.tb18137.x

Bowlby, J. (1969). *Attachment and loss*. New York, NY: Basic Books.

Boyd, H. (2009). Preparing your child for the birth of a sibling | Education.com. Retrieved June 16, 2015, from https://www.education.com/magazine/article/Preparing_Child_Birth_Sibling/

Braiker, H. B., & Kelley, H. H. (1979). Conflict in the development of close relationships. In R. L. Burgess & T. L. Huston (Eds.), *Social exchange in developing relationships* (pp. 135–168). New York, NY: Academic Press.

Breiman, L. (2001). Random forests. *Machine Learning*, **45**(1), 5–32. https://doi.org/10.1023/A:1010933404324

Breiman, L., Friedman, J., Stone, C. J., & Olshen, R. A. (1984). *Classification and regression trees* (1st ed.). Boca Raton, FL: Chapman and Hall/CRC.

Broeren, S., Muris, P., Diamantopoulou, S., & Baker, J. R. (2013). The course of childhood anxiety symptoms: Developmental trajectories and child-related factors in normal children. *Journal of Abnormal Child Psychology*, **41**(1), 81–95. https://doi.org/10.1007/s10802-012-9669-9

Bronfenbrenner, U. (1979). *The ecology of human development: Experiments by nature and design.* Cambridge, MA: Harvard University Press.

Brown, D. D., Weatherhol, T. N., & Burns, B. M. (2010). Understanding parent reports of children's attention behaviors: Role of children's attention skills, temperament, and home environment. *Journal of Early Childhood and Infant Psychology, 6,* 41.

Brownell, C. A., & Kopp, C. B. (2007). *Socioemotional development in the toddler years: Transitions and transformations.* New York: Guilford Press.

Buist, K. L., Deković, M., & Prinzie, P. (2013). Sibling relationship quality and psychopathology of children and adolescents: A meta-analysis. *Clinical Psychology Review, 33*(1), 97–106. https://doi.org/10.1016/j.cpr.2012.10.007

Buist, K. L., & Vermande, M. (2014). Sibling relationship patterns and their associations with child competence and problem behavior. *Journal of Family Psychology, 28*(4), 529–537. https://doi.org/10.1037/a0036990

Burr, W. R., & Klein, S. R. (1994). *Reexamining family stress: New theory and research.* Thousand Oaks, CA: Sage Publications.

Calkins, S. D. (1994). Origins and outcomes of individual differences in emotion regulation. *Monographs of the Society for Research in Child Development, 59*(2–3), 53–72. https://doi.org/10.1111/j. 1540-5834.1994.tb01277.x

Calkins, S. D., & Fox, N. A. (1992). The relations among infant temperament, security of attachment, and behavioral inhibition at twenty-four months. *Child Development, 63*(6), 1456–1472. https://doi.org/10.1111/j. 1467-8624.1992.tb01707.x

Campbell, S. B. (2002). *Behavior problems in preschool children: Clinical and developmental issues.* New York: Guilford Press.

Campbell, S. B. (2006). Maladjustment in preschool children: A developmental psychopathology perspective. In K. McCartney & D. Phillips (Eds.), *Blackwell handbook of early childhood development* (pp. 358–377). Malden, MA: Blackwell Publishing.

Campbell, S. B. (2011). A developmental and family systems perspective on mental health in young children. In C. Groark (Ed.), *Early childhood intervention: Shaping the future for children with special needs and their families* (Vol. 2, pp. 205–229). Santa Barbara, CA: Praeger.

Campbell, S. B., Matestic, P., von Stauffenberg, C., Mohan, R., & Kirchner, T. (2007). Trajectories of maternal depressive symptoms, maternal sensitivity, and children's functioning at school entry. *Developmental Psychology, 43*(5), 1202–1215. https://doi.org/10.1037/0012-1649.43.5.1202

Campis, L. K., Lyman, R. D., & Prentice-Dunn, S. (1986). The parental locus of control scale: Development and validation. *Journal of Clinical Child Psychology, 15*(3), 260–267. https://doi.org/10.1207/s15374424jccp1503_10

Campo, J. V., & Fritsch, S. L. (1994). Somatization in children and adolescents. *Journal of the American Academy of Child & Adolescent Psychiatry, 33*(9), 1223–1235. https://doi.org/10.1097/00004583-199411000-00003

Carter, A. S., Godoy, L., Wagmiller, R. L., Veliz, P., Marakovitz, S., & Briggs-Gowan, M. J. (2010). Internalizing trajectories in young boys and girls: The whole is not a simple sum of its parts. *Journal of Abnormal Child Psychology, 38*(1), 19–31. https://doi.org/10.1007/s10802-009-9342-0

Caspi, A., Harrington, H., Milne, B., Amell, J. W., Theodore, R. F., & Moffitt, T. E. (2003). Children's behavioral styles at age 3 are linked to their adult personality traits at age 26. *Journal of Personality, 71*(4), 495–514. https://doi.org/10.1111/1467-6494.7104001

Census Bureau, U. S. American FactFinder. Retrieved May 13, 2015, from https://factfinder. census.gov/faces/nav/jsf/pages/index.xhtml

Chao, E. L., & Utgoff, K. P. (2003). *The National Compensation Survey: Employee benefits in private industry in the United States, 2000.* Washington, DC: US Department of Labor. Retrieved from https://stats.bls.gov/ncs/ebs/sp/ebbl0021.pdf

Chen, N., Deater-Deckard, K., & Bell, M. A. (2014). The role of temperament by family environment interactions in child maladjustment. *Journal of Abnormal Child Psychology,* **42**(8), 1251–1262. https://doi.org/10.1007/s10802-014-9872-y

Chen, X., Wang, L., & Cao, R. (2011). Shyness-sensitivity and unsociability in rural Chinese children: Relations with social, school, and psychological adjustment. *Child Development,* **82**(5), 1531–1543. https://doi.org/10.1111/j.1467-8624.2011.01616.x

Choe, D. E., Olson, S. L., & Sameroff, A. J. (2013). The interplay of externalizing problems and physical and inductive discipline during childhood. *Developmental Psychology,* **49**(11), 2029–2039. https://doi.org/10.1037/a0032054

Cicchetti, D. (1984). The emergence of developmental psychopathology. *Child Development,* **55**(1), 1–7. https://doi.org/10.2307/1129830

Ciechanowski, P. S., Walker, E., Katon, W., & Russo, J. (2002). Attachment theory: A model for health care utilization and somatization. *Psychosomatic Medicine,* **64**(4), 660–667. https://doi.org/10.1097/01.PSY.0000021948.90613.76

Collins, W. A., Maccoby, E. E., Steinberg, L., Hetherington, E. M., & Bornstein, M. H. (2000). Contemporary research on parenting: The case for nature and nurture. *American Psychologist,* **55**(2), 218–232. https://doi.org/10.1037/0003-066X.55.2.218

Combs-Ronto, L. A., Olson, S. L., Lunkenheimer, E. S., & Sameroff, A. J. (2009). Interactions between maternal parenting and children's early disruptive behavior: Bidirectional associations across the transition from preschool to school entry. *Journal of Abnormal Child Psychology,* **37**(8), 1151–1163. https://doi.org/10.1007/s10802-009-9332-2

Connell, A. M., & Goodman, S. H. (2002). The association between psychopathology in fathers versus mothers and children's internalizing and externalizing behavior problems: A meta-analysis. *Psychological Bulletin,* **128**(5), 746–773. https://doi.org/10.1037/0033-2909.128.5.746

Coplan, R. J., Arbeau, K. A., & Armer, M (2007). Don't fret, be supportive! Maternal characteristics linking child shyness to psychosocial and school adjustment in kindergarten. *Journal of Abnormal Child Psychology,* **36**(3), 359–371. https://doi.org/10.1007/s10802-007-9183-7

Coplan, R. J., Hughes, K., Bosacki, S., & Rose-Krasnor, L. (2011). Is silence golden? Elementary school teachers' strategies and beliefs regarding hypothetical shy/quiet and exuberant/ talkative children. *Journal of Educational Psychology,* **103**(4), 939–951. https://doi.org/10.1037/a0024551

Cowan, C. P., & Cowan, P. A. (2000). *When partners become parents: The big life change for couples.* Mahwah, NJ: Lawrence Erlbaum.

Cox, M. J., & Paley, B. (2003). Understanding families as systems. *Current Directions in Psychological Science,* **12**(5), 193–196. https://doi.org/10.1111/1467-8721.01259

Crawford, N. A., Schrock, M., & Woodruff-Borden, J. (2010). Child internalizing symptoms: Contributions of child temperament, maternal negative affect, and family functioning. *Child Psychiatry & Human Development,* **42**(1), 53–64. https://doi.org/10.1007/s10578-010-0202-5

Crick, N. R., & Dodge, K. A. (1994). A review and reformulation of social information-processing mechanisms in children's social adjustment. *Psychological Bulletin*, **115**(1), 74–101. https://doi.org/10.1037/0033-2909.115.1.74

Crnic, K. A., Gaze, C., & Hoffman, C. (2005). Cumulative parenting stress across the preschool period: Relations to maternal parenting and child behaviour at age 5. *Infant and Child Development*, **14**(2), 117–132. https://doi.org/10.1002/icd.384

Crnic, K. A., & Greenberg, M. T. (1990). Minor parenting stresses with young children. *Child Development*, **61**(5), 1628–1637. https://doi.org/10.1111/j.1467-8624.1990.tb02889.x

Cummings, E. M., & Davies, P. T. (1994). Maternal depression and child development. *Journal of Child Psychology and Psychiatry*, **35**(1), 73–122. http://doi.org/10.1111/j.1469-7610.1994.tb01133.x

Cummings, E. M., & Davies, P. T. (2002). Effects of marital conflict on children: Recent advances and emerging themes in process-oriented research. *Journal of Child Psychology and Psychiatry*, **43**(1), 31–63. https://doi.org/10.1111/1469-7610.00003

Cummings, E. M., & Davies, P. T. (2011). *Marital conflict and children: An emotional security perspective.* New York, NY: Guilford Press.

Cummings, E. M., Davies, P. T., & Campbell, S. B. (2000). *Developmental psychopathology and family process: Theory, research, and clinical implications.* New York, NY: Guilford Press.

Cummings, E. M., Goeke-Morey, M. C., & Papp, L. M. (2004). Everyday marital conflict and child aggression. *Journal of Abnormal Child Psychology*, **32**(2), 191–202. https://doi.org/10.1023/B:JACP0000019770.13216.be

Cummings, E. M., Merrilees, C. E., & George, M. W. (2010). Fathers, marriages, and families: Revisiting and updating the framework for fathering in family context. In *The role of the father in child development* (5th ed.) (pp. 154–176). Hoboken, NJ: John Wiley & Sons.

Dahl, R. E., & El-Sheikh, M. (2007). Considering sleep in a family context: Introduction to the special issue. *Journal of Family Psychology*, **21**(1), 1–3. https://doi.org/10.1037/0893-3200.21.1.1

Dallaire, D. H., & Weinraub, M. (2005). Predicting children's separation anxiety at age 6: The contributions of infant-mother attachment security, maternal sensitivity, and maternal separation anxiety. *Attachment & Human Development*, **7**(4), 393–408. https://doi.org/10.1080/14616730500365894

Davies, P. T., Cicchetti, D., & Martin, M. J. (2012). Toward greater specificity in identifying associations among interparental aggression, child emotional reactivity to conflict, and child problems. *Child Development*, **83**(5), 1789–1804. https://doi.org/10.1111/j.1467-8624.2012.01804.x

Davies, P. T., & Cummings, E. M. (1994). Marital conflict and child adjustment: An emotional security hypothesis. *Psychological Bulletin*, **116**(3), 387–411. https://doi.org/10.1037/0033-2909.116.3.387

Davies, P. T., Sturge-Apple, M. L., Winter, M. A., Cummings, E. M., & Farrell, D. (2006). Child adaptational development in contexts of interparental conflict over time. *Child Development*, **77**(1), 218–233. https://doi.org/10.1111/j.1467-8624.2006.00866.x

Davies, P. T., Sturge-Apple, M. L., Woitach, M. J., & Cummings, M. (2009). A process analysis of the transmission of distress from interparental conflict to parenting: Adult relationship security as an explanatory mechanism. *Developmental Psychology*, **45**(6), 1761–1773. https://doi.org/10.1037/a0016426

Deater-Deckard, K., Dodge, K. A., Bates, J. E., & Pettit, G. S. (1998). Multiple risk factors in the development of externalizing behavior problems: Group and individual differences. *Development and Psychopathology*, **10**(03), 469–493.

DeGarmo, D. S., Patras, J., & Eap, S. (2008). Social support for divorced fathers' parenting: Testing a stress-buffering model. *Family Relations*, **57**(1), 35–48. https://doi.org/10.1111/j.1741-3729.2007.00481.x

Degnan, K. A., & Fox, N. A. (2007). Behavioral inhibition and anxiety disorders: Multiple levels of a resilience process. *Development and Psychopathology*, **19**(03), 729–746. https://doi.org/10.1017/S0954579407000363

Degnan, K. A., Henderson, H. A., Fox, N. A., & Rubin, K. H. (2008). Predicting social wariness in middle childhood: The moderating roles of childcare history, maternal personality and maternal behavior. *Social Development*, **17**(3), 471–487. https://doi.org/10.1111/j.1467-9507.2007.00437.x

DeKlyen, M., Biernbaum, M. A., Speltz, M. L., & Greenberg, M. T. (1998). Fathers and preschool behavior problems. *Developmental Psychology*, **34**(2), 264–275. https://doi.org/10.1037/0012-1649.34.2.264

DeKlyen, M., Speltz, M. L., & Greenberg, M. T. (1998). Fathering and early onset conduct problems: Positive and negative parenting, father-son attachment, and the marital context. *Clinical Child and Family Psychology Review*, **1**(1), 3–21. https://doi.org/10.1023/A:1021844214633

DeLeon, C. W., & Karraker, K. H. (2007). Intrinsic and extrinsic factors associated with night waking in 9-month-old infants. *Infant Behavior and Development*, **30**(4), 596–605. https://doi.org/10.1016/j.infbeh.2007.03.009

Denham, S. A. (1986). Social cognition, prosocial behavior, and emotion in preschoolers: Contextual validation. *Child Development*, **57**(1), 194–201. https://doi.org/10.2307/1130651

De Wolff, M. S., & van Ijzendoorn, M. H. (1997). Sensitivity and attachment: A meta-analysis on parental antecedents of infant attachment. *Child Development*, **68**(4), 571–591. https://doi.org/10.1111/j.1467-8624.1997.tb04218.x

Dhossche, D., Ferdinand, R., van der Ende, J., & Verhulst, F. (2001). Outcome of self-reported functional-somatic symptoms in a community sample of adolescents. *Annals of Clinical Psychiatry*, **13**(4), 191–199. https://doi.org/10.3109/10401230109147383

Dirks, M. A., Persram, R., Recchia, H. E., & Howe, N. (2015). Sibling relationships as sources of risk and resilience in the development and maintenance of internalizing and externalizing problems during childhood and adolescence. *Clinical Psychology Review*, **42**, 145–155. https://doi.org/10.1016/j.cpr.2015.07.003

Dishion, T. J., & Patterson, G. R. (2006). The development and ecology of antisocial behavior in children and adolescents. In D. Cicchetti & D. J. Cohen (Eds.), *Developmental psychopathology, vol 3: Risk, disorder, and adaptation* (2nd ed.) (pp. 503–541). Hoboken, NJ: John Wiley & Sons.

Dix, T., & Yan, N. (2014). Mothers' depressive symptoms and infant negative emotionality in the prediction of child adjustment at age 3: Testing the maternal reactivity and child vulnerability hypotheses. *Development and Psychopathology*, **26**(01), 111–124. https://doi.org/10.1017/S0954579413000898

Domènech-Llaberia, E., Jané, C., Canals, J., Ballesp, S., Esparó, G., & Garralda, E. (2004). Parental reports of somatic symptoms in preschool children: Prevalence and associations in a Spanish sample. *Journal of the American Academy of Child & Adolescent Psychiatry*, **43**(5), 598–604. https://doi.org/10.1097/00004583-200405000-00013

Dunn, J. (1983). Sibling relationships in early childhood. *Child Development*, **54**(4), 787–811. https://doi.org/10.2307/1129886

Dunn, J. (1988). Sibling influences on childhood development. *Journal of Child Psychology and Psychiatry*, **29**(2), 119–127. https://doi.org/10.1111/j.1469-7610.1988.tb00697.x

Dunn, J., Brown, J., Slomkowski, C., Tesla, C., & Youngblade, L. (1991). Young children's understanding of other people's feelings and beliefs: Individual differences and their antecedents. *Child Development*, **62**(6), 1352–1366. https://doi.org/10.2307/1130811

Dunn, J., & Kendrick, C. (1980). The arrival of a sibling: Changes in patterns of interaction between mother and first-born child. *Journal of Child Psychology and Psychiatry*, **21**(2), 119–132. https://doi.org/10.1111/j.1469-7610.1980.tb00024.x

Dunn, J., & Kendrick, C. (1982). *Siblings: Love, envy, & understanding.* Cambridge, MA: Harvard University Press.

Dunn, J., Kendrick, C., & MacNamee, R. (1981). The reaction of first-born children to the birth of a sibling: Mothers' reports. *Journal of Child Psychology and Psychiatry*, **22**(1), 1–18. https://doi.org/10.1111/j.1469-7610.1981.tb00527.x

Dunn, J., & Munn, P. (1985). Becoming a family member: Family conflict and the development of social understanding in the second year. *Child Development*, **56**(2), 480–492. https://doi.org/10.2307/1129735

Dunn, J., & Munn, P. (1986). Siblings and the development of prosocial behaviour. *International Journal of Behavioral Development*, **9**(3), 265–284. https://doi.org/10.1177/016502548600900301

Dunn, J., Slomkowski, C., & Beardsall, L. (1994). Sibling relationships from the preschool period through middle childhood and early adolescence. *Developmental Psychology*, **30**(3), 315–324. https://doi.org/10.1037/0012-1649.30.3.315

Dunst, C., Trivette, C., & Deal, A. (1988). *Enabling and empowering families: Principles and guidelines for practice.* Cambridge, MA: Brookline Books.

Egger, H. L., & Angold, A. (2006). Common emotional and behavioral disorders in preschool children: Presentation, nosology, and epidemiology. *Journal of Child Psychology and Psychiatry*, **47**(3–4), 313–337. https://doi.org/10.1111/j.1469-7610.2006.01618.x

Egger, H. L., Costello, E. J., Erkanli, A., & Angold, A. (1999). Somatic complaints and psychopathology in children and adolescents: Stomach aches, musculoskeletal pains, and headaches. *Journal of the American Academy of Child & Adolescent Psychiatry*, **38**(7), 852–860. https://doi.org/10.1097/00004583-199907000-00015

Eggum, N. D., Eisenberg, N., Spinrad, T. L., Valiente, C., Edwards, A., Kupfer, A. S., et al. (2009). Predictors of withdrawal: Possible precursors of avoidant personality disorder. *Development and Psychopathology*, **21**(Special Issue 03), 815–838. https://doi.org/10.1017/S0954579409000443

Ehrenberg, M. F., Gearing-Small, M., Hunter, M. A., & Small, B. J. (2001). Childcare task division and shared parenting attitudes in dual-earner families with young children. *Family Relations*, **50**(2), 143–153. https://doi.org/10.1111/j.1741-3729.2001.00143.x

Eisenberg, N., & Fabes, R. A. (2006). Emotion regulation and children's socioemotional competence. In L. Balter & C. S. Tamis-LeMonda (Eds.), *Child psychology: A handbook of contemporary issues* (2nd ed.) (pp. 357–381). New York, NY: Psychology Press.

Elder Jr. G. H., & Caspi, A. (1988). Human development and social change: An emerging perspective on the life course. In N. Bolger, A. Caspi, G. Downey, & M. Moorehouse (Eds.), *Persons in context: Developmental processes* (pp. 77–113). New York, NY: Cambridge University Press.

El-Sheikh, M., Buckhalt, J. A., Cummings, E., & Keller, P. (2007). Sleep disruptions and emotional insecurity are pathways of risk for children. *Journal of Child Psychology and Psychiatry*, **48**(1), 88–96. https://doi.org/10.1111/j.1469-7610.2006.01604.x

El-Sheikh, M., Hinnant, J. B., & Erath, S. A. (2015). Marital conflict, vagal regulation, and children's sleep: A longitudinal investigation. *Monographs of the Society for Research in Child Development*, **80**(1), 89–106. https://doi.org/10.1111/mono.12146

El-Sheikh, M., & Sadeh, A. (2015). I. Sleep and development: Introduction to the Monograph. *Monographs of the Society for Research in Child Development*, **80**(1), 1–14. https://doi.org/10.1111/mono.12141

Eminson, D. M. (2007). Medically unexplained symptoms in children and adolescents. *Clinical Psychology Review*, **27**(7), 855–871. https://doi.org/10.1016/j.cpr.2007.07.007

Fearon, R. P., Bakermans-Kranenburg, M. J., Van IJzendoorn, M. H., Lapsley, A.-M., & Roisman, G. I. (2010). The significance of insecure attachment and disorganization in the development of children's externalizing behavior: A meta-analytic study. *Child Development*, **81**(2), 435–456. https://doi.org/10.1111/j.1467-8624.2009.01405.x

Fearon, R. P., & Belsky, J. (2004). Attachment and attention: Protection in relation to gender and cumulative social-contextual adversity. *Child Development*, **75**(6), 1677–1693. https://doi.org/10.1111/j.1467-8624.2004.00809.x

Fearon, R. P., & Belsky, J. (2011). Infant-mother attachment and the growth of externalizing problems across the primary-school years. *Journal of Child Psychology and Psychiatry*, **52**(7), 782–791. https://doi.org/10.1111/j.1469-7610.2010.02350.x

Feng, X., Shaw, D. S., & Silk, J. S. (2008). Developmental trajectories of anxiety symptoms among boys across early and middle childhood. *Journal of Abnormal Psychology*, **117**(1), 32–47. https://doi.org/10.1037/0021-843X.117.1.32

Field, T. (1992). Infants of depressed mothers. *Development and Psychopathology*, **4**(01), 49–66. https://doi.org/10.1017/S0954579400005551

Field, T., & Reite, M. (1984). Children's responses to separation from mother during the birth of another child. *Child Development*, **55**(4), 1308–1316. https://doi.org/10.2307/1130000

Fox, N. A., Henderson, H. A., Marshall, P. J., Nichols, K. E., & Ghera, M. M. (2005). Behavioral inhibition: Linking biology and behavior within a developmental framework. *Annual Review of Psychology*, **56**(1), 235–262. https://doi.org/10.1146/annurev.psych.55.090902.141532

Fox, N. A., Henderson, H. A., Rubin, K. H., Calkins, S. D., & Schmidt, L. A. (2001). Continuity and discontinuity of behavioral inhibition and exuberance: Psychophysiological and behavioral influences across the first four years of life. *Child Development*, **72**(1), 1–21. https://doi.org/10.1111/ 1467-8624. 00262

Galli, F., D'Antuono, G., Tarantino, S., Viviano, F., Borrelli, O., Chirumbolo, A., et al. (2007). Headache and recurrent abdominal pain: A controlled study by the means of the Child Behaviour Checklist (CBCL). *Cephalalgia*, **27**(3), 211–219. https://doi.org/10.1111/ j.1468-2982.2006.01271.x

Garber, J., Zeman, J., & Walker, L. S. (1990). Recurrent abdominal pain in children: Psychiatric diagnoses and parental psychopathology. *Journal of the American Academy of Child &*

Adolescent Psychiatry, **29**(4), 648–656. https://doi.org/10.1097/00004583-199007000-00021

Garcia, M. M., Shaw, D. S., Winslow, E. B., & Yaggi, K. E. (2000). Destructive sibling conflict and the development of conduct problems in young boys. *Developmental Psychology*, **36**(1), 44–53. https://doi.org/10.1037/0012-1649.36.1.44

Gardner, F., & Shaw, D. S. (2008). Behavioral problems of infancy and preschool children (0–5). In M. Rutter (Ed.), *Child and adolescent psychiatry* (pp. 882–893). Malden, MA: Blackwell Publishing.

Gartstein, M. A., Putnam, S. P., & Rothbart, M. K. (2012). Etiology of preschool behavior problems: Contributions of temperament attributes in early childhood. *Infant Mental Health Journal*, **33**(2), 197–211. https://doi.org/10.1002/imhj.21312

Gazelle, H., & Ladd, G. W. (2003). Anxious solitude and peer exclusion: A diathesis-stress model of internalizing trajectories in childhood. *Child Development*, **74**(1), 257–278. https://doi.org/10.1111/1467-8624.00534

Gershoff, E. T., & Grogan-Kaylor, A. (2016). Spanking and child outcomes: Old controversies and new meta-analyses. *Journal of Family Psychology*, **30**, 453–469. https://doi.org/10.1037/fam0000191

Gilliom, M., & Shaw, D. S. (2004). Codevelopment of externalizing and internalizing problems in early childhood. *Development and Psychopathology*, **16**(2), 313–333. https://doi.org/10.1017/S0954579404044530

Goeke-Morey, M. C., & Cummings, E. M. (2007). Impact of father involvement: A closer look at indirect effects models involving marriage and child adjustment. *Applied Developmental Science*, **11**(4), 221–225. https://doi.org/10.1080/10888690701762126

Goeke-Morey, M. C., Papp, L. M., & Cummings, E. M. (2013). Changes in marital conflict and youths' responses across childhood and adolescence: A test of sensitization. *Development and Psychopathology*, **25**, 241–251. https://doi.org/10.1017/S0954579412000995

Goodman, S. H., Rouse, M. H., Connell, A. M., Broth, M. R., Hall, C. M., & Heyward, D. (2011). Maternal depression and child psychopathology: A meta-analytic review. *Clinical Child and Family Psychology Review*, **14**(1), 1–27. https://doi.org/10.1007/s10567-010-0080-1

Gordis, F. W., & Others, A. (1989). Young children's understanding of simultaneous conflicting emotions. Retrieved from https://eric.ed.gov/?id=ED306038

Gottlieb, L. N., & Mendelson, M. J. (1990). Parental support and firstborn girls' adaptation to the birth of a sibling. *Journal of Applied Developmental Psychology*, **11**(1), 29–48. https://doi.org/10.1016/0193-3973(90)90030-N

Gottlieb, L. N., & Mendelson, M. J. (1995). Mothers' moods and social support when a second child is born. *Maternal-Child Nursing Journal*, **23** (1), 3–14.

Graham, A. A., & Coplan, R. J. (2012). Shyness, sibling relationships, and young children's socioemotional adjustment at preschool. *Journal of Research in Childhood Education*, **26**(4), 435–449. https://doi.org/10.1080/02568543.2012.711802

Gregory, A. M., Eley, T. C., O'Connor, T. G., Rijsdijk, F. V., & Plomin, R. (2005). Family influences on the association between sleep problems and anxiety in a large sample of preschool aged twins. *Personality and Individual Differences*, **39**(8), 1337–1348. https://doi.org/10.1016/j.paid.2005.06.008

Grist, R. M., & Field, A. P. (2012). The mediating effect of cognitive development on children's worry elaboration. *Journal of Behavior Therapy and Experimental Psychiatry*, **43**(2), 801–807. https://doi.org/10.1016/j.jbtep.2011.11.002

Groh, A. M., Roisman, G. I., van IJzendoorn, M. H., Bakermans-Kranenburg, M. J., & Fearon, R. P. (2012). The significance of insecure and disorganized attachment for children's internalizing symptoms: A meta-analytic study. *Child Development, 83*(2), 591–610. https://doi.org/10.1111/j.1467-8624.2011.01711.x

Gross, D. D., & Tucker, S. M. S. (1994). Parenting confidence during toddlerhood: A comparison of mothers and fathers. *Nurse Practitioner, 19*(10), 25, 29–30, 33–34.

Grunau, R., Whitfield, M., Petrie, J., & Fryer, L. (1993). Extremely low birth weight (ELBW) toddlers are relatively responsive to pain at 18 months corrected age compared to larger birth weight children. *Early Human Development, 35*(3), 232–233. https://doi.org/10.1016/0378-3782(93)90126-F

Gullicks, J. N., & Crase, S. J. (1993). Sibling behavior with a newborn: Parents' expectations and observations. *Journal of Obstetric, Gynecologic, & Neonatal Nursing, 22*(5), 438–444. https://doi.org/10.1111/j.1552-6909.1993.tb01827.x

Guralnick, M. J., Hammond, M. A., Neville, B., & Connor, R. T. (2008). The relationship between sources and functions of social support and dimensions of child- and parent-related stress. *Journal of Intellectual Disability Research, 52*(12), 1138–1154. https://doi.org/10.1111/j.1365-2788.2008.01073.x

Haan, L. D., Hawley, D. R., & Deal, J. E. (2002). Operationalizing family resilience: A methodological strategy. *The American Journal of Family Therapy, 30*(4), 275–291. https://doi.org/10.1080/01926180290033439

Hall, W. A., Zubrick, S. R., Silburn, S. R., Parsons, D. E., & Kurinczuk, J. J. (2007). A model for predicting behavioural sleep problems in a random sample of Australian pre-schoolers. *Infant and Child Development, 16*(5), 509–523. https://doi.org/10.1002/icd.527

Hart, M. S., & Kelley, M. L. (2006). Fathers' and mothers' work and family issues as related to internalizing and externalizing behavior of children attending day care. *Journal of Family Issues, 27*(2), 252–270. https://doi.org/10.1177/0192513×05280992

Hastings, P. D., Nuselovici, J. N., Rubin, K. H., & Cheah, C. (2010). Shyness, parenting, and parent-child relationships. In K. H. Rubin, & R. J. Coplan (Eds.), *The development of shyness and social withdrawal* (pp. 107–130). New York, NY, US: Guilford Press.

Hastings, P. D., Ruttle, P. L., Serbin, L. A., Mills, R. S. L., Stack, D. M., & Schwartzman, A. E. (2011). Adrenocortical responses to strangers in preschoolers: Relations with parenting, temperament, and psychopathology. *Developmental Psychobiology, 53*(7), 694–710. https://doi.org/10.1002/dev.20545

Hay, D. F., Waters, C. S., Perra, O., Swift, N., Kairis, V., Phillips, R., et al. (2014). Precursors to aggression are evident by 6 months of age. *Developmental Science, 17*(3), 471–480. https://doi.org/10.1111/desc.12133

Heinicke, C. M., & Westheimer, I. (1966). *Brief separations.* Oxford, England: International U. Press.

Herba, C. M., Tremblay, R. E., Boivin, M., Liu, X., Mongeau, C., Séguin, J. R., et al. (2013). Maternal depressive symptoms and children's emotional problems: Can early child care help children of depressed mothers? *JAMA Psychiatry, 70*(8), 830–838. https://doi.org/10.1001/jamapsychiatry.2013.1361

Herbert, S. D., Harvey, E. A., Lugo-Candelas, C. I., & Breaux, R. P. (2013). Early fathering as a predictor of later psychosocial functioning among preschool children with behavior problems. *Journal of Abnormal Child Psychology, 41*(5), 691–703. https://doi.org/10.1007/s10802-012-9706-8

Herrera, C., & Dunn, J. (1997). Early experiences with family conflict: Implications for arguments with a close friend. *Developmental Psychology, 33*(5), 869–881. https://doi.org/10.1037/ 0012-1649.33.5.869

Hill, A. L., Degnan, K. A., Calkins, S. D., & Keane, S. P. (2006). Profiles of externalizing behavior problems for boys and girls across preschool: The roles of emotion regulation and inattention. *Developmental Psychology, 42*(5), 913–928. https://doi.org/10.1037/0012-1649.42.5.913

Hill, N. E., & Bush, K. R. (2001). Relationships between parenting environment and children's mental health among African American and European American mothers and children. *Journal of Marriage and Family, 63*(4), 954–966. https://doi.org/10.1111/j.1741-3737.2001.00954.x

Hill, R. (1958). Generic features of families under stress. *Social Casework, 39,* 139–150.

Hinde, R. A., & Stevenson-Hinde, J. (1988). Interpersonal relationships and child development. In S. Chess, A. Thomas, & M. E. Hertzig (Eds), *Annual progress in child psychiatry & child development* (pp. 5–26). New York, NY: Brunner/Mazel.

Hinde, R. A., Stevenson-Hinde, J., & Tamplin, A. (1985). Characteristics of 3- to 4-year-olds assessed at home and their interactions in preschool. *Developmental Psychology, 21*(1), 130–140. https://doi.org/10.1037/0012-1649.21.1.130

Hoagwood, K. E., Cavaleri, M. A., Olin, S. S., Burns, B. J., Slaton, E., Gruttadaro, D., et al. (2010). Family support in children's mental health: A review and synthesis. *Clinical Child and Family Psychology Review, 13*(1), 1–45. https://doi.org/10.1007/s10567-009-0060-5

Holden, G. W., & Zambarano, R. J. (1992). Passing the rod: Similarities between parents and their young children in orientations toward physical punishment. In I. E. Sigel, A. V. McGillicuddy-DeLisi, & J. J. Goodnow (Eds.), *Parental belief systems: The psychological consequences for children* (2nd ed.) (pp. 143–172). Hillsdale, NJ: Lawrence Erlbaum.

Ivanova, M. Y., Achenbach, T. M., Rescorla, L. A., Harder, V. S., Ang, R. P., Bilenberg, N., et al. (2010). Preschool psychopathology reported by parents in 23 societies: Testing the seven-syndrome model of the Child Behavior Checklist for ages 1.5-5. *Journal of the American Academy of Child & Adolescent Psychiatry, 49*(12), 1215–1224. https://doi.org/10.1016/j.jaac.2010.08.019

Jacobvitz, D., Hazen, N., Curran, M., & Hitchens, K. (2004). Observations of early triadic family interactions: Boundary disturbances in the family predict symptoms of depression, anxiety, and attention-deficit/hyperactivity disorder in middle childhood. *Development and Psychopathology, 16*(03), 577–592. https://doi.org/10.1017/S0954579404004675

Jamshidian, M., & Jalal, S. (2010). Tests of homoscedasticity, normality, and missing completely at random for incomplete multivariate data. *Psychometrika, 75*(4), 649–674. https://doi.org/10.1007/s11336-010-9175-3

Jenni, O. G., Achermann, P., & Carskadon, M. A. (2005). Homeostatic sleep regulation in adolescents. *Sleep-New York Then Westchester, 28* (11), 1446.

Jenni, O. G., & Carskadon, M. A. (2007). Sleep behavior and sleep regulation from infancy through adolescence: Normative aspects. *Sleep Medicine Clinics, 2*(3), 321–329. https://doi.org/10.1016/j.jsmc.2007.05.001

Jenni, O. G., Fuhrer, H. Z., Iglowstein, I., Molinari, L., & Largo, R. H. (2005). A longitudinal study of bed sharing and sleep problems among Swiss children in the first 10 years of life. *Pediatrics, 115,* 233–240. https://doi.org/10.1542/peds.2004-0815E

Johnston, J. R., Gonzàlez, R., & Campbell, L. E. G. (1987). Ongoing postdivorce conflict and child disturbance. *Journal of Abnormal Child Psychology, 15*(4), 493–509. https://doi.org/10.1007/BF00917236

Jones, D. C., Abbey, B. B., & Cumberland, A. (1998). The development of display rule knowledge: Linkages with family expressiveness and social competence. *Child Development, 69*(4), 1209–1222. https://doi.org/10.1111/j.1467-8624.1998.tb06168.x

Jones, L. B., Rothbart, M. K., & Posner, M. I. (2003). Development of executive attention in preschool children. *Developmental Science, 6*(5), 498–504. https://doi.org/10.1111/1467-7687.00307

Jordan, P. L. (1989). Support behaviors identified as helpful and desired by second-time parents over the perinatal period. *Maternal-Child Nursing Journal, 18*(2), 133–145.

Jouriles, E. N., & Farris, A. M. (1992). Effects of marital conflict on subsequent parent-son interactions. *Behavior Therapy, 23*(3), 355–374. https://doi.org/10.1016/S0005-7894(05)80163-7

Kaczynski, K. J., Lindahl, K. M., Malik, N. M., & Laurenceau, J.-P. (2006). Marital conflict, maternal and paternal parenting, and child adjustment: A test of mediation and moderation. *Journal of Family Psychology, 20*(2), 199–208. https://doi.org/10.1037/0893-3200.20.2.199

Kagan, J. (1997). Temperament and the reactions to unfamiliarity. *Child Development, 68*(1), 139–143. https://doi.org/10.1111/j.1467-8624.1997.tb01931.x

Kagan, J., Reznick, J. S., & Snidman, N. (1987). The physiology and psychology of behavioral inhibition in children. *Child Development, 58*(6), 1459–1473.

Kagan, J., Reznick, J. S., & Snidman, N. (1988). Biological bases of childhood shyness. *Science, 240*(4849), 167–171. https://doi.org/10.1126/science.3353713

Kagan, J., & Snidman, N. (1991). Temperamental factors in human development. *American Psychologist, 46*(8), 856–862. https://doi.org/10.1037/0003-066X.46.8.856

Kataria, S., Swanson, M. S., & Trevathan, G. E. (1987). Persistence of sleep disturbances in preschool children. *The Journal of Pediatrics, 110*(4), 642–646. https://doi.org/10.1016/S0022-3476(87)80571-1

Kearney, C. A., Sims, K. E., Pursell, C. R., & Tillotson, C. A. (2003). Separation anxiety disorder in young children: A longitudinal and family analysis. *Journal of Clinical Child & Adolescent Psychology, 32*(4), 593–598. https://doi.org/10.1207/S15374424JCCP3204_12

Keenan, K., & Shaw, D. (1997). Developmental and social influences on young girls' early problem behavior. *Psychological Bulletin, 121*(1), 95–113. https://doi.org/10.1037/0033-2909.121.1.95

Kelloway, E. K., Gottlieb, B. H., & Barham, L. (1999). The source, nature, and direction of work and family conflict: A longitudinal investigation. *Journal of Occupational Health Psychology, 4*(4), 337–346. https://doi.org/10.1037/1076-8998.4.4.337

Kendrick, C., & Dunn, J. (1982). Protest or pleasure? The response of first-born children to interactions between their mothers and infant siblings. *Journal of Child Psychology and Psychiatry, 23*(2), 117–129. https://doi.org/10.1111/j.1469-7610.1982.tb00057.x

Kingston, L., & Prior, M. (1995). The development of patterns of stable, transient, and school-age onset aggressive behavior in young children. *Journal of the American Academy of Child & Adolescent Psychiatry, 34*(3), 348–358. https://doi.org/10.1097/00004583-199503000-00021

Klackenberg, G. (1982). Sleep behaviour studied longitudinally. *Acta Pædiatrica*, **71**(3), 501–506. https://doi.org/10.1111/j.1651-2227.1982.tb09459.x

Kline, G. H., Julien, D., Baucom, B., Hartman, S., Gilbert, K., Gonzales, T., et al. (2004). The interactional dimensions coding system: A global system for couple interactions. In P. K. Kerig, & D. H. Baucom (Eds.), *Couple observational coding systems* (pp. 113–126). Mahwah, NJ: Lawrence Erlbaum.

Kochanska, G. (1993). Toward a synthesis of parental socialization and child temperament in early development of conscience. *Child Development*, **64**(2), 325–347. https://doi.org/10.2307/1131254

Kochanska, G., & Kim, S. (2012). Toward a new understanding of legacy of early attachments for future antisocial trajectories: Evidence from two longitudinal studies. *Development and Psychopathology*, **24**(3), 783–806. https://doi.org/10.1017/S0954579412000375

Kojima, Y., Irisawa, M., & Wakita, M. (2005). The impact of a second infant on interactions of mothers and firstborn children. *Journal of Reproductive and Infant Psychology*, **23**(1), 103–114. https://doi.org/10.1080/02646830512331330910

Kolak, A. M., & Volling, B. L. (2011). Sibling jealousy in early childhood: Longitudinal links to sibling relationship quality. *Infant and Child Development*, **20**(2), 213–226. https://doi.org/10.1002/icd.690

Kolak, A. M., & Volling, B. L. (2013). Coparenting moderates the association between firstborn children's temperament and problem behavior across the transition to siblinghood. *Journal of Family Psychology*, **27**(3), 355–364. https://doi.org/10.1037/a0032864

Koos, E. L. (1946). *Families in trouble.* Morningside Heights, NY: King's Crown Press.

Kopp, C. B. (1989). Regulation of distress and negative emotions: A developmental view. *Developmental Psychology*, **25**(3), 343–354. https://doi.org/10.1037/0012-1649.25.3.343

Kramer, L., & Gottman, J. M. (1992). Becoming a sibling: "With a little help from my friends." *Developmental Psychology*, **28**(4), 685–699. https://doi.org/10.1037/0012-1649.28.4.685

Kramer, L., & Kowal, A. K. (2005). Sibling relationship quality from birth to adolescence: The enduring contributions of friends. *Journal of Family Psychology*, **19**(4), 503–511. https://doi.org/10.1037/0893-3200.19.4.503

Kreppner, K., Paulsen, S., & Schuetze, Y. (1982). Infant and family development: From triads to tetrads. *Human Development*, **25**(6), 373–391. https://doi.org/10.1159/000272821

Lagattuta, K. H. (2007). Thinking about the future because of the past: Young children's knowledge about the causes of worry and preventative decisions. *Child Development*, **78**(5), 1492–1509. http://doi.org/10.1111/j.1467-8624.2007.01079.x

Lam, P., Hiscock, H., & Wake, M. (2003). Outcomes of infant sleep problems: A longitudinal study of sleep, behavior, and maternal well-being. *Pediatrics*, **111**(3), e203–e207. https://doi.org/10.1542/peds.111.3.e203

Lane, J. D., & Song, J.-H. (2015). Behavioral inhibition and social withdrawal across cultures. In *International encyclopedia of social and behavioral sciences* (2nd ed.) (Vol. 2, pp. 456–462). Oxford, England: Elsevier.

Leahy-Warren, P., McCarthy, G., & Corcoran, P. (2012). First-time mothers: Social support, maternal parental self-efficacy and postnatal depression. *Journal of Clinical Nursing*, **21**(3–4), 388–397. https://doi.org/10.1111/j.1365-2702.2011.03701.x

Lee, C.-Y. S., Anderson, J. R., Horowitz, J. L., & August, G. J. (2009). Family income and parenting: The role of parental depression and social support. *Family Relations*, **58**(4), 417–430. https://doi.org/10.1111/j.1741-3729.2009.00563.x

Legg, M. C., Sherick, D. I., & Wadland, W. (1974). Reaction of preschool children to the birth of a sibling. *Child Psychiatry and Human Development, 5*(1), 3–39. https://doi.org/10.1007/BF01441311

Lemerise, E. A., & Arsenio, W. F. (2000). An integrated model of emotion processes and cognition in social information processing. *Child Development,* **71** (1), 107–118.

Letourneau, N. L., Dennis, C.-L., Benzies, K., Duffett-Leger, L., Stewart, M., Tryphonopoulos, P. D., et al. (2012). Postpartum depression is a family affair: Addressing the impact on mothers, fathers, and children. *Issues in Mental Health Nursing, 33*(7), 445–457. https://doi.org/10.3109/01612840.2012.673054

Leve, L. D., Kim, H. K., & Pears, K. C. (2005). Childhood temperament and family environment as predictors of internalizing and externalizing trajectories from ages 5 to 17. *Journal of Abnormal Child Psychology, 33*(5), 505–520. https://doi.org/10.1007/s10802-005-6734-7

Levy, D. M. (1934). Rivalry between children in the same family. *Child Study,* **11**, 233–261.

Levy, D. M. (1937). *Studies in sibling rivalry.* New York, NY: American Orthopsychiatric Association.

Lindsey, E. W., Caldera, Y. M., & Tankersley, L. (2009). Marital conflict and the quality of young children's peer play behavior: The mediating and moderating role of parent-child emotional reciprocity and attachment security. *Journal of Family Psychology, 23*(2), 130–145. https://doi.org/10.1037/a0014972

Little, R. J. A., & Rubin, D. B. (2014). *Statistical analysis with missing data.* Hoboken, NJ: John Wiley & Sons.

Liu, L., & Wang, M. (2014). Parenting stress and children's problem behavior in China: The mediating role of parental psychological aggression. *Journal of Family Psychology, 29*(1), 20–28. https://doi.org/10.1037/fam0000047

Löhr, B., & Siegmund, R. (1999). Ultradian and orcadian rhythms of sleep-wake and food-intake behavior during early infancy. *Chronobiology International, 16*(2), 129–148. https://doi.org/10.3109/07420529909019081

Lovejoy, M. C., Graczyk, P. A., O'Hare, E., & Neuman, G. (2000). Maternal depression and parenting behavior: A meta-analytic review. *Clinical Psychology Review, 20*(5), 561–592. http://doi.org/10.1016/S0272-7358(98)00100-7

Mackenbach, J. D., Ringoot, A. P., van der Ende, J., Verhulst, F. C., Jaddoe, V. W. V., Hofman, A., et al. (2014). Exploring the relation of harsh parental discipline with child emotional and behavioral problems by using multiple informants. The Generation R study. *PLoS ONE,* **9**(8), e104793. https://doi.org/10.1371/journal.pone.0104793

Maguire, M. C., & Dunn, J. (1997). Friendships in early childhood and social understanding. *International Journal of Behavioral Development, 21*(4), 669–686. https://doi.org/10.1080/016502597384613

Margolin, G., Gordis, E. B., & John, R. S. (2001). Coparenting: A link between marital conflict and parenting in two-parent families. *Journal of Family Psychology, 15*(1), 3–21. http://doi.org/10.1037/0893-3200.15.1.3

Mathiesen, K. S., & Sanson, A. (2000). Dimensions of early childhood behavior problems: Stability and predictors of change from 18 to 30 months. *Journal of Abnormal Child Psychology, 28*(1), 15–31. https://doi.org/10.1023/A:1005165916906

McArdle, J. J., & Ritschard, G. (2013). *Contemporary issues in exploratory data mining in the behavioral sciences.* NY: Routledge.

McCubbin, H. I., & Patterson, J. M. (1983). The family stress process. *Marriage & Family Review,* **6**(1–2), 7–37. https://doi.org/10.1300/J002v06n01_02

McElwain, N. L., & Volling, B. L. (2005). Preschool children's interactions with friends and older siblings: Relationship specificity and joint contributions to problem behavior. *Journal of Family Psychology,* **19**(4), 486–496. https://doi.org/10.1037/0893-3200.19.4.486

McShane, K. E., & Hastings, P. D. 2009). The New Friends Vignettes: Measuring parental psychological control that confers risk for anxious adjustment in preschoolers. *International Journal of Behavioral Development,* **33**(6), 481–495. https://doi.org/10.1177/0165025409103874

Meijer, A. M., & van den Wittenboer, G. L. H. (2007). Contribution of infants' sleep and crying to marital relationship of first-time parent couples in the 1st year after childbirth. *Journal of Family Psychology,* **21**(1), 49–57. https://doi.org/10.1037/0893-3200.21.1.49

Melnick, S. M., & Hinshaw, S. P. (2000). Emotion regulation and parenting in AD/HD and comparison boys: Linkages with social behaviors and peer preference. *Journal of Abnormal Child Psychology,* **28**(1), 73–86. https://doi.org/10.1023/A:1005174102794

Meltzer, L. J., & Mindell, J. A. (2007). Relationship between child sleep disturbances and maternal sleep, mood, and parenting stress: A pilot study. *Journal of Family Psychology,* **21**(1), 67–73. https://doi.org/10.1037/0893-3200.21.1.67

Mercer, R. T. R. N. (1979). "She's a multip …. She knows the ropes." *Journal of Maternal Child Nursing,* **4**(5), 301–304.

Mesman, J., Stoel, R., Bakermans-Kranenburg, M. J., van IJzendoorn, M. H., Juffer, F., Koot, H. M., et al. (2009). Predicting growth curves of early childhood externalizing problems: Differential susceptibility of children with difficult temperament. *Journal of Abnormal Child Psychology,* **37**(5), 625–636. https://doi.org/10.1007/s10802-009-9298-0

Mezulis, A. H., Hyde, J. S., & Clark, R. (2004). Father involvement moderates the effect of maternal depression during a child's infancy on child behavior problems in kindergarten. *Journal of Family Psychology,* **18**(4), 575–588. https://doi.org/10.1037/0893-3200.18.4.575

Mikami, A. Y., & Pfiffner, L. J. (2008). Sibling relationships among children with ADHD. *Journal of Attention Disorders,* **11**(4), 482–492. https://doi.org/10.1177/1087054706295670

Mindell, J. A., Sadeh, A., Kohyama, J., & How, T. H. (2010). Parental behaviors and sleep outcomes in infants and toddlers: A cross-cultural comparison. *Sleep Medicine,* **11**(4), 393–399. https://doi.org/10.1016/j.sleep.2009.11.011

Miner, J. L., & Clarke-Stewart, K. A. (2008). Trajectories of externalizing behavior from age 2 to age 9: Relations with gender, temperament, ethnicity, parenting, and rater. *Developmental Psychology,* **44**(3), 771–786. https://doi.org/10.1037/0012-1649.44.3.771

Moffitt, T. E. (1990). Juvenile delinquency and attention deficit disorder: Boys' developmental trajectories from age 3 to age 15. *Child Development,* **61**(3), 893–910. https://doi.org/10.1111/j.1467-8624.1990.tb02830.x

Morris, N., Keane, S., Calkins, S., Shanahan, L., & O'Brien, M. (2014). Differential components of reactivity and attentional control predicting externalizing behavior. *Journal of Applied Developmental Psychology,* **35**(3), 121–127. http://doi.org/10.1016/j.appdev.2014.02.002

Moss, E., Bureau, J.-F., Cyr, C., & Dubois-Comtois, K. (2006). Is the maternal Q-Set a valid measure of preschool child attachment behavior? *International Journal of Behavioral Development,* **30**(6), 488–497. http://doi.org/10.1177/0165025406071908

Mulvaney, S., Lambert, E. W., Garber, J., & Walker, L. S. (2006). Trajectories of symptoms and impairment for pediatric patients with functional abdominal pain: A 5-year longitudinal study. *Journal of the American Academy of Child & Adolescent Psychiatry*, **45**(6), 737–744. https://doi.org/10.1097/10.chi.0000214192.57993.06

Muris, P., Merckelbach, H., Gadet, B., & Moulaert, V. (2000). Fears, worries, and scary dreams in 4- to 12-year-old children: Their content, developmental pattern, and origins. *Journal of Clinical Child Psychology*, **29**(1), 43–52. https://doi.org/10.1207/S15374424jccp2901_5

Muris, P., Merckelbach, H., Meesters, C., & van den Brand, K. (2002). Cognitive development and worry in normal children. *Cognitive Therapy and Research*, **26**(6), 775–787. https://doi.org/10.1023/A:1021241517274

Muthén, B. (2004). Latent variable analysis: Growth Mixture Modeling and related techniques for longitudinal data. In D. Kaplan (Ed.), *The Sage handbook of quantitative methodology for the social sciences* (pp. 345–68). Thousand Oaks, CA: Sage Publications.

Muthén, B., & Muthén, L. K. (2000). Integrating person-centered and variable-centered analyses: Growth mixture modeling with latent trajectory classes. *Alcoholism: Clinical and Experimental Research*, **24**(6), 882–891. https://doi.org/10.1111/j.1530-0277.2000.tb02070.x

Muthén, L. K., & Muthén, B. O. (1998–2012). *Mplus user's guide* (7th ed.). Los Angeles, CA: Muthén & Muthén.

Nadelman, L., & Begun, A. (1982). The effect of the newborn on the older sibling: Mothers' questionnaires. In M. E. Lamb & B. Sutton-Smith (Eds.), *Sibling relationships: Their nature and significance across the lifespan* (pp. 13–38). Hillsdale, NJ: Erlbaum.

Nagin, D. S. (1999). Analyzing developmental trajectories: A semiparametric, group-based approach. *Psychological Methods*, **4**(2), 139–157. https://doi.org/10.1037/1082-989X.4.2.139

Nylund, K. L., Asparouhov, T., & Muthén, B. O. (2007). Deciding on the number of classes in latent class analysis and growth mixture modeling: A Monte Carlo simulation study. *Structural Equation Modeling: A Multidisciplinary Journal*, **14**(4), 535–569. https://doi.org/10.1080/10705510701575396

Oh, W., Rubin, K. H., Bowker, J. C., Booth-LaForce, C., Rose-Krasnor, L., & Laursen, B. (2008). Trajectories of social withdrawal from middle childhood to early adolescence. *Journal of Abnormal Child Psychology*, **36**(4), 553–566. https://doi.org/10.1007/s10802-007-9199-z

Oh, W., Volling, B. L., & Gonzalez, R. (2015). Trajectories of children's social interactions with their infant sibling in the first year: A multidimensional approach. *Journal of Family Psychology*, **29**(1), 119–129. https://doi.org/10.1037/fam0000051

Owens, E. B., & Shaw, D. S. (2003). Predicting growth curves of externalizing behavior across the preschool years. *Journal of Abnormal Child Psychology*, **31**(6), 575–590. https://doi.org/10.1023/A:1026254005632

Owens-Stively, J. M. D., Frank, N., Smith, A. M. S., Hagino, O. M. D., Spirito, A., Arrigan, M. B. S., et al. (1997). Child temperament, parenting discipline style, and daytime behavior in childhood sleep disorders. *Journal of Developmental and Behavioral Pediatrics*, **18**(5), 314–321.

Patterson, G. R. (1986). Performance models for antisocial boys. *American Psychologist*, **41**(4), 432–444. https://doi.org/10.1037/0003-066X.41.4.432

Paulus, F. W., Backes, A., Sander, C. S., Weber, M., & von Gontard, A. (2015). Anxiety disorders and behavioral inhibition in preschool children: A population-based study. *Child Psychiatry & Human Development*, **46**(1), 150–157. https://doi.org/10.1007/s10578-014-0460-8

Perlman, M., & Ross, H. S. (1997). The benefits of parent intervention in children's disputes: An examination of concurrent changes in children's fighting styles. *Child Development*, **68**(4), 690–700. http://doi.org/10.1111/j.1467-8624.1997.tb04230.x

Peterson, J. L., & Zill, N. (1986). Marital disruption, parent-child relationships, and behavior problems in children. *Journal of Marriage and Family*, **48**(2), 295–307. https://doi.org/10.2307/352397

Petras, H., & Masyn, K. (2010). General growth mixture analysis with antecedents and consequences of change. In A. R. Piquero & D. Weisburd (Eds.), *Handbook of quantitative criminology* (pp. 69–100). New York, NY: Springer.

Petty, T. A. (1953). The tragedy of Humpty Dumpty. *Psychoanalytic Study of the Child*, **8**, 404–412.

Pons, F., Harris, P. L., & de Rosnay, M. (2004). Emotion comprehension between 3 and 11 years: Developmental periods and hierarchical organization. *European Journal of Developmental Psychology*, **1**(2), 127–152. https://doi.org/10.1080/17405620344000022

Quine, L. (1992). Severity of sleep problems in children with severe learning difficulties: Description and correlates. *Journal of Community & Applied Social Psychology*, **2**(4), 247–268. https://doi.org/10.1002/casp.2450020404

Renk, K., Roddenberry, A., Oliveros, A., & Sieger, K. (2007). The relationship of maternal characteristics and perceptions of children's emotional and behavioral problems. *Child and Family Behavior Therapy*, **29**(1), 37–57. https://doi.org/10.1300/J019v29n01_03

Richardson, P. (1983). Women's perceptions of change in relationships shared with children during pregnancy. *Maternal-Child Nursing Journal*, **12** (2), 75–88.

Robertson, J., & Robertson, J. (1971). Young children in brief separation: A fresh look. *The Psychoanalytic Study of the Child*, **26**, 264–315.

Rocha, E. M., & Prkachin, K. M. (2007). Temperament and pain reactivity predict health behavior seven years later. *Journal of Pediatric Psychology*, **32**(4), 393–399. https://doi.org/10.1093/jpepsy/jsl036

Rothbart, M. K., Ahadi, S. A., Hershey, K. L., & Fisher, P. (2001). Investigations of temperament at three to seven years: The children's behavior questionnaire. *Child Development*, **72**(5), 1394–1408. https://doi.org/10.1111/1467-8624.00355

Rothbart, M. K., & Bates, J. E. (1998). Temperament. In N. Eisenberg (Ed.), *Handbook of child psychology: Vol 3. Social, emotional, and personality development* (5th ed., Vol. 3, pp. 105–176). Hoboken, NJ: John Wiley & Sons.

Rothbart, M. K., & Bates, J. E. (2006). Temperament in children's development. In W. Damon & R. Lerner (Eds.), *Handbook of child psychology: Vol. 3. Social, emotional, and personality development* (6th ed., Vol. 3, pp. 99–166). New York, NY: Wiley.

Rothbart, M. K., Sheese, B. E., Rueda, M. R., & Posner, M. I. (2011). Developing mechanisms of self-regulation in early life. *Emotion Review*, **3**(2), 207–213. https://doi.org/10.1177/1754073910387943

Rubin, K. H., Burgess, K. B., & Hastings, P. D. (2002). Stability and social-behavioral consequences of toddlers' inhibited temperament and parenting behaviors. *Child Development*, **73**(2), 483–495.

Rubin, K. H., Burgess, K. B., Kennedy, A. E., & Stewart, S. L. (2003). Social withdrawal in childhood. In E. J. Mash & R. A. Barkley (Eds.), *Child psychopathology* (2nd ed.) (pp. 372–406). New York, NY: Guilford Press.

Rubin, K. H., Chen, X., McDougall, P., Bowker, A., & McKinnon, J. (1995). The Waterloo longitudinal project: Predicting internalizing and externalizing problems in adolescence.

Development and Psychopathology, 7(04), 751–764. https://doi.org/10.1017/S0954579400006829

Rubin, K. H., Coplan, R. J., & Bowker, J. C. (2009). Social withdrawal in childhood. *Annual Review of Psychology, 60*(1), 141–171. https://doi.org/10.1146/annurev.psych.60.110707.163642

Rubin, K. H., Hastings, P. D., Stewart, S. L., Henderson, H. A., & Chen, X. (1997). The consistency and concomitants of inhibition: Some of the children, all of the time. *Child Development, 68*(3), 467–483. https://doi.org/10.1111/j.1467-8624.1997.tb01952.x

Ruff, H. A., & Rothbart, M. K. (1996). *Attention in early development: Themes and variations.* New York, NY: Oxford University Press. Retrieved from https://proxy.lib.umich.edu/login?url=https://search.ebscohost.com/login.aspx?direct=true&db=psyh&AN=1996-98232-000&site=ehost-live&scope=site

Rushton, P. J., Brainerd, C. J., & Pressley, M. (1983). Behavioral development and construct validity: The principle of aggregation. *Psychological Bulletin, 94*(1), 18–38. https://doi.org/10.1037/0033-2909.94.1.18

Rutter, M. (1996). Transitions and turning points in developmental psychopathology: As applied to the age span between childhood and mid-adulthood. *International Journal of Behavioral Development, 19*(3), 603–626. https://doi.org/10.1177/016502549601900309

Rydell, A.-M., Bohlin, G., & Thorell, L. B. (2005). Representations of attachment to parents and shyness as predictors of children's relationships with teachers and peer competence in preschool. *Attachment & Human Development, 7*(2), 187–204. https://doi.org/10.1080/14616730500134282

Sadeh, A., Lavie, P., & Scher, A. (1994). Sleep and temperament: Maternal perceptions of temperament of sleep-disturbed toddlers. *Early Education and Development, 5*(4), 311–322. https://doi.org/10.1207/s15566935eed0504_6

Sadeh, A., Mindell, J. A., Luedtke, K., & Wiegand, B. (2009). Sleep and sleep ecology in the first 3 years: A web-based study. *Journal of Sleep Research, 18*(1), 60–73. https://doi.org/10.1111/j.1365-2869.2008.00699.x

Sadeh, A., Raviv, A., & Gruber, R. (2000). Sleep patterns and sleep disruptions in school-age children. *Developmental Psychology, 36*(3), 291–301. https://doi.org/10.1037/0012-1649.36.3.291

Sameroff, A. J. (2000). Developmental systems and psychopathology. *Development and Psychopathology, 12*, 297–312.

Sanders, M. R., & Woolley, M. L. (2005). The relationship between maternal self-efficacy and parenting practices: Implications for parent training. *Child: Care, Health and Development, 31*(1), 65–73. https://doi.org/10.1111/j.1365-2214.2005.00487.x

Schacht, P. M., Cummings, E. M., & Davies, P. T. (2009). Fathering in family context and child adjustment: A longitudinal analysis. *Journal of Family Psychology, 23*(6), 790–797. https://doi.org/10.1037/a0016741

Schaefer, C. (1990). Night waking and temperament in early childhood. *Psychological Reports, 67*(1), 192–194.

Schafer, J. L., & Graham, J. W. (2002). Missing data: Our view of the state of the art. *Psychological Methods, 7*(2), 147–177. https://doi.org/10.1037/1082-989X.7.2.147

Scher, A., & Asher, R. (2004). Is attachment security related to sleep-wake regulation?: Mothers' reports and objective sleep recordings. *Infant Behavior and Development, 27*(3), 288–302. https://doi.org/10.1016/j.infbeh.2003.12.002

Schoppe, S. J., Mangelsdorf, S. C., & Frosch, C. A. (2001). Coparenting, family process, and family structure: Implications for preschoolers' externalizing behavior problems. *Journal of Family Psychology, 15*(3), 526–545. https://doi.org/10.1037/0893-3200.15.3.526

Schoppe-Sullivan, S. J., Mangelsdorf, S. C., Frosch, C. A., & McHale, J. L. (2004). Associations between coparenting and marital behavior from infancy to the preschool years. *Journal of Family Psychology, 18*(1), 194–207. https://doi.org/10.1037/0893-3200.18.1.194

Schoppe-Sullivan, S. J., Weldon, A. H., Claire Cook, J., Davis, E. F., & Buckley, C. K. (2009). Coparenting behavior moderates longitudinal relations between effortful control and preschool children's externalizing behavior. *Journal of Child Psychology and Psychiatry, 50*(6), 698–706. https://doi.org/10.1111/j.1469-7610.2008.02009.x

Schwarz, G. (1978). Estimating the dimension of a model. *The Annals of Statistics, 6*(2), 461–464. https://doi.org/10.1214/aos/1176344136

Sclove, S. L. (1987). Application of model-selection criteria to some problems in multivariate analysis. *Psychometrika, 52*(3), 333–343. https://doi.org/10.1007/BF02294360

Seidman, E., & French, S. E. (2004). Developmental trajectories and ecological transitions: A two-step procedure to aid in the choice of prevention and promotion interventions. *Development and Psychopathology, 16*, 1141–1159. https://doi.org/10.1017/S0954579404040179

Seifer, R., Sameroff, A. J., Dickstein, S., & Hayden, L. C. (1996). Parental psychopathology and sleep variation in children. *Child and Adolescent Psychiatric Clinics of North America, 5*(3), 715–727.

Shapiro, A. F., & Gottman, J. M. (2005). Effects on marriage of a psycho-communicative-educational intervention with couples undergoing the transition to parenthood: Evaluation at 1-year post intervention. *The Journal of Family Communication, 5*(1) 1–24.

Shaw, D. S., Keenan, K., & Vondra, J. I. (1994). Developmental precursors of externalizing behavior: Ages 1 to 3. *Developmental Psychology, 30*(3), 355–364. https://doi.org/10.1037/0012-1649.30.3.355

Shaw, D. S., Keenan, K., Vondra, J. I., Delliquardi, E., & Giovannelli, J. (1997). Antecedents of preschool children's internalizing problems: A longitudinal study of low-income families. *Journal of the American Academy of Child & Adolescent Psychiatry, 36*(12), 1760–1767. https://doi.org/10.1097/00004583-199712000-00025

Shaw, D. S., Owens, E. B., Giovannelli, J., & Winslow, E. B. (2001). Infant and toddler pathways leading to early externalizing disorders. *Journal of the American Academy of Child & Adolescent Psychiatry, 40*(1), 36–43. https://doi.org/10.1097/00004583-200101000-00014

Song, J.-H., & Volling, B. L. (2015). Coparenting and children's temperament predict firstborns' cooperation in the care of an infant sibling. *Journal of Family Psychology, 29*(1), 130–135. https://doi.org/10.1037/fam0000052

Sroufe, L. A., & Rutter, M. (1984). The domain of developmental psychopathology. *Child Development, 55*(1), 17–29. https://doi.org/10.2307/1129832

Staples, A. D., Bates, J. E., & Petersen, I. T. (2015). IX. Bedtime routines in early childhood: Prevalence, consistency, and associations with nighttime sleep. *Monographs of the Society for Research in Child Development, 80*(1), 141–159. https://doi.org/10.1111/mono.12149

Steinhausen, H.-C. (2006). Developmental psychopathology in adolescence: Findings from a Swiss study—The NAPE lecture 2005. *Acta Psychiatrica Scandinavica, 113*(1), 6–12. https://doi.org/10.1111/j.1600-0447.2005.00706.x

Stevenson-Hinde, J., Shouldice, A., & Chicot, R. (2011). Maternal anxiety, behavioral inhibition, and attachment. *Attachment & Human Development*, **13**(3), 199–215. https://doi.org/10.1080/14616734.2011.562409

Stevenson, M. M., Fabricius, W. V., Cookston, J. T., Parke, R. D., Coltrane, S., Braver, S. L., et al. (2014). Marital problems, maternal gatekeeping attitudes, and father-child relationships in adolescence. *Developmental Psychology*, **50**(4), 1208–1218. https://doi.org/10.1037/a0035327

Stewart, R. B. (1990). *The second child: Family transition and adjustment.* Thousand Oaks, CA: Sage Publications.

Stewart, R. B., Mobley, L. A., van Tuyl, S. S., & Salvador, M. A. (1987). The firstborn's adjustment to the birth of a sibling: A longitudinal assessment. *Child Development*, **58**(2), 341–355. https://doi.org/10.2307/1130511

Stillwell, R., & Dunn, J. (1985). Continuities in sibling relationships: Patterns of aggression and friendliness. *Journal of Child Psychology and Psychiatry*, **26**(4), 627–637. https://doi.org/10.1111/j.1469-7610.1985.tb01645.x

Strobl, C., Malley, J., & Tutz, G. (2009). An introduction to recursive partitioning: Rationale, application, and characteristics of classification and regression trees, bagging, and random forests. *Psychological Methods*, **14**(4), 323–348. https://doi.org/10.1037/a0016973

Stuart, S., & Noyes, Jr., R. (1999). Attachment and interpersonal communication in somatization. *Psychosomatics*, **40**(1), 34–43. https://doi.org/10.1016/S0033-3182(99)71269-7

Tarabulsy, G. M., Provost, M. A., Larose, S., Moss, E., Lemelin, J.-P., Moran, G., et al. (2008). Similarities and differences in mothers' and observers' ratings of infant security on the Attachment Q-Sort. *Infant Behavior and Development*, **31**(1), 10–22. https://doi.org/10.1016/j.infbeh.2007.05.002

Terre, L., & Ghiselli, W. (1997). A developmental perspective on family risk factors in somatization. *Journal of Psychosomatic Research*, **42**(2), 197–208. https://doi.org/10.1016/S0022-3999(96)00237-1

Teti, D. M., & McGourty, S. (1996). Using mothers versus trained observers in assessing children's secure base behavior: Theoretical and methodological considerations. *Child Development*, **67**(2), 597–605. https://doi.org/10.1111/j.1467-8624.1996.tb01753.x

Teti, D. M., Sakin, J. W., Kucera, E., Corns, K. M., & Eiden, R. D. (1996). And baby makes four: Predictors of attachment security among preschool-age firstborns during the transition to siblinghood. *Child Development*, **67**(2), 579–596.

Teubert, D., & Pinquart, M. (2010). The association between coparenting and child adjustment: A meta-analysis. *Parenting*, **10**(4), 286–307. https://doi.org/10.1080/15295192.2010.492040

Tharner, A., Luijk, M. P. C. M., van IJzendoorn, M. H., Bakermans-Kranenburg, M. J., Jaddoe, V. W. V., Hofman, A., et al. (2012). Infant attachment, parenting stress, and child emotional and behavioral problems at age 3 years. *Parenting*, **12**(4), 261–281. https://doi.org/10.1080/15295192.2012.709150

Thomason, E., Volling, B. L., Flynn, H. A., McDonough, S. C., Marcus, S. M., Lopez, J. F., et al. (2014). Parenting stress and depressive symptoms in postpartum mothers: Bidirectional or unidirectional effects? *Infant Behavior and Development*, **37**(3), 406–415. https://doi.org/10.1016/j.infbeh.2014.05.009

Thompson, R. A., & Meyer, S. (2007). Socialization of emotion regulation in the family. In J. J. Gross & J. J. Gross (Eds.), *Handbook of emotion regulation* (pp. 249–268). New York, NY: Guilford Press.

Tikotzky, L., & Sadeh, A. (2009). Maternal sleep-related cognitions and infant sleep: A longitudinal study from pregnancy through the 1st Year. *Child Development*, **80**(3), 860–874. https://doi.org/10.1111/j.1467-8624.2009.01302.x

Tikotzky, L., Sadeh, A., Volkovich, E., Manber, R., Meiri, G., & Shahar, G. (2015). VII. Infant sleep development from 3 to 6 months postpartum: Links with maternal sleep and paternal involvement. *Monographs of the Society for Research in Child Development*, **80**(1), 107–124. https://doi.org/10.1111/mono.12147

Touchette, É., Petit, D., Paquet, J., Boivin, M., Japel, C., Tremblay, R. E., et al. (2005). Factors associated with fragmented sleep at night across early childhood. *Archives of Pediatrics & Adolescent Medicine*, **159** (3), 242–249.

Towe-Goodman, N. R., & Teti, D. M. (2008). Power assertive discipline, maternal emotional involvement, and child adjustment. *Journal of Family Psychology*, **22**(4), 648–651. https://doi.org/10.1037/a0012661

Trause, M. A. (1978). Birth in the hospital: The effect on the sibling. *Birth*, **5**(4), 207–210. https://doi.org/10.1111/j.1523-536X1978.tb01281.x

Trause, M. A., Voos, D., Rudd, C., Klaus, M., Kennell, J., & Boslett, M. (1981). Separation for childbirth: The effect on the sibling. *Child Psychiatry and Human Development*, **12**(1), 32–39. https://doi.org/10.1007/BF00706671

Tremblay, R. E., Japel, C., Perusse, D., Mcduff, P., Boivin, M., Zoccolillo, M., et al. (1999). The search for the age of "onset" of physical aggression: Rousseau and Bandura revisited. *Criminal Behaviour and Mental Health*, **9**(1), 8–23. https://doi.org/10.1002/cbm.288

Tremblay, R. E., Nagin, D. S., Séguin, J. R., Zoccolillo, M., Zelazo, P. D., Boivin, M., et al. (2004). Physical aggression during early childhood: Trajectories and predictors. *Pediatrics*, **114**(1), e43–e50. https://doi.org/10.1542/peds.114.1.e43

van Aken, C., Junger, M., Verhoeven, M., van Aken, M. A. G., & Deković, M. (2008). The longitudinal relations between parenting and toddlers' attention problems and aggressive behaviors. *Infant Behavior and Development*, **31**(3), 432–446. https://doi.org/10.1016/j.infbeh.2007.12.016

Vasey, M. W., Crnic, K. A., & Carter, W. G. (1994). Worry in childhood: A developmental perspective. *Cognitive Therapy and Research*, **18**(6), 529–549. https://doi.org/10.1007/BF02355667

Vinden, P. G. (1999). Children's understanding of mind and emotion: A multi-culture study. *Cognition & Emotion*, **13**(1), 19–48. https://doi.org/10.1080/026999399379357

Volling, B. L. (2005). The transition to siblinghood: A developmental ecological systems perspective and directions for future research. *Journal of Family Psychology*, **19**(4), 542–549. https://doi.org/10.1037/0893-3200.19.4.542

Volling, B. L. (2012). Family transitions following the birth of a sibling: An empirical review of changes in the firstborn's adjustment. *Psychological Bulletin*, **138**(3), 497–528. https://doi.org/10.1037/a0026921

Volling, B. L., & Elins, J. L. (1998). Family relationships and children's emotional adjustment as correlates of maternal and paternal differential treatment: A replication with toddler and preschool siblings. *Child Development*, **69**(6), 1640–1656. https://doi.org/10.2307/1132137

Volling, B. L., McElwain, N. L., & Miller, A. L. (2002). Emotion regulation in context: The jealousy complex between young siblings and its relations with child and family characteristics. *Child Development*, **73** (2), 581–600.

Volling, B. L., Oh, W., & Gonzalez, R. (2012). *Attachments to mother and father predict sibling relationship quality following the birth of a sibling*. In J. Mesman (Chair), Observing mothers and fathers with their young children: Unique patterns, predictors, and consequences, presented at the International Society for the Study of Behavioral Development, Edmonton, Canada.

Volling, B. L., Yu, T., Gonzalez, R., Kennedy, D. E., Rosenberg, L., & Oh, W. (2014). Children's responses to mother-infant and father-infant interaction with a baby sibling: Jealousy or joy? *Journal of Family Psychology*, **28**(5), 634–644. https://doi.org/10.1037/a0037811

Walcott, C. M., & Landau, S. (2004). The relations between disinhibition and emotion regulation in boys with attention deficit hyperactivity disorder. *Journal of Clinical Child & Adolescent Psychology*, **33**(4), 772–782. https://doi.org/10.1207/s15374424jccp3304_12

Walker, L. S., Garber, J., & Greene, J. W. (1993). Psychosocial correlates of recurrent childhood pain: A comparison of pediatric patients with recurrent abdominal pain, organic illness, and psychiatric disorders. *Journal of Abnormal Psychology*, **102**(2), 248–258. https://doi.org/10.1037/0021-843X.102.2.248

Walker, L. S., & Greene, J. W. (1989). Children with recurrent abdominal pain and their parents: More somatic complaints, anxiety, and depression than other patient families? *Journal of Pediatric Psychology*, **14**(2), 231–243. https://doi.org/10.1093/jpepsy/14.2.231

Warren, S. L., & Simmens, S. J. (2005). Predicting toddler anxiety/depressive symptoms: Effects of caregiver sensitivity on temperamentally vulnerable children. *Infant Mental Health Journal*, **26**(1), 40–55. https://doi.org/10.1002/imhj.20034

Waters, E., & Deane, K. E. (1985). Defining and assessing individual differences in attachment relationships: Q-methodology and the organization of behavior in infancy and early childhood. *Monographs of the Society for Research in Child Development*, **50**(1/2), 41–65. https://doi.org/10.2307/3333826

Weinraub, M., Bender, R. H., Friedman, S. L., Susman, E. J., Knoke, B., Bradley, R., et al. (2012). Patterns of developmental change in infants' nighttime sleep awakenings from 6 through 36 months of age. *Developmental Psychology*, **48**(6), 1511–1528. https://doi.org/10.1037/a0027680

Wellman, H. M., & Liu, D. (2004). Scaling of theory-of-mind tasks. *Child Development*, **75**(2), 523–541. https://doi.org/10.1111/j.1467-8624.2004.00691.x

Wellman, H. M., & Woolley, J. D. (1990). From simple desires to ordinary beliefs: The early development of everyday psychology. *Cognition*, **35**(3), 245–275. https://doi.org/10.1016/0010-0277(90)90024-E

Whalen, C. K., & Henker, B. (1992). The social profile of attention deficit hyperactivity disorder: Five fundamental facets. *Child and Adolescent Psychiatric Clinics of North America*, **1**, 395–410.

Wheeler, J., & Carlson, C. L. (1994). The social functioning of children with ADD with hyperactivity and ADD without hyperactivity: A comparison of their peer relations and social deficits. *Journal of Emotional and Behavioral Disorders*, **2**(1), 2–12. https://doi.org/10.1177/106342669400200101

Williams, L. R., Degnan, K. A., Perez-Edgar, K. E., Henderson, H. A., Rubin, K. H., Pine, D. S., et al. (2009). Impact of behavioral inhibition and parenting style on internalizing and externalizing problems from early childhood through adolescence. *Journal of Abnormal Child Psychology*, **37**(8), 1063–1075. https://doi.org/10.1007/s10802-009-9331-3

Wilson, S., & Durbin, C. E. (2010). Effects of paternal depression on fathers' parenting behaviors: A meta-analytic review. *Clinical Psychology Review*, **30**(2), 167–180. https://doi.org/10.1016/j.cpr.2009.10.007

Winnicott, D. W. (1964). *The child, the family and the outside world.* Harmandswoth, Middlesex, England: Penguin Books.

Winnicott, D. W. (1978). *The piggle: An account of the psychoanalytic treatment of a little girl.* London: The Hogarth Press and the Institute of Psycho-Analysis.

Wolff, N., Darlington, A.-S., Hunfeld, J., Verhulst, F., Jaddoe, V., Hofman, A., et al. (2010). Determinants of somatic complaints in 18-month-old children: The Generation R study. *Journal of Pediatric Psychology*, **35**(3), 306–316. https://doi.org/10.1093/jpepsy/jsp058

Wolff, N. J., Darlington, A. S., Hunfeld, J. A., Verhulst, F. C., Jaddoe, V. W., Moll, H. A., et al. (2009). The association of parent behaviors, chronic pain, and psychological problems with venipuncture distress in infants: The Generation R study. *Health Psychology*, **28**(5), 605–613. https://doi.org/10.1037/a0015202

Youngblade, L. M., & Dunn, J. (1995). Individual differences in young children's pretend play with mother and sibling: Links to relationships and understanding of other people's feelings and beliefs. *Child Development*, **66**(5), 1472–1492. https://doi.org/10.1111/j.1467-8624.1995.tb00946.x

Zemp, M., Bodenmann, G., & Cummings, E.M. (2014). The role of skin conductance level reactivity in the impact of children's exposure to interparental conflict on their attention performance. *Journal of Experimental Child Psychology*, **118**, 1–12. https://doi.org/10.1016/j.jecp.2013.09.007

Zuckerman, B., Stevenson, J., & Bailey, V. (1987). Sleep problems in early childhood: Continuities, predictive factors, and behavioral correlates. *Pediatrics*, **80** (5), 664–671.

ACKNOWLEDGMENTS

This research was supported by grants from the *Eunice Kennedy Shriver* National Institute of Child Health and Human Development (NICHD: R01HD042607, K02HD047423) to Brenda L. Volling. Matthew M. Stevenson was supported by the Developmental Psychology Training Grant (T32HD007109) at the University of Michigan from NICHD during the writing of this project. We are grateful to the parents and children of the Family Transitions Study whose commitment and generosity of time made this research possible in the first place, and to the many valuable research staff and students over the years who spent their time traveling throughout southeast Michigan to visit families, coding videotapes, and managing multiple timepoints of data collection simultaneously so that we could deliver the final product you now have before you.

PREDICTING NORMATIVE AND PROBLEMATIC FAMILY PATHWAYS TO THE TRANSITION TO SIBLINGHOOD: COMMENTARY ON VOLLING ET AL.'S MONOGRAPH

Nina Howe

This article is part of the issue "Developmental Trajectories of Children's Adjustment across the Transition to Siblinghood: Pre-Birth Predictors and Sibling Outcomes at One Year" Volling, Gonzalez, Oh, Song, Yu, Rosenberg, Kuo, Thomason, Beyers-Carlson, Safyer, and Stevenson (Issue Authors). For a full listing of articles in this issue, see: http://onlinelibrary.wiley.com/doi/10.1111/mono.v82.3/issuetoc.

Volling et al.'s monograph provides a rich, thoughtful, and rigorous account of how the transition to siblinghood is experienced by the first-born child and the family. In their comprehensive longitudinal study, they followed 241 families from the prenatal period before the second-born's birth until this child was 12-months old. Siblings are a critical, but understudied, relationship in children's development; the challenges posed in researching sibling dynamics in the context of the family are discussed. Prior psychodynamic and developmental research literature is critiqued, which places the current study into perspective and indicates the important theoretical frameworks (i.e., developmental psychopathology and developmental ecological systems) employed by Volling et al. to advance our understanding of this critical transition in the life of the family. The longitudinal study design, sample characteristics, identification of possible trajectories of adjustment (or not) to the birth of the sibling, and selection of family and child variables are addressed. The sophisticated statistical methods (Growth Mixture Modeling and data mining procedures) employed to predict child adjustment in association with parenting variables over time and sibling relationship quality at 12 months identified low- and high-risk trajectories on the seven subscales of the Child Behavior Check List (CBCL). This afforded a nuanced investigation of a variety of potentially problematic child behaviors (e.g., aggression, withdrawal, negative emotionality, somatic problems) in association with parenting behaviors. A final discussion included study limitations, significant strengths, and implications for clinicians and other professionals. The study's conclusion is that most children and families are resilient, take the birth of a sibling in their stride, and do not exhibit empirical evidence of a developmental crisis, as argued by earlier psychodynamic authors.

One of the greatest challenges for young children is to develop close, positive, and intimate relationships with significant others in their lives, in particular parents, siblings, and friends. As a number of key developmental theorists such as Carpendale and Lewis (2015), Dunn (1983, 2002, 2015), Hartup (1989), and Hinde (1979) have argued it is within the context of these significant relationships that children's social, cognitive, emotional, and moral development is facilitated. In particular, these close relationships afford a meaningful, coherent, and relevant context for children to acquire knowledge and understanding about their social worlds. Fundamental to this process is developing an understanding of the dynamics of different relationships and how one can best manage them to co-construct a positive context for development. These theorists emphasize the bi-directional nature of relationships and that their quality is co-constructed via a history of frequent and affectively varied interactions with one's partners over a significant period of time.

The research literatures on parent–child relationships and relationships with friends and peers are vast compared with the literature on sibling relationships. Yet, approximately 80% of North American children have at least one sibling and these relationships may be the longest that individuals form over their lifetime. Why has not the sibling relationship received more attention? Certainly, there are many reasons to focus on the primacy of parent–child relations in fostering children's development. Moreover, given children's widening social experiences with peers and friends by the time they enter middle childhood and beyond, it is a natural decision for researchers to focus on understanding individual differences in development and outcomes associated with patterns of positive well-being or at-risk behavior with peers. Yet, we know that young children spend a great deal of time interacting with their siblings, and that families are an interconnected set of parent–child, marital, and sibling subsystems. Clearly, what happens in one subsystem influences and is influenced by what happens in other subsystems. Thus, the study of family dynamics cannot be considered complete and valid without the inclusion of siblings into the research literature.

Studying siblings presents a number of challenges that may have dissuaded researchers from investigating this fascinating relationship, for example, the structural features (e.g., age, age gap, birth order, gender composition of dyads) associated with developmental differences, as well as individual

Social Sciences and Humanities Research Council of Canada

Corresponding author: Dr. Nina Howe, Department of Education, Concordia University, 1455 de Maisonneuve West, H3G 1M8, Montreal, QC, Canada, e-mail: nina.howe@concordia.ca

DOI: 10.1111/mono.12319

185

differences (e.g., temperament, aggression, attention) and characteristics inherent to studying relationship dynamics (e.g., interdependence of partners' interactions). These issues can make it a conceptual and methodological nightmare for researchers to know where to start in attempting to understand the role of these variables in the life of siblings within the context of the family. Where does one begin the process of untangling patterns of influence and development associated with the sibling relationship?

The current monograph by Brenda Volling and colleagues is to be commended for rising to the challenge of studying the relationship dynamics that develop between young siblings before and after the transition to siblinghood and over the ensuing year. The authors provide a thorough and critical review of the relatively few older studies addressing this question, which suffer from a number of methodological problems (e.g., small samples, psychometrically suspect measures, no prebirth observations, and/or reliance on retrospective parent reports), a lack of sophisticated statistical methods to study change, and the conceptual framework guiding their investigation. In particular, Volling et al. are especially careful to discuss the issue of the conceptual frameworks guiding previous studies and critique ideas following from the psychodynamic tradition of conceptualizing the birth of a younger sibling as a traumatic event for the older child and as a time of confusion and stress for the family. This emphasis has long historical roots in psychoanalytic theorists such as Alfred Adler (1927) and David Levy (1941). It has colored much of the earlier empirical research and writings on siblings designed either to validate or dispute this view. Moreover, this perspective still has a strong hold on current popular literature available in books, websites, and blogs designed for parents regarding the transition to siblinghood, a point I return to below.

By the 1980s, Dunn and Kendrick (1982), Stewart (1990), and others chose to use a developmental rather than psychodynamic approach to study the transition to siblinghood and its association with family dynamics. Part of their motivation may have been to debunk older ideas and to move the field forward based on more recent ideas about relationships as articulated by theorists such as Hinde (1979) and Hartup (1989). This step was a major advance in our understanding of sibling relations within the context of the family and provided an appropriate springboard for the current monograph.

Volling et al. have moved beyond a purely developmental approach by integrating ideas from developmental psychopathology and developmental ecological systems perspectives. The integration of these two recent theoretical advances results in a convincing framework that stands to contribute significantly to our understanding of sibling relations.

These frameworks allow the reader to put the child's and family's transition to siblinghood into a broader and more meaningful developmental context so as to assess the trajectories of the older sibling's adjustment, which family factors predict the trajectories, and which factors are associated with sibling relationship quality 12 months after the birth of the younger sibling. These theoretical perspectives also allow us to consider what might be normative, maladaptive, and resilient patterns of children's behavior before and after the birth of the sibling and how the nature of the wider family dynamics may be of importance in understanding children's (and parents') adjustment to having a younger sibling.

The authors note that many children gain a sibling in the toddler or early preschool years (ages 2–3), which is a period of great developmental change in learning social skills, emotional regulation, and understanding social relations. Often labeled by the lay public as the "terrible twos" for the seeming challenges children can present, they can also be considered, as my son's day care teacher called them, the "terrific twos" because of all the exciting social and cognitive developments that occur in this period. The question then arises: Are these normative developments influenced (or not) by the birth of a younger sibling? Is there evidence that children's responses can be understood as examples of typical behavior or are they symptomatic of some deeper psychological disturbance? The developmental psychopathology perspective allows us to consider maladaptive and pathological development and outcomes in relation to normative development. This is an important question for clinicians and other professionals: How do we know what is maladaptive or problematic unless we know what is normal and typical of children of particular ages and how they and the family as a unit might possibly respond to stress, transitions, disruptions, and find ways to adapt (or not) and demonstrate resilience? Why might some children adjust easily and positively and others not? What constitutes a pattern of behavior that puts a child into an at-risk or high-risk category? Identifying maladaptive patterns should then enlighten clinicians about how to design appropriate interventions for families.

To address these questions, Volling et al. also are guided by the family risk and resilience literature, which they use to identify potential maladaptive and adaptive trajectories after the birth of a sibling. This provides a way to understand the patterns over time in family adjustment and to trace trajectories of children's behavior that may be amenable to change in positive ways, demonstrate resilience, or which are problematic. One can also examine if there are periods of adjustment, recovery, and adaptation. Apriori, Volling, and colleagues defined possible trajectories to address the question of individual responses and pathways to relationship difficulties or well-adjusted outcomes and then tested these trajectories. They outline a number of possible trajectories, some of which follow a linear path (i.e., low stable indicating few problems over time; high stable, where problems were evident before the sibling's birth and continue over the first year after the sibling's birth; a gradual linear increase in problems over the first year; initial adjustment postbirth indicative of some problems but adaptation over time).

They also hypothesize possible curvilinear trajectories (i.e., sudden persistent change and problems after the sibling's birth, which are immediate and persistent over time; growth and maturity showing initial problems that decline as children mature; delayed impact when problems appear only after 6 months). Of course, the related issue is which family factors might be protective or indicate risk? The authors selected prebirth child, parent, and family variables as protective or risk factors that might predict sibling adjustment by 12 months (e.g., attachment, parenting efficacy). The selection was systematic, based on theoretical considerations and empirical evidence, to provide a nuanced picture that may allow for individual differences and patterns to emerge from the data.

The monograph reports the extensive and rich findings from a longitudinal study designed to address these questions and employed a community-based and larger number of families ($n = 241$) than in previous studies, which typically included about 40 families (e.g., Dunn & Kendrick, 1982). Families were studied 1 month before and 1 month after the birth of the second child, then again at 4, 8, and 12 months after the birth of the sibling, so as to determine short- and long-term patterns of adaptation (or not) for the family, if prebirth difficulties persist over time, and to predict sibling relationship dynamics. The five time points were chosen carefully and represent periods of theoretically important development changes/transitions in the lives of both siblings and the family. Moreover, the time periods also coincide with those in Stewart's (1990) study of the transition to siblinghood, thus, allowing for a comparison of the findings from both studies.

Multiple sources of data (child, parent, family) were included and a variety of methods such as questionnaires (e.g., child temperament, child care responsibilities), attachment q-sorts, observations of marital interaction and parenting, and parent interviews were used. In particular, the Child Behavior Check List (CBCL), which includes seven types of problem behaviors, provided the structure for identifying the trajectories of child behavior; it has strong psychometric properties thus making it a solid choice for the study. Although the CBCL is typically used to create measures of internalizing and externalizing behavior that are aggregated across multiple subscales, Volling et al. chose to look at the trajectories associated with each of the seven subscales individually (aggression, attention, withdrawal, etc). Earlier literature on the transition to siblinghood indicates that some children respond aggressively and others withdraw, but a number of different components define these rather broad categories of response. By examining each of the seven CBCL subscales separately, it was possible to identify different trajectories and which types of behavior were more or less problematic over time in predicting outcomes. This decision allowed for a nuanced investigation of children's patterns of behavior over time rather than providing an aggregated approach that may have hidden more subtle patterns. As was evident in the report of the findings for the seven subscales, this was a wise decision.

Since the earlier studies on the transition to siblinghood (e.g., Dunn & Kendrick, Stewart) conducted several decades ago, there have been major advances in the sophistication of statistical methods available for researchers. These newer methods allow for the analysis of more complex questions and different levels of data (e.g., child, family variables). Volling et al. make excellent use of these sophisticated methods in their analyses. Also, to their credit, the different steps in the analyses are quite clearly explained and relatively easy to follow. Employing Growth Mixture Modeling (a combination of Latent Growth Modeling and group-based trajectory analysis) revealed the various classes of trajectories and individual differences evident within trajectory groups. This approach allows for a nuanced understanding of the patterns of various trajectories, namely, which group adjusts quickly, slowly, not at all, or increases in specific behaviors over time. Importantly, one can test for the various apriori trajectories based on theory (i.e., sudden and persistent patterns of maladjustment; delayed impact, adjustment, and adaptation response) within each of the seven CBCL subscales.

The next step in the analytic plan was to determine which prenatal child, parent, and family variables were associated with the different classes of trajectories. Given the large amount of data and the number of possible variables to wade through this could have been an overwhelming process; however, data mining procedures were employed to identify specific predictor variables for each CBCL subscale. The data mining process was new to me, but this productive process revealed a relatively consistent pattern of child, parent, and family variables previously nominated as possible predictors, which discriminated the classes of trajectories, specifically child temperament, co-parenting, parental self-efficacy, and parent–child attachment. These variables reveal the different levels of influence, ranging from individual child characteristics to dyadic interactions, and emphasizes the bi-directional nature of the family subsystems in predicting how older siblings adjusted to the birth of a sibling. Interestingly, the data mining process revealed a pattern of predictor variables that are those often seen as most influential in the literature. I found this reassuring in the sense that the choice of predictor variables was not just based on a statistical method, but was justified and guided by the theoretical and empirical literature. Researchers who are seduced by the apparent advantages of the newest statistical methods can lose sight of the theoretical and conceptual framework that should have guided their study. This criticism cannot be applied to the present monograph.

The authors organized the order of the chapters by arranging findings for the seven CBCL subscales into the three larger categories of external, internalizing, and physical problems, which makes conceptual sense and a coherent way to guide the reader through the mass of findings. A separate chapter is allotted to each subscale and is organized in the same way, starting with a review of pertinent literature to place the behavior into context. Next, the analytic plan is presented, which first identified trajectories for the subscales indicating the variability and individual differences in trajectories. At this point, the reader is directed to "spaghetti plots" for the pattern of trajectories for each subscale, which are plotted against the CBCL criteria for normative, borderline, or clinical scores. This visual representation is very informative and a means to identify which children and how many who may be at-risk (e.g., for aggression). The visual representation of the different trajectories was particularly helpful in providing insight into the patterns for each subscale. The next analyses identified which child, parenting, and/or family variables were significant in predicting the trajectories by comparing the trajectory group low on the specific behavior to other trajectories and sometimes mid- to high-level trajectories. This systematic approach revealed which variables were significant predictors of the most at-risk compared to low-risk or mid-level groups of children, a question of relevance to parents and clinicians. Finally, regression analyses focused on which variables predicted sibling relationship quality 12 months after the birth of the younger sibling.

What emerged from this sophisticated analytical approach? Overall, the news is positive in that most children demonstrated little evidence of a severe psychologically stressful response to the birth of a younger sibling. In fact, the vast majority of children did not exhibit a sudden stressful response to the birth of their sibling at one month and were members of the low-stable trajectory for each of the seven CBCL behaviors. The one exception to this pattern was aggression, which showed an increase for many children at 1 month but declined by 4 months. The authors argue that aggression may be a relatively normative response to the transition to siblinghood. Given the age of many of the older siblings (2–3 years) and their still developing language and cognitive skills, aggression may not be an unreasonable response to the changing dynamics and disruptions that occur at home and family life. The finding also replicates a similar report by Stewart (1990) and suggests aggression may be a short-term but normative response.

The Growth Mixture Modeling analyses revealed different trajectories emanating from their prenatal level within each of the seven behaviors and the number of trajectories varied across the seven behaviors from three to five. The presence of this variability allowed for an examination of individual differences in terms of where children started and where they fell out over the next year resulting in a complex and rich set of findings. One consistent, significant, and clinically important pattern showed that children who were initially high on any of the seven CBCL behaviors at the prenatal point generally continued to show high rates at one month postbirth and for the ensuing period of the study. There was no evidence that children exhibited a sudden increase in problematic behavior or signs of a developmental crisis after the birth of the sibling, contrary to psychodynamic perspectives or popular belief. Also, few children fell into the at-risk (borderline-clinical) or high-risk (clinical) trajectories. Although this general finding is reassuring, it nevertheless indicates that these families may eventually require some kind of intervention. The authors acknowledge that since they only conducted one prenatal measurement, which was close to the actual birth, it is not possible to know if these high rates of problematic difficulties were accentuated by the impending event or if these patterns had a longer history that began earlier in the pregnancy or even predated it. The authors are appropriately cautious in interpreting the origins of this high-risk pattern. One could argue that the persistence of these (clinically) problematic behaviors such as aggression or emotional reactivity or withdrawal, may have had a history that long predated the pregnancy. On the other hand, changes in family dynamics and awareness of physical changes in the household (e.g., preparing a room for the baby) over the course of the pregnancy may have exacerbated some behaviors to the point where they were observed at problematic levels one month prior to the sibling's birth. Of course, future research is required to test these speculations.

The earlier literature reported that siblings often respond to the birth of a younger child in problematic ways such as behaving aggressively, but also by withdrawing, or regressing (toileting, illness, and sleep problems), showing a lack of attention, and being anxious or depressed. The current study indicated that most children showed little evidence of responding to the birth by suddenly withdrawing, exhibiting somatic complaints, having sleep problems, or showing signs of anxiety. In terms of attention, most children showed a decline in attention issues over the year (except for the group that was initially high and stayed that way), suggesting a pattern of normative development. Only a small minority of children demonstrated any evidence of difficulties, but again the high levels of difficult behavior were evident even before the birth, and therefore, apparently not a consequence of the presence of a new family member.

We know that children's behavior cannot be seen in isolation from that of other family members leading the authors to assess a large number of parenting and family variables. The findings regarding predictors of the trajectories of children's behavior provide a rich picture, while the patterns of interaction between the child and parenting variables are key to advancing our understanding of family dynamics. For example, it was not surprising that child temperament as assessed by negative emotionality and behavioral inhibition predicted high-risk behaviors at all points in the study. But it is in combination with other parenting variables that the outcomes become worrisome. Children demonstrated the highest rates of aggression when mother–child attachment was insecure and they had difficult temperaments, in combination with fathers who had low parenting self-efficacy and when mothers and fathers engaged in undermining one another in their parenting.

Considering this complex and ineffective pattern of dynamics, it is no wonder these children exhibited high rates of aggression. Further, when parents engaged in a parenting style of undermining one another, children demonstrated mid-stable rates of withdrawal, whereas children who were in the low-stable withdrawal group had parents reporting a positive marital relationship. While insecure attachment to the mother was a predictor of poor child adjustment, a secure attachment to father was apparently a buffer against children's somatic problems. These findings are only some examples that provide support for the notion that family dynamics are never simple or straightforward and one must take account of all partners. It was rather reassuring that the best predictors of child problem trajectories that might be amenable to intervention were the classic factors of temperament and attachment security coupled with family factors (i.e., fathers' parenting efficacy, co-parenting). From a conceptual point of view, the consistent interrelations among these factors provides a framework for considering whether there is a need for intervention and if it might benefit some families.

What about the role of fathers in helping their children to make a smooth transition after the birth of the sibling? One of the strengths of the current study is the inclusion of fathers as important members of the family system, which may reflect contemporary paternal involvement, at least in some families. Although there can be methodological challenges of recruiting fathers and maintaining their participation, the authors overcame these challenges. The findings suggest fathers' ratings of low self-efficacy regarding their parenting, often in combination with difficult child temperament, was a factor in predicting more child problems (e.g., aggression). Certainly temperamentally difficult children can be hard to manage and sooth and it may be that if fathers take less responsibility or initiative for child management than mothers, they may feel less competent. Interestingly, regarding withdrawal trajectories, children in the high-decreasing group who initially showed high rates of withdrawal before the sibling's birth, had fathers (and mothers) who were less likely to engage in an undermining parenting style and had more positive marital relations. Perhaps fathers were active in somehow drawing their child into more frequent and positive family interactions, thus acting as a protective buffer so that withdrawal decreased over time. Further evidence that fathers may play a buffering role for children was the finding that even when children were high in negative emotionality, if they had a secure father attachment, they were likely to be in the low trajectory for somatic problems. Clearly, fathers have an important role to play in affording opportunities to facilitate both positive and sometimes more negative patterns of children's behavior. One question that arose for me was the father's role when mothers suffer from severe postpartum depression or the second child is born with developmental issues, but this is a question for future studies.

The final set of research questions focused on the predictors of sibling relationship quality when the younger child was 12 months old. One-year-olds are interesting people—they are mobile, determined, interested in social interactions, vocal about their desires and needs although not yet talking, emotional, thinking, and agentic individuals. Furthermore, they are deeply interested in their older siblings. Of course, whether older siblings return the interest varies across families from hostile, conflictual to playful, happy to ambivalent interactions. A relatively clear pattern of findings significantly predicted the relationship at 12 months. Specifically, indices of externalizing behavior (i.e., high trajectories of aggression, attention problems, and emotional negativity) predicted greater sibling conflict and less frequent positive interactions at 12 months. Whereas anxiety, somatic complaints, sleep problems, and withdrawal did not predict sibling relationship quality indicating that these internalizing and physical problems were not prominent factors. Certainly, older siblings who actively engage in high levels of aggression, have poor attention spans, and react in emotionally intense ways would not facilitate conditions conducive for co-constructing a positive relationship with their younger sibling. At 12 months, the younger sibling does not yet have the social, cognitive, and emotional competence to change the tone of the interactions in an effective way. Whether this pattern of more hostile sibling relations will develop into more positive exchanges or possibly into avoidance as the younger sibling matures is an open question that would be interesting to pursue with these data. A stable pattern of hostile sibling relations that threatens the emotional climate of the family and the well-being of the children may eventually require parental and/or professional intervention. I would be curious to know if the children in the at-risk and high-risk trajectories in fact, receive professional help in later years. This question assumes the longitudinal study will continue, which I encourage the authors to seriously consider.

As I read the monograph, I wondered if the same children were consistently identified in the at-risk or high-risk trajectories across the seven behaviors. The authors address this question in the final chapter and indicate that different children were observed in the high-risk groups across the seven behaviors. Thus, examining each of the seven separate CBCL subscales was a more effective way to assess the degree of possible difficulties than a broad-band approach of only determining scores on the aggregated externalizing or internalizing scales. Volling et al.'s approach should have application for clinicians working with families seeking help after the birth of a sibling. By assessing the patterns of behavior specific to a particular child, one could determine which behaviors to target. For example, by assessing if the child is exhibiting very high levels of aggression or withdrawal or emotional reactivity, the clinician could tailor the intervention to the needs of the child and family. The withdrawn child may benefit from strategies to increase responsive and sensitive parenting so as to promote positive sibling interaction, whereas the aggressive or emotionally reactive child may require different methods of parenting and intervention.

A few final comments are in order. The lack of child age and gender findings as significant predictors was somewhat surprising, but the age range between children was somewhat restricted. Although the community-based sample was an important strength in investigating children's typical transitions to siblinghood, the lack of diversity in the Caucasian, middle-class sample restricts generalizations to more diverse populations. Similar studies in ethnically and culturally diverse or low-SES populations would enrich our understanding of early sibling and family dynamics. Future work should also compare community samples with clinical samples to provide a better understanding of the diversity of responses to the birth of a sibling. The lack of more than one prenatal observation was noted earlier. These limitations are overcome by the theoretically rich framework guiding the longitudinal study, the large sample, the multitude of child, parenting, and family variables, psychometrically validated measures, multiple informants, sophisticated statistics, and a well-organized presentation. Volling et al., give much attention to advancing theory, which is critical for guiding future research and an important strength of this monograph. Implications of the findings for parenting and professional intervention are interwoven into the final chapter, but might have also been repeated in a separate section on recommendations for easier access for interested parties.

In conclusion, the bottom line is that most children are more resilient than we give them credit for and take the birth of a sibling in their stride and over time sometimes come to love and cherish their sibling and sometimes not. In any case, it is a relationship that will continue to be a significant context for their development, certainly in the early years and often over a lifetime. Clearly, the birth of a sibling is not a developmental crisis for the vast majority of older siblings as is believed by advocates of the psychodynamic perspective, the writers of parenting books, and the public. It is time to debunk these popular, but erroneous beliefs!

ACKNOWLEDGMENTS

The author is supported by a Strategic Research Grant from the Social Sciences and Humanities Research Council of Canada and the Concordia University Research Chair in Early Childhood Development and Education.

REFERENCES

Adler, A. (1927). *Understanding human nature.* London, UK: Allen & Unwin.

Carpendale, J. I., & Lewis, C. (2015). The development of social understanding. In R. M. Lerner, L. S. Liben, & U. Mueller (Eds.), *Handbook of child psychology and developmental science: Cognitive processes* (pp. 381–424). Hoboken, NJ: Wiley.

Dunn, J. (1983). Sibling relationships in early childhood. *Child Development, 54,* 787–811.

Dunn, J. (2002). Sibling relationships. In P. K. Smith, & C. H. Hart (Eds.), *Blackwell handbook of childhood social development* (pp. 223–237). Malden, MA: Blackwell.

Dunn, J. (2015). Sibling relationships. In J. Grusec & P. Hastings (Eds). *Handbook of socialization: Theory and research* (pp. 182–201). New York, NY: Guilford Press.

Dunn, J., & Kendrick, C. (1982). *Siblings: Love, envy, and understanding.* Cambridge, MA: Harvard University Press.

Hartup, W.W. (1989). Social relationships and their developmental significance. *American Psychologist Psychologist, 44,* 120–126.

Hinde, R. A. (1979). *Towards understanding relationships.* London, UK: Academic Press.

Levy, D. (1941). The hostile act. *Psychological Review, 48,* 356–361.

Stewart R. B. (1990). *The second child: Family transition and adjustment.* Newbury Park, CA: Sage.

CONTRIBUTORS

This article is part of the issue "Developmental Trajectories of Children's Adjustment across the Transition to Siblinghood: Pre-Birth Predictors and Sibling Outcomes at One Year" Volling, Gonzalez, Oh, Song, Yu, Rosenberg, Kuo, Thomason, Beyers-Carlson, Safyer, and Stevenson (Issue Authors). For a full listing of articles in this issue, see: http://onlinelibrary.wiley.com/doi/10.1111/mono.v82.3/issuetoc.

Emma Beyers-Carlson, M.S., is a doctoral student in Developmental Psychology at the University of Michigan. Her research interests center on typical and atypical families and how family members interact in systemic and interrelated ways. Specifically, her work focuses on how the interconnected relationships in the family system impact prosocial development in early childhood.

Richard Gonzalez, Ph.D., is Professor of Psychology, Statistics, and Integrative Systems & Design; Research Professor in the Research Center for Group Dynamics and the Center for Human Growth and Development, and Director of the Research Center for Group Dynamics. He is also Director of the Biosocial Methods Collaborative. His research is in the area of judgment and decision making. He is interested in applied statistical models, longitudinal designs, data mining techniques, and research designs that integrate biological and behavioral processes.

Patty X. Kuo, Ph.D., is currently a post-doctoral research associate in the Department of Anthropology at the University of Notre Dame. She received her Ph.D. in Developmental Psychology at the University of Michigan. Her

DOI: 10.1111/mono.12320

research interests focus on father involvement in families with infants and young children from a biopsychosocial perspective.

Wonjung Oh, Ph.D., is an Assistant Professor of Human Development and Family Studies at Texas Tech University. Her research focuses on the role of individual, relational, peer, and family factors in developmental trajectories of adaptive and maladaptive social behavior and relationships. She actively seeks novel, innovative approaches to basic and applied research questions pertaining to developmental and family processes across various transitions.

Lauren Rosenberg, M.S., is the Project Coordinator for the Family Transitions Study. She received her Master's Degree in Developmental Psychology from Teacher's College, Columbia University and her undergraduate degree in Psychology and Women's Studies from the University of Michigan. She has interests in early childhood and family relationships.

Paige Safyer, M.S., M.S.W., is a doctoral student in Developmental Psychology and Social Work at the University of Michigan. Her research focuses on infant social–emotional development within the parenting context. She is also interested in interventions that strengthen the parent–infant attachment relationship.

Ju-Hyun Song, Ph.D., is currently a post-doctoral fellow in the Department of Psychology at the University of Toronto. She received her Ph.D. in Developmental Psychology from the University of Michigan. Her research focuses on the roles of children's social–emotional and social–cognitive characteristics for the development of prosocial behavior and aggression.

Matthew M. Stevenson, Ph.D., is a Postdoctoral Research Fellow at the Center for Human Growth and Development at the University of Michigan. He received his Ph.D. in Clinical Psychology from Arizona State University in 2014. He is interested in the role of fathers in child development and developmental psychopathology.

Elizabeth Thomason, Ph.D., is a data analyst for the Depression Center in the Department of Psychiatry and a lecturer in the School of Social Work at the University of Michigan. She received her Ph.D. in Psychology and Social work from the University of Michigan. Her interests center around women's depression in the perinatal period.

Brenda L. Volling, Ph.D., is Professor of Psychology, and Director and Research Professor of the Center for Human Growth and Development at the University of Michigan. Her research focuses on the role of family relationships for early social and emotional development. She is the Principal Investigator of the Family Transitions Study, a longitudinal investigation of child and family functioning after the birth of a second child, which provided the data for the present monograph.

Tianyi Yu, Ph.D., is an associate research scientist at the Center for Family Research, University of Georgia. She received her Ph.D. in Human Development and Family Studies at Auburn University, and was a former post-doctoral fellow on the Family Transitions Study. Her major research goal is to identify factors and processes associated with resiliency and vulner-abilities in children as well as young adults who experience family stress and transitions.

Nina Howe, Ph.D., holds the Concordia University Research Chair in Early Childhood Development and Education and is a Professor in the Department of Education, Concordia University, Montreal, Quebec, Canada. Her areas of research include relationships (particularly sibling pretense, conflict, teaching, imitation), the social–cognitive development of preschool and school-aged children, children's play, and early childhood education.

STATEMENT OF EDITORIAL POLICY

The SRCD *Monographs* series aims to publish major reports of developmental research that generates authoritative new findings and that foster a fresh perspective and/or integration of data/research on conceptually significant issues. Submissions may consist of individually or group-authored reports of findings from some single large-scale investigation or from a series of experiments centering on a particular question. Multiauthored sets of independent studies concerning the same underlying question also may be appropriate. A critical requirement in such instances is that the individual authors address common issues and that the contribution arising from the set as a whole be unique, substantial, and well integrated. Manuscripts reporting interdisciplinary or multidisciplinary research on significant developmental questions and those including evidence from diverse cultural, racial, and ethnic groups are of particular interest. Also of special interest are manuscripts that bridge basic and applied developmental science, and that reflect the international perspective of the Society. Because the aim of the *Monographs* series is to enhance cross-fertilization among disciplines or subfields as well as advance knowledge on specialized topics, the links between the specific issues under study and larger questions relating to developmental processes should emerge clearly and be apparent for both general readers and specialists on the topic. In short, irrespective of how it may be framed, work that contributes significant data and/or extends a developmental perspective will be considered.

Potential authors who may be unsure whether the manuscript they are planning wouldmake an appropriate submission to the SRCD *Monographs* are invited to draft an outline or prospectus of what they propose and send it to the incoming editor for review and comment.

Potential authors are not required to be members of the Society for Research in Child Development nor affiliated with the academic discipline of psychology to submit a manuscript for consideration by the *Monographs*. The significance of the work in extending developmental theory and in contributing new empirical information is the crucial consideration.

Submissions should contain a minimum of 80 manuscript pages (including tables and references). The upper boundary of 150–175 pages is more flexible, but authors should try to keep within this limit. Manuscripts must be double-spaced, 12pt Times New Roman font, with 1-inch margins. If color artwork is submitted, and the authors believe color art is necessary to the presentation of their work, the submissions letter should indicate that one or more authors or their institutions are prepared to pay the substantial costs associated with color art reproduction. Please submit manuscripts electronically to the SRCD *Monographs* Online Submissions and Review Site (Scholar One) at http://mc.manuscriptcentral.com/mono. Please contact the *Monographs* office with any questions at monographs@srcd.org.

The corresponding author for any manuscript must, in the submission letter, warrant that all coauthors are in agreement with the content of the manuscript. The corresponding author also is responsible for informing all coauthors, in a timely manner, of manuscript submission, editorial decisions, reviews received, and any revisions recommended. Before publication, the corresponding author must warrant in the submissions letter that the study has been conducted according to the ethical guidelines of the Society for Research in Child Development.

A more detailed description of all editorial policies, evaluation processes, and format requirements can be found under the "Submission Guidelines" link at http://srcd.org/publications/monographs.

Monographs Editorial Office
e-mail: monographs@srcd.org

Editor, Patricia J. Bauer
Department of Psychology, Emory University
36 Eagle Row
Atlanta, GA 30322
e-mail: pjbauer@emory.edu

Note to NIH Grantees

Pursuant to NIH mandate, Society through Wiley-Blackwell will post the accepted version of Contributions authored by NIH grantholders to PubMed Central upon acceptance. This accepted version will be made publicly available 12 months after publication. For further information, see http://www.wiley.com/go/nihmandate.

syndrome scales, 17, 41, 43, 46, *47*, 142, 147, 155, 184, 188–190 (*see also specific scales*)
withdrawal, 112
Child Behavior Questionnaire (CBQ), 33
child predictors, 8, 32–39. *See also specific predictors*
childcare, 28, 37, 75
class membership. *See* trajectories, classes
classification and regression trees (CART), 43–44
clinging, 7, 10, 16, 32, 82, 83, 89, 92, 147, 149
cognitive development, 10, 94, 102
communication, parent–child, 121
communicative development, 10
conflict-management skills, 22
conflict resolution, 58, 67
confrontation. *See* defiance
constipation, 119
coparenting. *See* parent/parenting/coparenting
Coparenting Questionnaire (CQ), 37
CQ. *See* Coparenting Questionnaire
crying, 131, 134, 140, 147
culture and sleep, 131

D
Daily Hassles Scale, 37
data mining procedures, 8, 20–21, 99, 137, 142, 148, 153, 156, 184, 189
defiance, 10, 16, 32, 54
demanding behavior. *See* behavior
dependency, 82
depression
    father's, 95
    mother's, 19, 56–57, 85, 91–92, 95–96, 102–103, 108, 121, 132, 134, 151–152
    parental, 34–35, 102–103
    See also anxiety-depression
diarrhea, 116
discipline, 74, 83, 121, 128, 150, 151
disruptive behavior. *See* behavior
distress, 107
dizziness, 119
dying/death, 94

E
eating behavior, 16, 119, 148
ecological systems model, 18, 19–21, 139, 184

internalizing behavior, 23, 24, 31, 46, 50–51, 58, 91, 95–96, 102–104, 107–109, 115, 117, 120, 145, 155, 188, 189
Intimate Relations Scale, 35
irritability, 97

J
jealousy, 75, 143, 150

L
language, 10
limb pain. *See* musculoskeletal pain
LMR. *See* Lo-Mendell-Rubin
Lo-Mendell-Rubin (LMR), 41, 76, 97, 111, 123, 135

M
marital relationship
    aggression, 57
    anxiety-depression, 87–88, 90, 92
    communication, 128
    conflict, 21, 115, 121–122, 133
    construct, 32
    ecological contexts, 19, 20
    equity, 57
    interaction, 31, 36, 113, 137, 157
    length, 27
    quality, 18, 35–36, 110, 113, 115, 116, 124–125, 140, 152, 158, 192
MCAR. *See* missing completely at random
missing completely at random (MCAR), 42
mobility, infant, 66, 67
mood/moodiness, 31, 93–94, 95, 97, 101, 121, 127, 140, 149, 152
mother. *See* marital relationship; parent efficacy; parent/parenting/coparenting
musculoskeletal pain, 119

N
napping, 131
nausea, 119
nightmares, 131
noncompliant behavior. *See* behavior

O
opposition. *See* defiance